Sudeshna Chatterjee, Alberto Minujin, and Katie Hodgkinson (Eds.)

Leaving No Child and No Adolescent Behind
A Global Perspective on Addressing Inclusion through the SDGs

CROP International Poverty Studies

Edited by Thomas Pogge

1 *Maria Petmesidou, Enrique Delamónica, Christos Papatheodorou, and Aldrie Henry-Lee (Eds.)*
 Child Poverty, Youth (Un)Employment, and Social Inclusion
 ISBN 978-3-8382-0912-8

2 *Alberto Minujin, Mónica González Contró, and Raúl Mercer (Eds.)*
 Tackling Child Poverty in Latin America
 Rights and Social Protection in Unequal Societies
 ISBN 978-3-8382-0917-3

3 *Mariano Féliz and Aaron L. Rosenberg (Eds.)*
 The Political Economy of Poverty and Social Transformations
 of the Global South
 ISBN 978-3-8382-0914-2

4 *Chris Tapscott, Tor Halvorsen, and Teresita Cruz-Del Rosario (Eds.)*
 The Democratic Developmental State: North-South Perspectives
 ISBN 978-3-8382-0915-9

5 *Enrique Delamonica, Gustave Nébié, Chinyere Emeka-Anuna, and Felix Fofana N'Zue (Eds.)*
 Child Poverty and Social Protection in Central and Western Africa
 ISBN 978-3-8382-1176-3

6 *Sofiya An, Tatiana Chubarova, Bob Deacon, and Paul Stubbs (Eds.)*
 Social Policy, Poverty, and Inequality in Central and Eastern Europe and the Former Soviet Union
 Agency and Institutions in Flux
 ISBN 978-3-8382-1308-8

7 *Keetie Roelen, Richard Morgan, and Yisak Tafere (Eds.)*
 Putting Children First
 New Frontiers in the Fight Against Child Poverty in Africa
 ISBN 978-3-8382-1317-0

8 *Sudeshna Chatterjee, Alberto Minujin, and Katie Hodgkinson (Eds.)*
 Leaving No Child and No Adolescent Behind
 A Global Perspective on Addressing Inclusion through the SDGs
 ISBN 978-3-8382-1547-1

Sudeshna Chatterjee, Alberto Minujin,
and Katie Hodgkinson (Eds.)

LEAVING NO CHILD AND NO ADOLESCENT BEHIND
A Global Perspective on Addressing
Inclusion through the SDGs

Bibliografische Information der Deutschen Nationalbibliothek
Die Deutsche Nationalbibliothek verzeichnet diese Publikation in der Deutschen Nationalbibliografie; detaillierte bibliografische Daten sind im Internet über http://dnb.d-nb.de abrufbar.

Bibliographic information published by the Deutsche Nationalbibliothek
Die Deutsche Nationalbibliothek lists this publication in the Deutsche Nationalbibliografie; detailed bibliographic data are available in the Internet at http://dnb.d-nb.de.

Cover picture: Tukaram.Karve /Shutterstock.com

ISBN-13: 978-3-8382-1547-1
© *ibidem*-Verlag, Stuttgart 2021
copyright © GRIP, 2021
Alle Rechte vorbehalten

Das Werk einschließlich aller seiner Teile ist urheberrechtlich geschützt. Jede Verwertung außerhalb der engen Grenzen des Urheberrechtsgesetzes ist ohne Zustimmung des Verlages unzulässig und strafbar. Dies gilt insbesondere für Vervielfältigungen, Übersetzungen, Mikroverfilmungen und elektronische Speicherformen sowie die Einspeicherung und Verarbeitung in elektronischen Systemen.

All rights reserved. No part of this publication may be reproduced, stored in or introduced into a retrieval system, or transmitted, in any form, or by any means (electronic, mechanical, photocopying, recording or otherwise) without the prior written permission of the publisher. Any person who does any unauthorized act in relation to this publication may be liable to criminal prosecution and civil claims for damages.

Printed in the EU

About CROP

CROP, the Comparative Research Programme on Poverty, was initiated in 1992, and the CROP Secretariat was officially opened in June 1993 by the Director General of UNESCO, Dr Frederico Mayor. The CROP network comprises scholars engaged in poverty-related research across a variety of academic disciplines and has been coordinated by the CROP Secretariat at the University of Bergen, Norway.

The CROP series on *International Studies in Poverty Research* presents expert research and essential analyses of different aspects of poverty worldwide. By promoting a fuller understanding of the nature, extent, depth, distribution, trends, causes and effects of poverty, this series has contributed to knowledge concerning the reduction and eradication of poverty at global, regional, national and local levels.

From CROP to GRIP

After a process of re-thinking CROP, 2019 marked the beginning of a transition from CROP to GRIP the Global Research Programme on Inequality. GRIP is a radically interdisciplinary research programme that views inequality as both a fundamental challenge to human well-being and as an impediment to achieving the ambitions of the 2030 Agenda. It aims to facilitate collaboration across disciplines and knowledge systems to promote critical, diverse and inter-disciplinary research on inequality. GRIP will continue to build on the successful collaboration between the University of Bergen and the International Science Council that was developed through the former Comparative Research Programme on Poverty.

For more information contact:

GRIP Secretariat
Faculty of Social Sciences
University of Bergen
PO Box 7802
5020 Bergen, Norway.
E-mail: gripinequality@uib.no
Web: www.gripinequality.org

For more information about CROP and previous publications in this series, please visit www.crop.org.

Contents

Introduction: Leaving No Child and No Adolescent Behind 9
Sudeshna Chatterjee, Alberto Minujin and Katie Hodgkinson

Part I: MAPPING AND MONITORING URBAN COMMUNITIES AND ADOLESCENTS IN POVERTY

Chapter 1
Monitoring Child Wellbeing and Inequality in Cities: A Model Developed in Colombia 39
Samantha Cocco-Klein and Alberto Minujin

Chapter 2
Capturing Children Left Behind in Urban Poor Communities: Lessons for Equity-Focused SDG Monitoring From the Bangkok Small Community MICS, Thailand 63
Tomoo Okubo, Ana Maria Restrepo, Chirawat Poonsab and Christina Popivanova

Chapter 3
A Safe and Inclusive City for Adolescents in Kolkata: Lessons From a Participatory Mapping of an Urban Ward in India 85
Sudeshna Chatterjee

Part II: MAKING INVISIBLE CHILDREN AND YOUTH VISIBLE

Chapter 4
Exploring and Addressing the Exclusion of "Invisible" Youth: Applying a Relational Framework to SDG 10.2 117
Katie Hodgkinson, Nicky Pouw and Marielle L.J. Le Mat

Chapter 5
Finding the Hard to Reach: A Mixed Methods Approach to Including Adolescents with Disabilities in Survey Research 145
Jennifer Seager, Sarah Baird, Joan Hamory Hicks, Sabina Faiz Rashid, Maheen Sultan, Workneh Yadete, and Nicola Jones

Chapter 6
The Role of Context in Social Exclusion of Children: Lessons From Children's Homes in Ghana 173
Ernest Darkwah and Marguerite Daniel

Part III: SOCIAL AND CHILD PROTECTION, CHILD WELL-BEING

Chapter 7
Child-Sensitive Non-Contributory Social Protection in the MENA Region 199
Anna Carolina Machado and Charlotte Bilo

Chapter 8
Child Poverty and Quality of Life: Material and Non-Material Domains of Well-Being 223
Ismael Cid Martinez, Enrique Delamonica, Jose Luis Espinoza Delgado, Aristide Kielem, Mohamed Obaidy

Chapter 9
Protection Risks and Protective Factors of Vulnerable Young Children Through the Study of Community-Based Child Protection (CBCP) in Rural Western Kenya 243
Martin Hayes, Melissa Kelly and Darcy Strouse

Contributor Biographies.. 271

Introduction:
Leaving No Child and No Adolescent Behind

Sudeshna Chatterjee,[1] Alberto Minujin[2] and Katie Hodgkinson[3]

The Promise of Agenda 2030 for Sustainable Development

Today's children and adolescents (0–19 years) are the first generation to be born entirely in the 21st century. They are widely acknowledged to be better educated, have better health and live longer than previous generations. They are also the most digitally connected generation. An estimated one in three internet users around the world is under 18 (UNICEF, 2017). Although the world is becoming a more prosperous place, however, there is also increasing prevalence of inequality (Alvaredo et al., 2018), which translates into deprivation and exclusion for disadvantaged children. In its State of the World's Children report of 2016, UNICEF suggested that based on current trends, by 2030 70 million children under five will die from mostly preventable causes; 167 million children will live in poverty; and a shocking 750 million women will have been married as children (UNICEF, 2016). By contrast, 2030 is also the target date for achieving the Sustainable Development Goals (SDGs) that promise to provide children and young people with the services, skills and opportunities they need to build better futures for themselves, their families, and their societies.

The future of our world over the next decade is thus being shaped by the Agenda 2030 for Sustainable Development, which was unanimously agreed by the 193 member states of the UN General Assembly in October 2015. Building on both the achievements and failures of the Millennium Development Goals (MDGs), the Agenda 2030 is the most ambitious global agreement to date. It takes on complex societal challenges such as poverty eradication, environmental protection and institution-building. It pledges to take bold and transformative steps to 'shift the world onto a sustainable and resilient path', and to crucially ensure that 'no one will be left behind'

---

[1] Founder and CEO, Action for Children's Environments. Consulting Senior Evaluation Specialist for Evaluation of UNICEF's Work for Children in Cities, UNICEF, New York
[2] Executive Director, Equity for Children. Professor at the Studley Graduate Program in International Affairs, The New School
[3] MSc in International Development Studies, Post-Graduate Researcher in the School of Languages, Cultures and Societies at the University of Leeds

(United Nations, n.d.). Any forward-looking development agenda must secure the future of millions of today's children and adolescents. The Sustainable Development Goals (SDGs) do that by seeking to uphold children's wellbeing. Indeed, the call to *leave no one behind* and to reach the furthest behind first, shines a spotlight on the world's most vulnerable populations including children and adolescents living in poverty and exclusion.

With 17 Goals, 169 Targets, and 232 Indicators linked to the Targets, this inter-governmental development agenda offers a pathway to a future by generating economic growth, achieving social justice, exercising environmental stewardship and strengthening governance. The goals and targets relate to both development outcomes and means of implementation (MoI). They are further designed to be integrated and indivisible, and to balance the social, economic and environmental dimensions of sustainable development. Mapping the critical connections between the different SDG goals and their targets suggest that not only do the SDGs explicitly reference one another (Le Blanc, 2015), they interact in one of three ways: interdependence, imposing conditions, and reinforcement (Weitz et al. 2018).

The SDGs offer a framework to strengthen and transform preventative action to build peaceful, just, and inclusive societies. They further seek to realise the human rights of all, and to achieve gender equality and the empowerment of all women and girls. Since people are at the core of such work, experts have pointed out that UN frameworks have to be translated into local action by encouraging grassroots civil society to get involved, strengthening partnerships with local stakeholders and allowing communities to own the process (Satterthwaite, 2018). This ambitious new universal agenda is intended to be implemented by all countries and all stakeholders, acting in collaborative partnership.

In October 2018, an international workshop was organised in New York by the Comparative Research Programme on Poverty—CROP (ISSC/UiB), Equity for Children/The New School and SOS Children's Villages, on 'Including Children and Adolescents in Progress for the SDGs: Understanding and Addressing Exclusion among Poor Children'. The workshop was supported by UNICEF, UNDP, Save the Children, the Global Coalition to End Child Poverty and ChildFund Alliance. Its purpose was to make a concrete contribution, within the context of the SDGs, to understanding, defining, measuring, and addressing social inclusion among children and young people living in poverty, in particular relation to:

- Target 10.2: By 2030, empower and promote the social, economic and political inclusion of all, irrespective of age, sex, disability, race, ethnicity, origin, religion or economic or other status
- Target 11.3: By 2030, enhance inclusive and sustainable urbanization and capacity for participatory, integrated and sustainable human settlement planning and management in all countries
- Target 11.7: By 2030, provide universal access to safe, inclusive and accessible, green and public spaces, in particular for women and children, older persons and persons with disabilities
- Target 16.2: End abuse, exploitation, trafficking and all forms of violence against and torture of children

The workshop sought to investigate how knowledge, information, data collection, measurement and monitoring can support strategies and innovations to prevent and effectively address the main drivers of poverty, exclusion and violence against children and adolescents. It had a particular focus on gathering information about 'invisible children', who were not covered or counted in standard surveys. Each of the 17 papers presented at the workshop made an effort to conceptualise the issues in different social contexts, explain them in causal terms, and find feasible solutions to the problems that affect the realization of the rights of an unacceptable number of children globally within the timeframe of the SDGs' targets. This book is based on a selection of the papers presented at the international workshop in New York selected by an academic committee. The authors of the various chapters in this book are tasked with explaining the meaning of 'inclusion' for children and adolescents within the context of the SDGs and to discuss how it could be better defined and measured in different contexts, in order to evaluate the progress being made towards achieving the targets most directly linked to children's well-being. The chapters in this book connect with the literature on inclusion and current policy challenges around poverty and inequities globally, regionally, nationally and locally to provide indepth analysis of rich empirical evidence from primarily low- and middle-income countries in Asia, Africa, Latin America and the Middle East.

Children and Adolescents in SDGs

The SDGs are designed to bring in changes for people, planet and prosperity and envisaged to have wide ranging impacts on future generations. Todays' children and adolescents are particularly important to the success of the SDGs as no sustainable development is possible without meeting their needs. In 2018, children (0–14 years) comprise 25.79 per cent of the global population or nearly 2 billion, and 42 per cent of the child population reside in low-income countries (World Bank, 2019). Children have more future years of life but they are also vulnerable to many risks while growing up and depend on adults for care and protection. Caring for children requires counting all children in social statistics and accounting for them in policies, as well as social progress plans that will protect these policies and provide the means for their realization. Several of the papers in this volume discuss how different surveys and census style approaches to sampling often miss the most vulnerable and furthest behind children (Muz et al.; Cocco-Klein et al.; Okubo et al.; and Chatterjee), which impedes progress on the issue of inclusion—a key goal of the SDGs—due to lack of high-quality, timely, reliable and disaggregated data on children and adolescents living in poverty.

Children's well-being has been mapped and monitored in statistical data and through indicators since at least the "State of the Child" reports published regularly from the 1940s (Ben-Arieh 2006; Ben-Arieh and Goerge 2001). Several of the SDG targets have indicators for children's wellbeing. 35 of these indicators are directly related to children and several more can be unpacked or modified to more directly include children. For example, SDG indicator 1.2.1 ('proportion of population living below the national poverty line, by sex and age') has been adapted by UNICEF to 'proportion of children living below the national poverty line' (UNICEF, 2018a, p. 104). UNICEF in its first comprehensive assessment on progress towards achieving the global SDG targets for children, *Progress for Every Child in the SDG Era*, focused on 44 indicators situated under 9 goals that are linked to key children's rights that are integral to the UNICEF's Strategic Plan 2018–2021: the right to good health, to learn, to be protected from violence and exploitation, to live in a safe and clean environment, and to have a fair chance to succeed in life. Their analysis reveals that most countries have insufficient data to assess whether they are on track to achieve each of the SDG targets, and where data are available, an overwhelming number of countries need to speed up progress (UNICEF, 2018a).

Some 1.2 billion adolescents aged 10–19 years make up 16 per cent of the world's population (UNICEF, 2019). Even though the proportion of adolescents in the global population is on the decline, the absolute numbers are increasing particularly in Asia where more than half the world's adolescents live. South Asia has the largest adolescent population, around 340 million, followed by East Asia and the Pacific with around 277 million. Most adolescents, up to the age of 18 years are protected under the Convention on the Rights of the Child. Yet the vulnerabilities and needs of adolescents typically fall between the cracks as many interventions for children focus on early years and adolescents age out of paediatric health care just as they are often unreached by programmes for adults (UNICEF, 2019). A review of mortality patterns reveal road injuries, AIDS-related causes, suicide, lower respiratory infections and interpersonal violence as the leading causes of death among adolescents and young people in 2012 (WHO, 2014). The challenges facing adolescents include, among others, limited opportunities to gain skills and confidence, barriers to education, unsafe living environments, and lack of sexual and reproductive health information and services (Gold, 2015). Girls are disproportionately affected by these challenges. The SDGs bring a renewed and expanded focus on adolescent health and well-being such as through disease specific interventions, improving road safety, greater alcohol and tobacco taxation, and increased access to education (WHO, 2015).

The UN Statistical Commission (UNSC) has established an Inter-Agency and Expert Group on SDG Indicators (IAEG-SDG) 'to develop and implement the global indicator framework for the goals and targets of the 2030 Agenda' (United Nations Statistics Division, 2019a). The IAEG has identified UNICEF as the custodian or co-custodian for 17 global SDG indicators related to children (see table 1). These include indicators covering birth and early years such as those related to stunting, wasting and overweight children, skilled attendant at birth, under five mortality, neo natal mortality, full vaccination coverage, early childhood development, birth registration; indicators catering to adolescent issues related to violence against girls and harmful practices such as sexual violence by intimate partner, sexual violence by non-intimate partner, early marriage, *Female Genital Mutilation*/Cutting (FGM/C); indicators related to child protection such as child labour, child discipline and sexual violence against children; and two indicators for environmental conditions that impact health and well-being of children and adolescents such as safely managed drinking water and safely managed sanitation and hygiene. These indicators represent an important but limited range of issues impacting children and adolescent's lives covered by the SDGs. UNICEF had itself stated that in addition to the 17 global SDG indicators for which UNICEF is custodian or co-custodian, it supports the collection and reporting of a wide range of other child-related indicators relevant for monitoring progress at the national, regional and global levels (UNICEF, 2018b). For example, in the Strategic Plan 2018–2021, UNICEF has included some of the indicators under the urban SDG (11) to achieve its goal of 'Every child lives in a safe and clean environment' both as impact and output indicators. Several of the papers in this book report on UNICEF supported mapping projects in different countries but by looking at a wider range of SDG indicators and their interdependence to secure positive outcomes for children and adolescents in poverty (see table 2).

Table 1: Child related SDGs under the custodianship of UNICEF and other agencies

SDG	Indicator	Custodian	Co-custodian
1	1.2.1 National poverty line	National governments	UNICEF, World Bank, UNDP
	1.2.2 Multi-dimensional poverty		
2	2.2.1 Stunting	UNICEF, WHO	World Bank
	2.2.2 Wasting/overweight		
3	3.1.1 Maternal mortality	WHO	
	3.1.2 Skilled attendant at birth	UNICEF	WHO, UNFPA
	3.2.1 Under-five mortality	UNICEF	WHO, UN Population Division, World Bank Group
	3.2.2 Neonatal mortality	UNICEF	WHO, UN Population Division, World Bank Group
	3.8.1 Universal health coverage	WHO	UNICEF, UNFPA, UN Population Division
	3.b.1 Full vaccination coverage	UNICEF, WHO	

4*	4.2.1 Early childhood development	UNICEF	UNESCO-UIS, OECD
5	5.2.1 Sexual violence by intimate partner	UNICEF, UN Women, UNFPA, WHO, UN Statistics Division	UNDP
	5.2.2 Sexual violence by non-intimate partner	UNICEF, UN Women, UNFPA, WHO, UN Statistics Division	UNDP
	5.3.1 Early marriage	UNICEF	WHO, UNFPA, UN Women, UN Population Division
	5.3.2 FGM/C	UNICEF	UNFPA, WHO
6	6.1.1 Safely managed drinking water	UNICEF, WHO	UNEP
	6.2.1 Safely managed sanitation and hygiene	UNICEF, WHO	UNEP
8	8.7.1 Child labour	UNICEF, ILO	
16	16.2.1 Child discipline	UNICEF	
	16.2.3 Sexual violence against children	UNICEF	UN Statistics Division, UNODC
	16.9.1 Birth registration	UNICEF	UN Statistics Division
17	17.19.2 Census, birth and death registration	UN Stats	UNFPA, CRVS group (includes UNICEF), UN Population Division

*Note: While UNESCO Institute for Statistics is the custodian agency of most of the SDG 4 indicators, UNICEF plays an active role in SDG4 monitoring such as for 4.2.1.
Source: UNICEF (2018a); UNICEF (2018c); and United Nations (2019).

Table 2: SDGs and Targets discussed in this book

Authors	SDG	Target	Context
Samantha Cocco-Klein and Alberto Minujin	11	**11.3** (inclusive and sustainable urbanization, and capacity for participatory, integrated and sustainable human settlements) **11.7** (universal access to safe, inclusive and accessible, green and public spaces, in particular for women and children)	An approach to measuring and monitoring child wellbeing and inequity in cities
Tomoo Okubo, Ana Maria Restrepo, Chirawat Poonsab, Christina Popivanova	11	**11.1** (adequate, safe and affordable housing and basic services, and slum upgrading) **11.2** (safe, affordable, accessible and sustainable transport systems for all, improved road safety)	Equity-focused SDG monitoring focusing on families and children living in urban impoverished areas
Sudeshna Chatterjee	6 10 11 16 17	**6.1** (access to safe drinking water) **6.2** (adequate, equitable sanitation and hygiene) **10.2** (social, economic and political inclusion of all) **11.1** (adequate, safe and affordable housing and basic services, and slum upgrading) **11.3** (inclusive and sustainable urbanization, and capacity for participatory, integrated and sustainable human settlements) **11.7** (universal access to safe, inclusive and accessible, green and public spaces, in particular for women and children) **16.2** (End abuse, exploitation, trafficking and all forms of violence against and torture of children**)** **16.7** (responsive, inclusive, participatory and representative decision-making) **17.18** (high quality, timely, reliable data disaggregated by income, gender, age, migratory status, location ...)	Ward level mapping with adolescents and adults focusing on vulnerable and often invisible urban populations to support participatory planning for the local implementation of SDGs to create a safe and inclusive city for adolescents

Authors	SDGs	Targets	Topic
Katie Hodgkinson, Nicky Pouw and Marielle L.J. Le Mat	10	10.2 (social, economic and political inclusion of all)	Inclusion in the context of youth in institutional care organisations and leaving care
Jennifer Seager, Sarah Baird, Joan Hamory Hicks, Sabina Faiz Rashid, Maheen Sultan, Workneh Yadete, and Nicola Jones	4 10 11 16	4.5 (equal access to education and vocational training for vulnerable groups including persons with disabilities) 4.a (upgraded educational facilities that are child, disability, and gender sensitive) 10.2 (social, economic and political inclusion of all) 11.7 (universal access to safe, inclusive and accessible, green and public spaces, in particular for women and children) 16.1 (reduce violence related deaths) 16.7 (responsive, inclusive, participatory and representative decision-making)	Invisibility and social exclusion of adolescents with disability within international development research, policy, and practice
Ernest Darkwah and Marguerite Daniel	1 3 8 10	1.1 (Eradicate extreme poverty) 1.2 (Reduce poverty by at least 50%) 1.3 (Implement social protection systems) 3.4 (Reduce mortality from non-communicable diseases and promote mental health) 8.5 (Full employment and decent work with equal pay) 10.2 (social, economic and political inclusion of all)	Influence of children's socio-cultural context on social exclusion in residential institutional care
Anna Carolina Machado and Charlotte Bilo	1	1.3 (implementation of nationally-appropriate social protection systems and measures for all)	Assessing the child-sensitivity of non-contributory social protection in MENA region, identifying features that can improve the potential of programmes to enhance children's well-being

Ismael Cid Martinez, Enrique Delamonica, Jose Luis Espinoza Delgado. Aristide Kielem, and Mohamed Obaidy	16	16.2 (End abuse, exploitation, trafficking and all forms of violence against and torture of children)	Relationship between child poverty and non-material quality of life elements (including violence)
Martin Hayes, Melissa Kelly, and Darcy Strouse	1 5 16	1.3 (implementation of nationally-appropriate social protection systems and measures for all) 5.2 (eliminate all forms of violence against women and girls) 16.2 (End abuse, exploitation, trafficking and all forms of violence against and torture of children) 16.4 (combat organized crime) 16.5 (reduce bribery and corruption) 16.10 (access to information and protection of fundamental freedoms)	Community-level child protection issues, including risks and protective factors and rural child protection systems for infants and young children

(Source: own work by the authors)

Poverty and inclusion in childhood

Poverty is not merely the absence of wealth. It also has many dimensions that affect children and adolescents in different ways than they affect adults. Poverty also impacts children in different ages differently; even within the same family the needs of a three-year-old child are different from the needs of a ten-year-old. Falling into poverty in childhood has far deeper consequences which can last a lifetime and are likely to be passed on to future generations, entrenching and even exacerbating inequality in society. A child will not get a second chance at a healthy start in life or better early years education if these opportunities were not provided at the right time (Ortiz et al., 2012).

The major objective of measuring child poverty is to highlight the plight of children so that disadvantaged children are considered a priority, especially in the creation and implementation of poverty reduction strategies (Minujin, 2012). Typically, multidimensional poverty measures the extent to which households and children within them are deprived of capabilities and opportunities, financial security as well as the actual access of children to goods and services that are fundamental for their full development and essential for the fulfilment of their rights under the Convention on the Rights of the Child (CRC).

> **Target 1.2:** By 2030, reduce at least by half the proportion of men, women and children of all ages living in poverty in all its dimensions according to national definitions.
>
> **Indicator 1.2.1:** Proportion of population living below the national poverty line, by sex and age
>
> **Indicator 1.2.2:** Proportion of men, women and children of all ages living in poverty in all its dimensions according to national definitions.
>
> **Target 10.2:** By 2030, empower and promote the social, economic and political inclusion of all, irrespective of age, sex, disability, race, ethnicity, origin, religion or economic or other status
>
> **Indicator 10.2.1** Proportion of people living below 50 per cent of median income, by age, sex and persons with disabilities,

It is interesting to note that SDG 1 and its Target (1.2), including indicators 1.2.1 and 1.2.2 which aim to end poverty in all its forms everywhere, are considered important to children; while SDG 10 that deals with inequality and more specifically Target 10.2 and indicator 10.2.1 are not considered a child-related indicator by UNICEF despite the strong interdependence and reinforcing effects of these two SDGs. In this volume Darkwah and Daniel highlight how social exclusion (SDG 10) of children raised in children's homes in Ghana, may reinforce alienation and mental health problems (SDG 3), which in turn would make it harder for them to find employment (SDG 8), thus increasing the likelihood they will live in poverty (SDG 1). Similarly, Hodgkinson, Pouw & Le Mat report on the social exclusion of youth from care in six countries suggest that young people with limited connections and prejudicial images struggle to access the job market and find independent accommodation after leaving care, which in turn limits their ability to continue with their education and socialise with their peers, further deepening their experiences of exclusion while keeping them in poverty.

The two indicators 1.2.1 and 1.2.2 are both based on monetary poverty though the indicator 1.2.2 aims to capture the multidimensional nature of poverty by assessing the extent to which households are materially deprived in different countries. In order to address children in poverty and to leave no one behind, it is very important to consider the array of indicators linked to child well-being in the context of rising income. The

UNICEF Briefing Note# 2 (UNICEF, 2018c) on Child Poverty points out the strong inter-connections between child wellbeing issues embedded in the SDGs and the pitfalls of not considering them while looking at rising incomes:

> Household income could surpass the poverty line because children beg in the streets or are engaged in hazardous work. Household income could increase because parents work extremely long hours, leaving children abandoned, neglected, and without any adult supervision, comfort, or guidance. Household income may be above the poverty line, yet if social services are unavailable (e.g. in rural areas) or unaffordable, it does no good to children who will still be left without education or health care (UNICEF, 2018C, p. 7).

Inequality is concerned with the unevenness in the distribution of resources and opportunities among individuals, among groups in a population and/or among countries (Yang, 2017). Inequality impacts many aspects of our lives including wealth and income status, health and education outcomes, experiences of gender and ethnicity, as well as access to employment and social services (Cook, 2012). As Sarah Cook (2012) points out, poverty and inequality are part of the same problem and high levels of inequality are an obstacle to poverty reduction as they make it difficult to reduce poverty even when economies are growing. The very conditions of inequality such as insecure living environments, limited citizenships, spatial disadvantage, limited work opportunities and social discrimination are deepening the poverty trap (Harper et al., 2012).

The Young Lives project, which is a longitudinal child poverty study in Ethiopia, India, Peru and Vietnam, showed that inequalities contribute to multiple disadvantages in children's development, with compounding effects on children's long-term outcomes. The children who are most at risk come from the poorest households, from rural locations, belong to an ethnic/language minority or low-caste group and have low levels of maternal (and paternal) education. Children from disadvantaged families quickly fall behind and gender-based inequalities become more significant as children get older. Inequalities not only impact children in early childhood but also during middle and later childhood with caregivers adjusting their expectations for girls and boys according to their employment or marriage prospects, as well as household composition, financial circumstances and vulnerability to shocks (Woodhead et al., 2012). Young Lives concluded that since the consequences of inequality are multidimensional, so too must be the response.

Policies for economic growth, equitable education and health, and effective social protection floors can contribute to reducing inequalities. These ideas are reiterated in *Rethinking Poverty: Report on the World Social Situation* (United Nations, 2010). This report claims that key policies for poverty reduction must include macroeconomic policies focused on the stability of real output, incomes and employment; universal social policies must focus on the determinants of asset and income inequality as well as poverty, such as social protection floor; and the participation, inclusion and voice of poor people must be heard and promoted. These ideas are embedded in the SDGs, particularly SDG 1 'End poverty in all its forms everywhere'; and Target 1.3, which calls for the implementation of nationally-appropriate social protection systems and measures for all to achieve substantial coverage of poor and vulnerable populations, including children, by 2030. As social protection plays an important role in reducing inequality, their interdependence on SDG 10 needs to be strongly articulated. Machado and Bilo emphasize in this volume that to reduce inequality in children's lives and improve their prospects for human development it is essential to impose conditions of convergence and reinforcement. In their chapter, Machado and Bilo investigate the importance of social protection in poverty reduction in the Middle East and North Africa (MENA) and conclude that programmes are often not large enough to reach all vulnerable children in a context where an estimated one in four children suffers from acute multidimensional poverty.

Importance of Cities in the SDGs to end poverty and exclusion

By 2050, 70 per cent of the world's population will be living in cities. As higher income countries are already highly urbanized, most of the world's urban growth is now expected in less wealthy regions of the world, making child poverty and exclusion an increasingly urban phenomenon. The urban population of the world's two poorest regions, South Asia and Sub-Saharan Africa, is expected to double by 2030 (United Nations, 2014). Cities are recognized as the primary engines of economic growth and development. But over one billion people are living in slums throughout the world's cities. Though many argue that slums are not the only environments where the urban poor live, in the absence of well-defined spatial markers of deprivation, slums remain a good proxy for urban deprivation and inequality that greatly affect children of the urban poor including higher risk of ill-health, injury and pre-mature death (Jorgensen & Rice, 2012). The Sustainable Development Goals (SDGs) present a new opportunity to address urban exclusion by measuring and monitoring child wellbeing and inequity in cities as is discussed in detail by Cocco-Klein and Minujin in this volume.

Urban development is typically seen as the process of organizing a city's growth and structuring/restructuring of human settlements. Rising urban populations and expanding slums in fast urbanizing cities of the global south pose multidimensional challenges to formal urban development processes ranging across planning, investments, management and implementation. The threat of climate change further compounds the problem. The price of failure is too high; failure to provide adequate, safe and affordable housing and basic services and to upgrade slums (Target 11.1) as well as failure to generate the jobs necessary to improve livelihoods, may result in deepening inequalities, exclusion, and violence. For cities to reap the benefits of the post-2015 development agenda, 'business as usual' models of urban development may leave some people behind. Recognizing the essential role that urbanization must play in sustainable development, the SDGs included a standalone urban goal instead of treating urbanization as a "cross-cutting" issue. By getting urban development right, cities can substantially contribute to the economic, social and environmental aspects of sustainable development. It is believed that sound urban development will accelerate progress towards achieving SDGs, including the end of extreme poverty (Revi & Rosenzweig, 2014). However, a key challenge for inclusive urbanization is capturing data on vulnerable families and children who are very often invisible to formal planning processes. The NUA recommends creating, promoting and enhancing open, user friendly data

The Urban Goal in SDG

SDG 11: Make cities and human settlements inclusive, safe, resilient and sustainable

Direct mention of Children

11.2 By 2030, provide access to safe, affordable, accessible and sustainable transport systems for all, improving road safety, notably by expanding public transport, with special attention to the needs of those in vulnerable situations, women, children, persons with disabilities and older persons

11.7 By 2030, provide universal access to safe, inclusive and accessible, green and public spaces, in particular for women and children, older persons and persons with disabilities

platforms for sharing relevant knowledge among all tiers of government and other stakeholders. Okubo et al. discuss this in the context the Bangkok Small Community Multiple Indicator Cluster Surveys (BSC MICS) that was specifically designed to capture data from and about urban poor families who are otherwise invisible in large national survey analyses and thus also remain hidden from policy makers.

SDG 11 implicitly recognizes the need for safe, inclusive and resilient cities as the foundations for sustainable urban development. Children are mentioned twice: in Target 11.2 (convenient access to public transport), an important indicator particularly for adolescents given that road injuries are a major cause of death for this group (WHO, 2014); and Target 11.7 (access to safe, inclusive and green public spaces) with two indicators looking at the quantity of public space in cities for use by all age groups, and the instances of sexual harassment in public spaces in a year. Public open spaces such as parks, boulevards, gardens, playgrounds and streets are vital spaces for a community's social and economic life and for affording play, recreation and leisure activities for children and adolescents. Even though data from 231 cities in 2014 show 59% of the built-up area in cities across the world as urbanized open spaces (United Nations Statistics Division, 2019b) including streets, not all open spaces are safe spaces for children. Chatterjee's chapter in this volume strongly makes this case through safe and unsafe space mapping with adolescents in Kolkata. Public sexual harassment in public spaces is a major reason why girls and women find cities unsafe and to that effect monitoring the indicator 11.7.2 will be critical to creating safe inclusive cities.

Several other targets and indicators under SDG 11 have positive consequences for children even though children are not explicitly mentioned in them. These include:

Participatory planning and management: In the 1990s, with the almost universal ratification of the United Nations Convention on the Rights of the Child (1990) and a series of iconic global conferences such as the UN Conference on Environment and Development (also called Earth Summit) in 1992 and the Habitat Agenda coming out of the second UN Conference on Human Settlements in 1996 (also called the City Summit) a new vision of the urban child as an active agent emerged (Chawla & van Vliet, 2017). The message was clear: children and youth are a major demographic group with inalienable rights; they should be involved in participatory programs to improve their environment, including the urban environment. The Convention on the Rights of the Child specifies that children have a right to seek and communicate information and to express their views on all matters that concern them. As the quality of the place where children and adolescents live undeniably affects their lives and well-being, they must be involved in planning and shaping them. The New Urban Agenda (NUA, 2016), which sets out the guidelines for implementing the urban aspects of the SDGs, also recommends capacity building and participation of all stakeholders including children and youth in urban decision-making (NUA 15: *We will promote capacity development initiatives to empower and strengthen skills and abilities of women and girls, children and youth, older persons and persons with disabilities, indigenous peoples and local communities, as well as persons in vulnerable situations for shaping governance processes, engaging in dialogue, and promoting and protecting human rights and anti-discrimination, to ensure their effective participation in urban and territorial development decision-making.*)

Disaster: In 2011, the United Nations International Strategy for Disaster Reduction (UNISDR) called children and youth the largest group affected by disasters (UNISDR, 2011). Children and youth are recognized as critical stakeholders to support the implementation of the Sendai Framework that is referenced in Target 11b.

Targets and indicators with implied well-being of children in urban goal

11.3: By 2030, enhance inclusive and sustainable urbanization and capacity for participatory, integrated and sustainable human settlement planning and management in all countries

11.3.2: Proportion of cities with a direct participation structure of civil society in urban planning and management that operate regularly and democratically.

11.5: By 2030, significantly reduce the number of deaths and the number of people affected and substantially decrease the direct economic losses relative to global gross domestic product caused by disasters, including water-related disasters, with a focus on protecting the poor and people in vulnerable situations.

11.5.1: Number of deaths, missing persons and persons affected by disaster per 100,000 people

11.6: By 2030, reduce the adverse per capita environmental impact of cities, including by paying special attention to air quality and municipal and other waste management.

11.6.1: Proportion of urban solid waste regularly collected and with adequate final discharge out of total urban solid waste generated, by cities

11.6.2: Annual mean levels of fine particulate matter (e.g. PM2.5 and PM10) in cities (population weighted)

Safe drinking water, solid waste management and air quality: UNICEF is custodian of two indicators for environmental conditions that impact health and well-being of children and adolescents such as safely managed drinking water (indicator 6.1.1) and safely managed sanitation and hygiene (Target 11.6.1). However, in the context of worsening air quality across the world, and in particular in cities, the indicator 11.6.2 'Annual mean levels of fine particulate matter (e.g. PM2.5 and PM10) in cities (population weighted)' was included in the 44 child-related indicators across five dimensions of child rights underpinning UNICEF's Strategic Plan 2018–2021.

Even though Goal 11 is considered to be the urban goal, given the social, economic and environmental dimensions of sustainability as well as of safety and inclusion, for SDG 11 to succeed in integrating all these dimensions, experts believe it has to be interlinked with other urban-critical SDGs such as poverty (SDG 1), health (SDG 3), and inequality (SDG 10); water and sanitation (SDG6) and energy (SDG7); employment and economic growth (SDG8) and infrastructure (SDG9); sustainable consumption and production (SDG12) and climate change (SDG13); and accountable and inclusive institutions (SDG16) (Rudd et al., 2018).

Social and Child Protection

The SDGs directly address the issue of child protection through the inclusion of target 16.2: *End abuse, exploitation, trafficking and all forms of violence against and torture of children.* Unlike the MDGs, the SDGs firmly put key child protection issues including violence on the development agenda (Buchard n.d.). Know Violence in Childhood, an interdisciplinary global learning initiative, reveals that at least three out of four of the world's children—an estimated 1.7 billion—had experienced some form of inter-personal violence in a previous year. This estimate includes child homicide, violent discipline (or corporal punishment) at the hands of caregivers, peer violence (including bullying and physical fights), and sexual and physical violence experienced mostly by adolescent girls. This implies that almost no children, irrespective of where they live in the global North or South experience violence-free childhoods (Know Violence in Childhood, 2017). All forms of violence have harmful effects on children and their families, the communities and societies in which they live with often long-term societal consequences that persist beyond the immediate experience. It could affect every aspect of a child's life, affecting her or his health and education, and restricting future life opportunities (Know Violence in Childhood, 2017).

Violence is considered to be inseparably linked to poverty and inequality (Moser & McIlwaine, 2014). Family violence has been seen as most common among low-income groups and as the possible contributor to higher rates of child abuse (Akmatov, 2011). However, others have refuted this claim and suggested that even though poverty and inequality are harmful in all kinds of ways for children and families, they are at best mediating factors that explain their association with maltreatment (Bartlett, 2018). From another angle, Ismael Cid Martinez, Enrique Delamonica, Jose Luis Espinoza Delgado. Aristide Kielem, and Mohamed Obaidy analyse data on children's quality of life, merging information on child poverty (material deprivation) and non-material deprivations such as children suffering disciplinary violence at home (emotional or physical, including severe physical violence) as well as neglect and lack of interaction with parents.

Social protection is fundamental to preventing and reducing poverty for children and families and addressing inequality. Increasing evidence shows that social protection has important outcomes for children's lives, ranging from poverty reduction to improved education and health outcomes and, in general, realizing children's rights (Roelen, 2015). A new approach, child-sensitive social protection, suggests responding to children's vulnerabilities in any social protection programme even if children are not the intended recipients. Anna Carolina Machado and Charlotte Bilo in their chapter discuss the findings of a joint research programme on child-sensitive non-contributory social protection programmes in the MENA region where an estimated one in four children suffers from acute multidimensional poverty. The MENA region has also recently seen a dramatic increase in the number of internally displaced persons and refugees; conflicts and violence are widespread in parts of the region, leaving millions of children in need of humanitarian assistance. Children in humanitarian settings are presumed to face an increased risk of exposure to child protection issues due to the disruption of the functioning of their community or society (Stark & Landis, 2016) such as during a refugee crisis. Machado and Bilo report how in some countries, such as Iraq, Syria, Turkey and Yemen, humanitarian cash assistance programmes have been designed to make use of parts of national social protection systems. Yet, most social protection programmes in MENA are not accessible to refugees, leaving vulnerable families largely dependent on temporary humanitarian support (Machado et al., 2018). Machado & Bilo argue in their chapter in this volume that national social protection systems can respond effectively in times of crisis through the inclusion of shock-responsive measures and through the establishment of appropriate regulatory frameworks that ensure access to a baseline level of social protection by refugees to minimize potential adverse consequences for the most vulnerable children.

SDGs and Violence

Target 5.2 Eliminate all forms of violence against women and girls

Target 5.3 Eliminate all harmful practices, such as child, early and forced marriage, and female genital mutilation

Target 16.1 Significantly reduce all forms of violence and related death rates everywhere

Target 16.2 End abuse, exploitation, trafficking and all forms of violence against children

Risk factors in violence prevention that are targeted in SDGs include:

Poverty reduction and social protection systems and measures for all (SDG 1)

Mental health and wellbeing, and the prevention and treatment of substance abuse (SDG 3)

Safe, non-violent, inclusive and effective learning environments (SDG 4)

Ending all forms of discrimination against all women and girls everywhere (SDG 5)

Social, economic and political inclusion of all and greater equality (SDG 10)

Safe housing & urbanization (SDG 11)

Rule of law and justice for all (SDG 16)

The United Nations Convention on the Rights of the Child (UNCRC 1989) promotes protecting children and adolescents from all forms of violence, abuse, exploitation, cruelty, and neglect, while also providing protection from abuse in the criminal justice system as well as from manmade and natural emergencies. Keeping children safe from harm is both a private and public responsibility. Both preventive and responsive child protection measures are the responsibility of various sectors. Increasingly, a systems approach is being used to create a framework for child protection requiring both prevention and response involving different sectors such as health, education, social welfare, justice and security as well as civil society (NGOs, private sectors, community) (UNICEF, 2008). This approach to violence prevention is adopted in the SDGs.

In this book, the chapter by Martin Hayes, Melissa Kelly, and Darcy Strouse discusses both prevention and response strategies for the local level action planning based on the findings of their study in rural Kenya.

Structure of the book

The book is divided into three sections that respectively discuss the following issues:

1. **Mapping and monitoring urban communities, children and adolescents in poverty:** The challenges of urbanization in deepening inequality and deprivation and the ongoing efforts across the world to map and monitor the progress on the SDGs for urban children and adolescents in poverty
2. **Making invisible children and youth visible:** The deep challenges of addressing social exclusion by making invisible children and adolescents such as disabled children, children and adolescents in state care visible for greater societal integration, inclusion and development
3. **Social and Child Protection, Child Well-being**: The challenges for inclusion through social protection and child protection for children and adolescents living in multi-dimensional poverty who are especially vulnerable to abuse, exploitation, trafficking and all forms of violence.

Each of the three sections includes three chapters, whose themes and concerns are briefly outlined below.

1. **Mapping and monitoring urban communities, children and adolescents in poverty**

In **Monitoring Child Wellbeing and Inequality in Cities: A model developed in Colombia,** Samantha Cocco-Klein and Alberto Minujin discuss child poverty and exclusion in cities, as more than 1 billion children now live in cities and towns—a figure set to rise in coming decades. In this chapter they examine an approach to measuring and monitoring child wellbeing and inequity in cities that was developed by Equity for Children in Colombia, which potentially provides a model and lessons for the SDGs. The approach rests on two foundations. The first is disaggregating local data to reveal the often-hidden inequities experienced by urban children and families. The second is social accountability, fostered through the active engagement of urban communities with local authorities. The ultimate objective is to spark policies and programs for children that are sensitive to the local context. They illustrate the building blocks of the approach, while also taking a critical look at the challenges and lessons learned in using evidence to incentivize government action.

In **Capturing children left behind in urban poor communities: Lessons for equity-focused SDG monitoring from the Bangkok Small Community MICS, Thailand**, Tomoo Okubo, Ana Maria Restrepo, Chirawat Poonsab, Christina Popivanova introduce a case study where a standard MICS survey was tailored to capture data on some of the most vulnerable and often invisible groups of children and women living in urban poor communities in Bangkok. During 2015–2016, MICS-5 was conducted nationally in Thailand. The Bangkok Small Community MICS (BSC-MICS) with a separate sampling framework and analysis was carried out in urban poor areas in Bangkok at the same time in order to enumerate the families who would otherwise not have been included in the national analysis. The BSC-MICS used over 80 indicators and collected information from 2,707 households including data on children under 5 years of age, and women and men aged 15–49 years. This paper analyses the results from the BSC MICS and compares them with the national MICS and highlights the specific challenges families face in the more disadvantaged areas of Bangkok.

In **A Safe and Inclusive City for Adolescents in Kolkata: Lessons from a participatory mapping of an urban ward in India,** Sudeshna Chatterjee writes about a ward (the smallest administration unit for local governance decentralization in an Indian city) level participatory mapping led by UNICEF India and technical partner Action for Children's Environments (ACE) with the cooperation of the Kolkata Municipal Corporation (KMC). This is the first phase of an urban program called "A Safe and Inclusive City for Adolescents in Kolkata" that is being implemented by local NGO partners. The purpose of the mapping was to collect and analyse disaggregated local data on several indicators based on the SDGs to understand the risks and vulnerabilities and everyday challenges in adolescents' lives across nine dimensions/These include: governance and planning; environment; safety and security; protection; health; education; play and recreation; and participation and empowerment. The mapping was designed to be participatory, involving adolescents and adults residing in the slums and other vulnerable pockets of Kolkata Municipal Corporation Ward no. 26. This was an attempt to understand inclusion of vulnerable populations in the local implementation of the SDGs. The chapter presents the findings of the ward level mapping, analyses them against the commitments in the SDGs and highlights the drivers of poverty, exclusion and violence against children and adolescents in an urban ward in Kolkata, India.

2. Making invisible children and youth visible

In **Exploring and addressing the exclusion of "invisible" youth: Applying a relational framework to SDG 10.2,** Katie Hodgkinson, Nicky Pouw and Marielle Le Mat discuss inclusion in the context of youth in institutional care organisations and leaving care. This is a relatively invisible group in many countries, largely missing in governmental and institutional statistics and agendas. This is despite evidence that these young people are particularly vulnerable and consistently have poorer outcomes in education, employment, housing and social integration. The Sustainable Development Goals' (SDGs) call to 'leave no one behind' makes the visibility and inclusion of youth from care a pertinent issue. This chapter presents the research findings of a two-year study on the social exclusion of youth from care in six countries: Côte d'Ivoire, Guatemala, Indonesia, Kenya, Malawi and the Netherlands. A relational framework is used to analyse the data. The authors recommend developing socialisation activities for youth, whilst still in care, involving relatives and caregivers in providing guidance and support to care leavers, and building constructive inter-connections with local employers and official institutions and organisations that have a stake in the societal integration of young people from care.

In **Finding the Hard to Reach: A Mixed Methods Approach to Including Adolescents with Disabilities in Survey Research,** Jennifer Seager, Sarah Baird, Joan Hamory Hicks, Sabina Faiz Rashid, Maheen Sultan, Workneh Yadete, and Nicola Jones discuss the invisibility and social exclusion of adolescents with disability. Both the Convention on the Rights of Persons with Disabilities (CRPD) and the SDGs, with its declared commitment to 'leave no one behind', have contributed to a greater focus on persons with disabilities, but adolescents with disabilities are rarely visible within international development research, policy, and practice. The chapter reports on the Gender and Adolescence: Global Evidence (GAGE) programme that used a multi-faceted approach to identify and include adolescents with disabilities, who are often hidden due to stigma and lack of accommodation in public spaces, in its baseline surveys in Bangladesh and Ethiopia during 2017–2018. After presenting the strategies implemented and challenges faced in identifying and working with adolescents with disabilities, this chapter presents findings on their experiences across the six GAGE capability areas. These findings contribute to the limited evidence base on how disability shapes the daily lives of adolescents.

In **The role of context in social exclusion of children: Lessons from children's homes in Ghana,** Ernest Darkwah and Marguerite Daniel discuss the social exclusion of children in residential care institutions in Ghana. The authors used qualitative exploratory techniques to gather and analyse data from residential child care workers on local perceptions and reactions to children in residential care to generate insights into their inclusion/exclusion chances. They found that the general perceptions of the children are negative often due to negative public perceptions of international child rights principles such as the United Nations Conventions on the Rights of the Child, which differ from local norms, but are strictly followed in raising them. Participant accounts also suggested that children in residential care face social rejection, alienation and stigma stemming from negative local reactions to their tendency to insist on their rights when interacting with other members of the local community, especially adults. They conclude that the clash between local socio-cultural expectations of children and the principles of child rights followed in raising children in residential care expose such children to higher risks of social exclusion within local communities. They consequently recommend to hold discussions on more effective ways of blending local norms and child rights, aimed at driving acceptance of rights-oriented child care in local communities and the increased inclusion chances of children.

3. Social and Child Protection, Child Well-being

In **Child-sensitive Non-contributory Social Protection in the MENA Region,** Anna Carolina Machado and Charlotte Bilo address the importance of social protection in poverty reduction in the Middle East and

North Africa (MENA), where an estimated one in four children suffers from acute multidimensional poverty. The chapter presents the findings of a joint research programme on child-sensitive non-contributory social protection undertaken by the International Policy Centre for Inclusive Growth (IPC-IG) and the UNICEF Middle East and North Africa Regional Office (MENARO). More than 100 non-contributory social protection programmes were mapped and classified, including: cash and in-kind transfers; school feeding programmes; public works programmes (cash-for-work—CFW); educational fee waivers; housing benefits; programmes facilitating access to health. The limited availability of data in MENA presents a great challenge for any incidence analysis of social protection schemes. An assessment based on the comparison between the child coverage estimations and the number of poor children in any given country shows that programmes are often not large enough to reach all vulnerable children.

In **Child Poverty And Quality Of Life: Material and Non-Material Domains of Well-Being,** Ismael Cid Martinez, Enrique Delamonica, Jose Luis Espinoza Delgado. Aristide Kielem, and Mohamed Obaidy argue that children's well-being and quality of life is comprised of two conceptually distinct groups of elements. The first corresponds with material deprivation and is associated with child poverty. The second is associated with non-material deprivations, i.e. problems or child rights violations which are not the direct result of lacking economic goods and services. One of these non-material elements is violence, in particular disciplinary violence at home which includes emotional/psychological violence as well as mild and severe physical violence. Most quality of life indices deal with national aggregates, not individual level data. Pursuing an innovative turn, the authors analyse the most recent Multiple Indicator Cluster Surveys (MICS) data for a few countries across all developing regions to estimate jointly (i.e. for the same child) the overall impact of material deprivations—such as lack of food, water, or proper housing—as well as the overall non-material deprivations, which includes physical punishment and/or psychological aggression by caregivers, neglect, and unhappiness.

In **Child Protection Risks and Protective Factors of Vulnerable Young Children through the Study of Community-Based Child Protection (CBCP) in rural Western Kenya**, Martin Hayes, Melissa Kelly, and Darcy Strouse report on ChildFund International studies that examined the community-level child protection issues in Kenya, including risks and protective factors and child protection systems for infants and young children (IYC). Despite the studies initially intending to focus on IYC, the authors acknowledge that much of the data in this paper includes the situation of children older than five years of age, as families tended to talk about children across age groups. The chapter discusses the stresses experienced by families and the corresponding impact on children, the roles of informal and formal child protective service providers and the barriers that prevent children and their families from accessing services. The qualitative findings of this study supplement quantitative research from Kenya's Violence against Children's 2010 National Survey which revealed high percentages of children nationwide experiencing various forms of violence, while very few were able to access protective services. The local level action planning based on the findings of this study included key thematic areas of action: integrated parenting education (including child development, health, and child protection); community sensitization on existing child protection services for IYC; activating non-functional community-based structures for child protection; improved coordination of child protection services; and capacity building. A critical component planning was to strengthen local child protection referral and service provision networks and mechanisms of accountability.

References

Akmatov, M. K. (2011). Child abuse in 28 developing and transitional countries—results from the Multiple Indicator Cluster Surveys', *International Journal of Epidemiology*, Volume 40, Issue 1, pp. 219–227,

Alvaredo, F., Chancel, L., Piketty, T., Saez, E., & Zucman, G. (2018). *PART V—TACKLING ECONOMIC INEQUALITY*. (Retrieved from World Inequality Database: https://wir2018.wid.world/part-5.html) (Accessed May 2020)

Bartlett, S. (2018). *Children and the Geography of Violence: Why space and place matter.* Oxon and New York: Routledge.

Ben-Arieh, A. (2006). 'Is the study of the "State of Our Children" changing? Revisiting after five years'. *Children and Youth Services Review*, Vol. 28 No. 7, pp. 799–811.

Ben-Arieh, A., Goerge, R. (2001). 'Beyond the numbers: How do we monitor the state of our children'. *Children and Youth Services Review*, Vol. 23 No. 8, pp. 603–631.

Chawla, L., & van Vliet, W. (2017). 'Children's Rights to Child-Friendly Cities'. In Ruck, M.D., Peterson-Badali, and M, Freeman, M. (eds) *Handbook of Children's Rights: Global Multidisciplinary Perspectives,* New York: Routledge, pp. 533–549.

Cook, S. (2012). 'Combating Poverty and Inequality: Structural Change, Social Policy and Politics'. In: Ortiz, I., Daniels, L.M. & Engilbertsdóttir, S. (eds.) *Child Poverty and Inequality: New Perspectives:* pp. 69–78, New York: United Nations Children's Fund (UNICEF), Division of Policy and Practice.

Gold, S. (2015). *'How Do We Make the 2030 Agenda Meaningful for Adolescents and Youth?'* (International Women's Health Coalition. Retrieved from: https://iwhc.org/2015/09/how-do-we-make-the-2030-agenda-meaningful-for-adolescents-and-youth/). (Accessed May 2020)

Harper, C., Alder, H., and Pereznieto, P. (2012). 'Escaping Poverty Traps: Children and Chronic Poverty.' In: Ortiz, I., Daniels, L.M. & Engilbertsdóttir, S. (eds). *Child Poverty and Inequality: New Perspectives*, New York: United Nations Children's Fund (UNICEF), Division of Policy and Practice, pp. 48–56.

Jorgensen, A., and Rice, J. (2012). 'Urban slums and children's health in less-developed countries' *American Sociological Association* Vol. 28 No. 1, pp. 103–116

Know Violence in Childhood. (2017). *Ending Violence in Childhood: Overview.* Global Report 2017. Available online at: https://resourcecentre.savethechildren.net/node/12380/pdf/global_report_2017_ending_violence_in_childhood_overview.pdf (Acessed May 2020)

Le Blanc, D. (2015). 'Towards Integration at Last? The Sustainable Development Goals as a Network of Targets.' *Sustainable Development* Vol. 23 No. 3, pp. 176–87.

Machado, A. C., Bilo, C., Soares, F. V., and Osorio, R. G. (2018). *Overview of Non-contributory Social Protection Programs in the Middle East and North Africa (MENA) Region through a Child and Equity Lens.* International Policy Centre for Inclusive Growth and UNICEF Middle East and North Africa Regional Office (Retrieved from: https://ipcig.org/pub/eng/JP18_Overview_of_Non_contributory_Social_Protection_Programsrs_in_MENA.pdf) (Accessed May 2020)

Minujin A., (2012). 'Making the Case for Child Poverty'. In: I. Ortiz, L. M. Daniels and S. Engilbertsdóttir, (eds). *Child Poverty and Inequality: New Perspectives,* New York: United Nations Children's Fund (UNICEF), Division of Policy and Practice, pp.: 14–17.

Moser C and McIlwaine C. (2014). New frontiers in twenty-first century urban conflict and violence, *Environment and Urbanization* 26 (2), pp. 331–344.

Ortiz, I., Daniels, L. M. & Engilbertsdóttir, S., (2012). 'Introduction'. In: I. Ortiz, L. M. Daniels & S. Engilbertsdóttir, (eds.) *Child Poverty and Inequality: New Perspectives.* New York, United Nations Children's Fund (UNICEF), Division of Policy and Practice, pp. 1–13.

Revi, A., and Rosenzweig, C. (2014). *Why the World Needs an Urban SDG?* (Retrieved from sustainabledevelopment.un.org: https://sustainabledevelopment.un.org/content/documents/5448revi.pdf) Accessed May 2020.

Roelen, K. (2015). *Commentaries.* (Retrieved from socialprotection-humanrights.org: https://socialprotection-humanrights.org/expertcom/challenging-assumptions-from-child-focused-to-child-sensitive-social-protection) Accessed May 2020

Rudd, A., Simon, D., Cardama, M., Birch, E. L., and Revi, A. (2018). 'The UN, the Urban Sustainable Development Goal, and the New Urban Agenda'. In Elmqvist, T., Bai, X., Frantzeskaki, N., Griffith, C., Maddox, D., McPhearson, T., and Watkins M. (Eds.) *Urban Planet: Knowledge towards Sustainable Cities*, Cambridge: Cambridge University Press, pp. 180–196.

Satterthwaite, D. (2018), *Transforming aid for urban areas* [Blog post September 4 2018]. (Retrieved from https://www.iied.org/transforming-aid-for-urban-areas) (Accessed May 2020)

Stark L, and Landis D. (2016). 'Violence against children in humanitarian settings: a literature review of population-based approaches'. *Soc Sci Med*. Vol. 152, pp. 125–37.

The United Nations. (1989). *Convention on the Rights of the Child*. Treaty Series, 1577, 3.

UNICEF (2016). *The State of the World's Children 2016: A fair chance for every child.* New York: Division of Communication, UNICEF.

UNICEF. (2017). *The State of the World's Children 2017: Children in a Digital World.* New York: Division of Communication, UNICEF.

UNICEF. (2018a). *Progress for Every Child in the SDG Era.* (Retrieved from UNICEF Data: https://data.unicef.org/resources/progress-for-every-child-2018/) (Accessed May 2020)

UNICEF. (2018b). *Briefing notes on SDG global indicators related to children.* (Retrieved from UNICEF.org: https://data.unicef.org/resources/sdg-global-indicators-related-to-children/) (Accessed May 2020)

UNICEF. (2018c). Briefing note #2 Child poverty: Briefing notes on SDG global indicators related to children. (Retrieved from UNICEF Data: Monitoring the situation of children and women: https://data.unicef.org/resources/sdg-global-indicators-related-to-children/). (Accessed May 2020)

UNICEF. (2019). *Adolescent demographics.* (Retrieved from https://data.unicef.org/: https://data.unicef.org/topic/adolescents/demographics/) (Accessed May 2020)

United Nations (2010). *Rethinking Poverty: Report on the World Social Situation 2010*. New York: UNDESA.

United Nations International Strategy for Disaster Reduction (UNISDR) (2011). *UNISDR says the young are the largest group affected by disasters.* (Retrieved from http://www.unisdr.org/archive/22742) (Accessed May 2020)

United Nations Statistics Division (UNSD). (2019a). *IAEG-SDGs.* (Retrieved from https://unstats.un.org/sdgs/: https://unstats.un.org/sdgs/iaeg-sdgs/). (Accessed May 2020)

United Nations Statistics Division (UNSD). (2019b). *Goal 11*. UN Statistics (Retrieved from: https://unstats.un.org/sdgs/report/2018/Goal-11/) (Accessed May 2020)

United Nations. (2019). *SDG Indicators.* United Nations Statistics Division (Retrieved from: https://unstats.un.org/sdgs/dataContacts/) (Accessed May 2020)

United Nations. (n.d.). *Transforming our world: the 2030 Agenda for Sustainable Development*. Sustainable Development Goals Knowledge Platform (Retrieved from: https://sustainabledevelopment.un.org/post2015/transformingourworld) (Accessed May 2020)

United Nations. (2014). *World Urbanization Prospects: The 2014 Revision*. New York: United Nations, Department of Economic and Social Affairs.

Weitz, N., Carlsen, H., Nilsson, M., & Skånberg, K. (2018). 'Towards systemic and contextual priority setting for implementing the 2030 Agenda'. *Sustainability Science* Vol. 13 No. 2, pp. 531–548.

Woodhead, M., Dornan, P., and Murray, H. (2012). *What inequality means for children: evidence from young lives*. Background paper for the Global Thematic Consultation "Addressing Inequalities" in the post-2015 Development Agenda. New York: UNICEF & UN Women (Retrieved from https://oro.open.ac.uk/35650/1/What%20Inequality%20Means%20for%20Children_corrected_17Dec2012.pdf) (Accessed May 2020)

World Bank. (2019). *Population ages 0–14 (% of total population)*. (Retrieved from data.worldbank.org: https://data.worldbank.org/indicator/SP.POP.0014.TO.ZS?display=3Dgr3D) (Accessed May 2020)

World Health Organization. (2015). *Health in 2015: from MDGs to SDGs*. Geneva: World Health Organization. Retrieved from https://www.who.int/gho/publications/mdgs-sdgs/MDGs-SDGs2015_chapter4_snapshot_adolescent_health.pdf) (Accessed May 2020)

World Health Organization. (2014), *Global Health Estimates (GHE) 2012*. Geneva: WHO.

Yang, L. (2017). 'The relationship between poverty and inequality: Concepts and measurement'. *CASE Discussion Paper No. 205*, Centre for Analysis of Social Exclusion, LSE, London.

PART I

MAPPING AND MONITORING URBAN COMMUNITIES AND ADOLESCENTS IN POVERTY

Monitoring Child Wellbeing and Inequality in Cities: A Model Developed in Colombia

Samantha Cocco-Klein[4] and Alberto Minujin[5]
Equity for Children/Equidad Para La Infancia[6]

Introduction

Global child poverty and exclusion is increasingly an urban phenomenon. Over half of the world's population, including more than 1 billion children, now live in cities and towns. As compares with their rural peers, urban children can at first appear to benefit from better socioeconomic conditions. However, when the urban data is disaggregated, greater income inequality emerges. Children and adolescents living in poor urban areas of Latin America, Africa and Asia-Pacific, are often unable to access the services and quality of living that the urban environment is expected to facilitate.

Motivated by the urban face of child poverty and exclusion, Equity for Children developed an approach to measuring and addressing child well-being and inequality in cities. Done in partnership with Red Latinoamericana por Ciudades y Territorios Justos, Democráticos y Sustentables, a civil society network that promotes quality of life in Latin American cities, the approach rests on two foundations. The first foundation is data; disaggregating local data to reveal the inequities experienced by children and families. As noted by Alberto Minujin, 'childhood inequities form part of an unseen and sometimes concealed reality. Documenting and demonstrating the extent of these inequalities can prompt action and ultimately change' (Nuestra Cordoba, Fundacion Arcor, 2016).

The second foundation is social accountability, fostered through the active participation of urban families and communities. Social accounta-

---

4   Senior Advisor, Equity for Children. PhD Candidate in Public and Urban Policy at the Milano School of Policy, Management and Environment, The New School
5   Executive Director, Equity for Children. Professor at the Studley Graduate Program in International Affairs, The New School
6   The authors thank Veronica Bagnoli from Equidad para la infancia for her insights on the Como Vamos initiative. We extend a special thank you to the Colombian Como Vamos network, Corona Foundation for their partnership and very especially to Angela Escallon Emiliani for her permanent support and participation on the experience in Colombia and her commitment in realizing child equity and rights.

bility is generally understood to be a bottom-up approach to improving government accountability—using civic engagement to stimulate improved provision of public goods and services (Malena et al., 2004). The data generated through the Equity for Children system generates public awareness of inequities, through public platforms and media coverage— and provides an evidence base for advocacy with local government.

This article describes Equity for Children's experience of implementing the approach in Colombia, as well as more recent efforts to implement the method in Argentina and Nigeria.[7] We illustrate the building blocks of the approach, from establishing partnerships with local research institutions and non-governmental organizations, to identifying and disaggregating a wide range of data on child and family wellbeing, and actively engaging with communities and policymakers. The article presents the process of developing indicators and data that reflect the global commitments articulated in the CRC and SDGs, while remaining relevant to local contexts and needs.

The article also takes a critical look at the challenges involved in implementing the model and rendering its applicability to it to new contexts. A salient challenge is the availability of local data on children, which is further complicated by a lack of data on urban environments. We share the different solutions participating cities have put forward, which provide lessons to improve progress tracking and reporting for the SDGs. Effective social accountability is also a challenge, and we look at the factors needed to translate an awareness of child inequities into policy commitments.

Background

Rapid urbanization is changing the nature and shape of poverty and exclusion in developing countries. Over half of the world's people—including more than one billion children—now live in cities and towns. These figures are set to increase in the coming years, with the lion's share of urban growth occurring in developing countries. By 2030, the majority of

---

[7] A Manual for Action presents the steps develop this model in urban areas: http://equidadparalainfancia.org/2017/02/manual-de-replica-monitoreo-local-de-bienestar-e-inequidades-en-la-infancia/ The manual enables cities to develop a social monitoring system based on regular measurement of child wellbeing and inequalities. In addition, the manual provides guidance on how to establish a child and equity-centered perspective within municipal governance and civil society activism.

the world's urban population will be under the age of 18—and concentrated in urban centers across Asia, Africa and Latin America (Tulchin et al. 2003; Ragan, 2012; UNFPA, 2012).

In comparison to their rural peers, urban children can at first appear to do better. Cities provide greater access to clean water and sanitation, and services such as health and education. When child wellbeing is assessed, urban children on average perform better than their rural counterparts. However, these averages often hide profound disparities (Bartlett, 2008). When disaggregated, the data shows that the urban poor can have health outcomes on par with the rural poor. Likewise, education attainment can be deeply unequal (Montgomery, 2009); (UNICEF, 2018).

Often, family incomes determine access to services in urban settings. In Latin American cities, one in three children grow up in precarious households (Born et al. 2012) a rate similar to New York, where 30 percent of all children live in monetary poverty (CCCNY, 2015). These children are subject to urban marginalization (Matthews, et al., 2010); they are unable to access the services and quality of living that urban life is expected to facilitate, specifically in the area of housing conditions, infrastructure and services. Everything is there, but not for them.

In other contexts, particularly sub-Saharan Africa and South Asia, mass exclusion is the driver of urban disparities. In these regions, the provision of services in urban areas has not kept pace with population growth. As a result, a majority of urban residents have inadequate access to protective infrastructure and health services. In a number of sub-Saharan African countries these conditions have contributed to stagnant or increasing infant and maternal mortality rates among the urban poor (Fotso et al., 2007; Matthews, et al., 2010; Buckley & Kallergis, 2014).

In turn, inadequate investment in urban planning and infrastructure heightens the environmental risks experienced by children. Crowded housing and unsanitary conditions increase the incidence of communicable diseases, such as diarrhea and pneumonia, and of chronic conditions, such as asthma. In addition, road traffic accidents have become the leading cause of death for children aged 10 to 19 (WHO and UNICEF, 2008). Informal settlements and urban poor neighborhoods around the world also face increased exposure to natural hazards and pollution. And the lack of safe, public spaces leaves children and adolescents with limited opportunities to play and socialize (Bartlett, 1999, 2008); Satterthwaite & Bartlett, 2017).

Rising income inequality in cities, and underinvestment in inclusive urban infrastructure, thus lead to spatial divisions, wherein the urban poor increasingly live in under-served and often inaccessible areas. This, in turn, further exacerbates exclusion and marginalization (UN-Habitat, 2013). The price of growing up in a marginalized urban neighborhood is paid most heavily by children, who grow up without the opportunities of their wealthier peers. However, increasingly it is argued that in the near future we all pay that price collectively, through higher rates of violence and lower overall growth (Glaeser et al., 2009; Stephens, 2011).

In spite of this, urban inequities are not inevitable. While inequality is growing in the cities of Africa and Asia, cities in Latin America and the Caribbean have narrowed the gap (UN-Habitat, 2013). In the U.S., progressive mayors have expressed their commitment to expanding early childhood education to all children (Paterson et al., 2017). This makes part of a growing recognition that cities can tackle the drivers of poverty through inclusive services (Schragger, 2016). With the introduction of the UN Sustainable Development Goals, this movement has formally moved into the forefront of global public policy.

Children, cities and the SDGs

The UN Sustainable Development Goals have renewed the focus on tackling the drivers of urban inequities and exclusion. A concerted campaign by urban activists and international organizations led to a dedicated urban goal, to 'Make cities and human settlements inclusive, safe, resilient and sustainable' (Simon, et al., 2015). Children are implicitly and explicitly included in Goal 11,[8] which presents a new opportunity to tackle urban child exclusion. At the same time, cities will play a central role in implementing the broader SDGS. Most of the goals that address child wellbeing and development, from providing clean water and sanitation to im-

---

8   Within Goal 11, specific targets are particularly relevant to urban child poverty and exclusion. These include: Target 11.3, which calls for 'inclusive and sustainable urbanization, and capacity for participatory, integrated and sustainable human settlements', and Target 11.7, which seeks to 'provide universal access to safe, inclusive and accessible, green and public spaces, in particular for women and children'.

proving education quality, will be financed and led by local governments (Biron, 2016; UN-Habitat, 2015).

However, there are concerns that development expectations from cities outstrip the local governmental capacity to plan, finance and implement urban development (Satterthwaite, 2015). For children and other vulnerable populations, such as the elderly and disabled, there is the added concern that their needs are only rarely considered in urban planning (Bartlett, 1999). While there is a growing movement calling for child-friendly urban design (ARUP, 2017)—it is making fewer inroads in the cities that are growing the fastest. Investment in urban children, like other dimensions of social spending, is often subjected to a 'Robin Hood paradox' (Lindert, 2004); it is the highest where it is least needed.

Monitoring SDG progress in urban areas is particularly challenging. When the drafting of Goal 11 was being finalized, creating a common set of indicators that apply to cities around the world proved to be difficult. There are too few standard metrics, inconsistent spatial analyses, and widely different capacities to regularly collect and report reliable data (Simon, et al., 2015). A recent attempt to compare progress across cities found that there was simply not enough data available at the city-level to make meaningful comparisons. Take Infant Mortality Rate for example. Of 178 cities reviewed, only 27 had available data—and the periodicity of reporting ranged from every year to twice in a decade (Cohen et al. 2018). The lack of data results from weak civil and administrative data systems. For example, less than half of Latin American countries have full civil registration systems; in sub-Saharan Africa only six percent do (World Bank n.d.; in OECD, 2013).

For the most part, reporting on children's wellbeing and inequities in developing countries is done through nationally representative surveys, which enable countries to study urban populations as a whole. However, sample sizes are rarely large enough to enable analysis of any given city. And three to ten years can pass between surveys, a time lag which is insufficient for routine monitoring (Montgomery, 2009; Lucci & Bhatkal, 2014). Measuring urban poverty and deprivations is complicated further by the difficulties in adequately counting and sampling urban slum dwellers, many of whom live in households that are not part of official records (Lucci et al., 2016). And household surveys often fail to capture the most vulnerable urban children, including street children and those living without parental care. Moving forward, new approaches are needed that provide granular data at the city-level—and capture the multiple, overlapping dimensions of childhood inequities.

Beyond monitoring, inclusive urban development requires governments that are accountable and responsive to their residents—a work in progress in many places (Satterthwaite, 2015). Urban childhood equity also requires a commitment by national and local governments to reducing barriers to quality services and infrastructure—together with active civic participation by families and advocates (UN-Habitat, 2013). A number of objectives and commitments have been declared at the global, national and municipal levels, but, as Satterthwaite and Bartlett ask, 'What will it take for governments to turn these pledges into action? Who will act locally to ensure that these pledges are kept?' (Satterthwaite & Bartlett, 2016).

Monitoring Urban Inequities and Child Wellbeing

Motivated by the urban face of child poverty and exclusion, Equity for Children (Equidad para la Infancia) developed a system in eight Latin American cities to measure and monitor child wellbeing and inequalities. The goal of the system is to establish a child and equity-centered perspective within municipal governance and civil society activism—and to improve the institutions and services meant to guarantee the rights of children and adolescents. The approach dovetails neatly with Agenda 2030—including the urban-specific targets within Goal 11 and the broader agenda for children—thus providing a child-sensitive way to monitor and implement the goals at the city-level.

The system was first developed and implemented in collaboration with Red Colombiana de Ciudades Cómo Vamos (The Colombian Network of Ciudades Cómo Vamos) programs, part of broader urban civil society network in Latin America.[9] Como Vamos, or 'how are we doing', monitors urban quality of life and provides feedback to local governments in 15 Columbian cities.[10] For Equity for Children, the collaboration provided an opportunity to use an in-depth and participatory model for evaluating the local quality of life. For

---

9   Red Latinoamericana por Ciudades y Territorios Justos, Democráticos y Sustentables
10 http://redcomovamos.org/

Como Vamos, the collaboration represented the first time the network looked specifically at urban children (Equity for Children, 2015).

A first phase, initiated in 2013, focused on early childhood wellbeing. This focus reflected the growing evidence and awareness that early years are critical to children's lifelong physical and mental growth—and was aligned with a new national policy, "From Zero to Always" (De Zero a Siempre). At the national level, Equity for Children worked with the country's Inter-Sectoral Commission for Comprehensive Care in Early Childhood. Baseline measurements and advocacy were carried out in seven cities: Bogota, Barranquilla, Bucaramanga, Cali, Cartagena, Manizales and Medellín (Minujin et al., 2015). In addition, the system examined national and local policies, and institutional capacity to address children's wellbeing. In a second phase, the indicators were expanded to cover later childhood (six to 12 years) and adolescence (13 to 17 years).

The following section provides a more in-depth look at the methodology developed in Colombia. Step-by-step, we explore how the approach works, the underlying assumptions, and what has been learnt in the process. At the same time, the methodology was designed to be adaptable—allowing researchers to generate statistical evidence relevant to different cities and settings. In Latin America, the system has been trialed in Peru, Brazil and Argentina, with varying degrees of success. In 2018, working with UNICEF, the model was introduced in Ondo State, Nigeria, providing a first application in sub-Saharan Africa. Building on these experiences, we consider how well the model translates to different countries and urban contexts.

Methodology

Step One: Local Partnerships and Viability

Determining the viability of the monitoring system is a critical first step. In line with the overall approach, viability rests on two foundations; data and local partners. In assessing data availability, Equity for Children looks at national and sub-national sources, mapping the extent to which disaggregated data on children is available at the city level and neighborhood level (Equity for Children, 2017). Generally, viability is linked with the maturity of national monitoring systems; in countries where administrative data on children is routinely collected and reported by government ministries and agencies, child rights monitoring becomes possible.

At the same time, there needs to be local partners, in civil society and academia, who can support the analysis of indicators and coordinate civic engagement. By grounding the initiative with city teams, the resulting research will better reflect the local context—and be more accessible to local discussions (Stren, 2008). At the city-level, Equity for Children starts by mapping and contacting child experts and advocates. Once a local team is assembled, roles are formally agreed, and the team is responsible for implementation, with technical support provided by Equity for Children (Equity for Children, 2017).

To a certain extent viability reflects the context in which the monitoring system was created. Colombia has relatively strong administrative and survey data on children and cities (Cohen et al. 2018) and a vibrant network of civil society organizations. Each of the cities that took part is a member of the Como Vamos network and the local cohort of affiliate formed the core of city teams. They were joined by academic partners from university departments and centers specializing in social research. The support of local foundations, such as the Corona Foundation in Colombia and the Arcor Foundation in Argentina, has been critical—a fact that reflects a growing trend of local and community philanthropy in middle-income countries (Hodgson, 2016).

Translating the approach to Nigeria has proven to be even more complicated. Local administrative data is available, but that availability ranges considerably across sectors. The strongest data system is health, followed by education and birth registration. In other sectors, including water and sanitation, child protection and environment, systems to aggregate data are weak. But even within the health data system, quality and consistency is a concern. For example, the 2016/17 MICS estimated an immunization rate of 45 percent for Ondo State (NBS and UNICEF, 2017), compared to 91 percent reported in the health system data. In light of data concerns and limitations, the first phase and piloting was framed as an exercise in strengthening data use and quality.

Step Two: Developing a Battery of Indicators

The starting point for monitoring child wellbeing and inequities is the Convention on the Rights of the Child (CRC), which provides a consistent, legal framework for engaging with governments, both national and local. Moreover, the CRC's principles of non-discrimination and best interest of the child provide a foundation for an equity-based and child-focused approach (Riggio, 2002). And monitoring grounded in the CRC requires governments to consider children's access to health, education, shelter, water, sanitation, nutrition and information. This multi-dimensional approach assumes that child well-being is based not just on what a family can purchase—but also the public goods and services afforded to them (Minujin, 2005; Minujin & Delamonica, 2012).

In developing a battery of indicators, Equity for Children, begins with *dimensions,* which reflect specific rights, such as the right to life and healthy development (CRC Article 6). In turn, each dimension is expanded into *components*, which articulate the complex set of elements needed to fulfill and monitor child rights. For example, the dimension of health expands to include child mortality, prevention of childhood disease, nutrition, and sexual and reproductive health. For each component, at least one indicator is selected (Equity for Children, 2017). In some cases, these are standard socio-economic indicators, such as Infant Mortality Rate. In other cases, the indicator may be specific to a country or city, such as coverage in national health insurance schemes, or access to city-sponsored health services.

Creating the battery is an iterative process reflecting, not only the CRC, but also national policies and commitments, and the situation of urban poor children. The process invariably creates a long list of indicators. In Colombia, the initial list ran to 90 components and indicators. Through dialogue with local teams, and the use of preexisting research on child wellbeing, the list was reduced to 18 components and 25 indicators (Minujin et al. 2015). In each city, it was necessary to adapt the indicators according to the available information, while maintaining the comparability as much as possible (See Annex 1 for an overview of the indicatory battery).

Children's physical environments
A particular challenge in developing the battery relates to the physical dimensions of child rights. The CRC has a strong focus on protection and participation, a focus reflected in the early Child Friendly City models which encouraged cities to develop child-friendly laws and institutional frameworks and to facilitate child participation in decision-making (Riggio, 2002). What this approach leaves out is connections to urban environments, and how these connections affect child wellbeing. For exam-

ple, there are no consistent efforts to measure children's access to play space, within households or in neighborhoods, or to understand their experience of hazardous urban environments. Household surveys do not look at a neighborhoods' overall exclusion from sewers and drainage systems or waste management systems (Bartlett, 1999; Bartlett, 2009).

In Colombia, indicators for children's physical environments were relatively strong; including 'access to public utilities', and 'meters squared available for game and recreation'. A household is defined as having full access to public utilities when connected to electricity, piped water, sewers and trash collection. Data on space for games and recreation, though available, did not note the quality or condition of the spaces. (Minujin, 2015). Without that information, it is difficult to assess whether the spaces meet the criteria for SDG 11, Target 11.7, which calls for green and safe public spaces. In Nigeria, information on access to public utilities and play spaces was not available. Instead, the number of road traffic accidents has been used as proxy for urban safety and planning, along with the extent to which schools have water, sanitation and electricity.

Taking a different approach, in Cordoba, Argentina a local NGO gathered data on play space, including quality and accessibility using an innovative survey of neighborhood parks (Nuestra Cordoba; Fundacion Arcor, 2016). The experience aligns with other initiatives to monitor children's urban environments. For example, an inter-generational survey in two Indian cities, Mumbai and Bhavnagar, collected data at scale across the cities' neighborhoods. The results showed that children and their families wanted safe play places, as well as access to basic services, and sparked community action and improved city planning (Wridt et al. 2015). Similar approaches have been undertaken in Turkey, France and 24 other countries, highlighting the value of participatory, inter-generational surveys for monitoring children' urban environments and progress towards SDG Target 11.7 (Wridt, 2015).

Step Three: Data Collection and Analysis

Once the battery of indicators is finalized, data is collected and analyzed for each city. Traditionally, monitoring of child wellbeing in low and middle-income countries has relied on periodic health surveys, such as DHS and MICS, along with census and income surveys (HIES). However, these surveys do not provide adequate data for monitoring within distinct urban areas (Montgomery, 2009) and contribute to a 'tyranny of averages', which mask the deprived areas (Custer et al., 2017). Instead, Equity for Children's system calls for teams to cast as wide a net as possible in looking for data sources on urban children, at the national, regional and local level. The challenge is to find data that can drill down to the level of neighborhoods, but also remain comparable across and between urban areas.

A core principle is that data should come from official sources, both national and local, to increase ownership and buy-in of the resulting analysis. Data sources included national statistics office and the government ministries and departments responsible for child wellbeing and development (for example, ministries of education, health and social welfare). In addition, other government offices, including environment, police and judiciary, planning and budget, provided information on the urban context. Experience has shown that geographically disaggregated data is available, but it requires a concerted effort to locate (Equity for Children, 2017).

Across the participating cities, the process itself revealed large gaps in data on children at the local level. Within cities, data on children can be inconsistent. For example in Cordoba, Argentina, education data is available by neighborhood, but health data is not (Nuestra Cordoba; Fundacion Arcor, 2016). An important, though initially unplanned result during this phase was the provision of recommendations to the government authorities and child advocates on improving data for children—specifically how national and local surveys could better capture information on the living standards of urban children. In Manizales, Colombia a lack of information on early childhood nutrition, and the ability to disaggregate the data, led to inclusion of questions on the next city survey. The experience highlights the value of monitoring for improving data availability and quality—an aspect that has been cited as of particular value to the participating cities.

Table 1: The measurement and analysis process

Selection of indicators	Compilation and request of information	Processing and analysis of the data
• Definition of the final battery of indicators • Inclusion of variables according to local needs	• Wide range of official sources • Relationship with the institutions that produce information • Application of information requests protocols	• Calculation of the indicators • Analysis of inequities • Contextual analysis/public policy

Source: Equity for Children (2017)

Analyzing Inequalities

Once data is available, city teams calculate the indicators. These baseline measures provide a snapshot of how children in the city are doing overall, demonstrating the extent and depth of poverty, along with overall health and access to services. The first round of monitoring in Colombia, which covered one in three children in the country, revealed that 60 percent of child deaths in cities could have been prevented through simple measures such as vaccinations and treatment of infections. When carried out across multiple cities, the baseline measures can reveal dramatic inter-city disparities. In Medellin, 65 percent of young children accessed free early childhood care compared to only 26 percent in Bogota (Minujin et al., 2015).

Children's well-being and holistic development is profoundly influenced by inequalities that put some at a disadvantage from the moment they are born. A number of factors, including place of residence, gender, ethnic group and disability status, shape a child's chances of achieving physical, emotional and material well-being, and of growing up in an environment where he or she is safe and protected. Equity for Children measures inequities using the 'relative inequality gap', which looks at the ratio between the most advantaged and disadvantaged groups.

In Colombia, place of residence proved to be a primary driver of urban inequities. In Bogota, young children living in the under-served periphery community of Sumapaz were five times more likely to die than children living in the central neighborhood of La Candelaria, where basic services are more widely available (Minujin et al., 2015). In Medellin, children from the most disadvantaged areas are four times more likely to die.

In some cases, residence and other variables interact to produce areas of profound inequities. In Cali, children from the county where the Embera Katio indigenous community live had a 17 times greater chance of dying before the age of five than those in areas without an indigenous population (Minujin, 2016). Until Equity for Children and the local teams undertook this analysis, these disparities had been largely invisible.

For some indicators, the disaggregation of data has led to the recognition of previously unrecognized problems. Adolescent pregnancy is one example, with overall city rates hiding concentrated areas with extraordinarily high rates. In Cali, 74 percent of adolescent pregnancies were concentrated in just four neighborhoods (*communas*). In one neighborhood (*Communa 13*), an adolescent girl had a 359 greater chance of becoming pregnant in comparison with a girl from *Communa 2* (Equity for Children, 2015).

Disparities in children's physical environments were pronounced between cities. In Bogota, 98 percent of households had access to the full set of public services, compared to 63 percent in Cartagena. The disparities within cities were even greater, particularly between the rural and urban areas. In Bucaramanga, households in the city center were 157 times more likely to have full access to utilities than outlying areas. Likewise, access to recreational spaces varied, from 53 meters squared in Cartagena to 15 meters squared in Cali. However, information on play spaces could not be broken down by neighborhood, or indicate the accessibility, safety or child-friendliness of the spaces (Minujin et al., 2015).

In Nigeria, among the salient findings was the poor performance across almost all local governments. For example, less than 20 percent of primary schools have toilet facilities, five percent have running water, and two percent electricity. Taken together, the data on children's physical environments confirmed a situation of mass exclusion, in which the large majority of children lack access to basic infrastructure and services.

Reporting the final results and findings

As a tool to raise awareness and actions on childhood inequities, it is essential that data analysis is reported in a user-friendly way. Spatial analysis, in which indicators are geo-referenced and plotted on city maps, allows an immediate visual understanding of the most disadvantaged areas. (An example from Bogota is provided in Annex 2). Traffic light systems provide another tool to highlight inequality gaps within a city (Equity for

Children, 2017). The end result is a report card showing how children fare within neighborhoods in each city.

Translating awareness of inequities into action also requires contextual analysis. Local teams are responsible for linking the data on inequities with public policies—and the local government institutions responsible for children. Inputs such as local development plans, sector plans and city reports provide a basis for understanding the local context. At the same time, teams should map the institutions and venues where policy and programs for children are determined. A useful methodology for this analysis entails cross-referencing results of each indicator with the local public policies which target children (Equity for Children, 2017).

Our experience in Latin America has revealed significant weaknesses in terms of urban policy for children. Cities simply don't have child-specific plans, relying instead on national and regional policies for children. However, we have discovered many forums at the city level that provide an opportunity to contribute evidence on how children's policies and programs can be improved. These include councils of mayors, city councils, district mayors, and school boards.

Step Four: Communication and Advocacy

In line with recognized approaches to social accountability, the final reports of the findings were widely communicated within the participating cities (Malena et al., 2004). Local teams in Colombia held public forums, involving city officials responsible for child and adolescent wellbeing, as well as social service providers in both the public and private sectors. These public presentations enabled debate and dialogue about the measurement and monitoring process—and generated concrete actions and commitments (Equity for Children, 2017). For example, in Bogota, a public debate with the mayoral candidates for the October 2015 election led to strategies for inequality reduction (Minujin, 2016).

In addition, local teams communicated the findings through the media, including traditional, online and social media. The aim was to reach as many stakeholders as possible, from public officials to families and children (Equity for Children, 2017). Media coverage plays a double role; on the one hand it can generate a demand for action among the public, and on the other hand it may help to define issues of importance to decision-makers (Baumgartner & Jones, 1993; Walgrave & Van Aelst, 2016). The

Como Vamos network played an important role in the communication of the findings. The organization's previous experience in monitoring and reporting urban quality of life—and its professional communication capacity—contributed to the overall impact of the child wellbeing monitoring.

Step Five: Monitoring and Participation

The final component in the system is the active engagement of affected citizens and communities. By disaggregating official data, urban communities can demonstrate the ways in which local governments are failing to provide their children with equitable opportunities to grow and thrive. This approach can help the urban poor to 'voice' their experiences and concerns in a way that improves governance, and in turn, leads to better outcomes for their children (Malena et al. 2004; O'Neill et al., 2007).

In Colombia, the local teams organized workshops with civil society and grassroots organizations for the communities with the most urgent cases of child inequality. The workshops provided an opportunity to discuss the findings—and connect them with the lived experience of the people in the communities. Participants in the workshops developed concrete plans to improve child well-being, linked to national and municipal policies. For example, in Cali, communities with high levels of adolescent pregnancy pressed for priority funding for pregnancy prevention and child protection programs. By bringing together the different citizens groups interested in children and adolescents, Equity for Children and the local teams, were able to foster new connections and coalitions. In Bogota, this led to creation of civic action committees in some of the most deprived communities in the cities (Minujin, 2016; Equity for Children, 2017).

Ongoing monitoring is essential to social accountability. One-off measures and situation analyses can highlight inequities and prompt action, but it is only through repeated rounds of measurement that communities can sustain government attention. In addition, monitoring should align with local administration's policy cycles so as to provide data and evidence when plans and budgets are being decided. If possible, monitoring should be done annually but at least every two years, to sustain government focus and action. Early childhood presents important milestones for human development, as well as very short periods to implement solutions. A child counted today as part of the early childhood population will have completed this phase in her life in three years (Equity for Children, 2017).

Over time, the local teams have had different experiences sustaining monitoring and civic engagement. In Cali, which is home to Equity for Children's primary research partner, the Pontifica Universidad Javeriana, the local team has facilitated three rounds of monitoring, whereas in Bogota, where Como Vamos has a sizeable field presence, the local team has fostered more dynamic civic engagement. Local foundations have played a central role in funding and expanding the monitoring system in Colombia and Argentina. Their support reflects the growing role of philanthropy in middle-income countries, which tends to be more flexible, long-term and locally focused (The Guardian, 2014).

Ultimately, the effectiveness of social accountability is not in the claims made by citizens—but in the response by governments (O'Neill et al. 2007). In some cities, there have been immediate shifts in policy and budgets as a result of the monitoring. However, the initiative has struggled to achieve consistent and ongoing improvements in governance for disadvantaged children. This struggle reflects a weakness shared by social accountability initiatives that focus largely on bottom-up approaches. Recent evaluations of social accountability highlight the importance of a multi-pronged approach, which improves citizen voice while also including reforms to improve government responsiveness (Fox, 2014).

An alternative approach is offered by UNICEF's Child Friendly Cities, which anchors child rights monitoring in local governments (Riggio, 2002). One of the most successful approaches to Child-Friendly Cities is Brazil's Municipal Seal, in which local governments compete to show improvements across multiple indicators of child wellbeing.[11] The Municipal Seal shares many of the same indicators as the Equity for Children approach, encompassing child health, education and protection. However,

---

11 UNICEF's Municipal Seal of Approval was launched in 1998 in the State of Ceará. In 2005, the strategy was expanded to the 11 states of the Semi-Arid region and, in 2009, it was extended to the Amazon region. The Seal is a certification process that stimulates positive competition among municipalities and rewards success with visibility for their achievements. Evidence indicates that municipalities with a high level of success in implementing the Seal methodology have seen faster improvements in their social indicators as compared to other regions and to national averages (UNICEF, 2013).

the Seal adds specific policy and participation actions for local governments, committing municipalities to concrete steps to improve child rights (Fuentes & Niimi, 2002; UNICEF, 2013). In Nigeria, Equity for Children is working with UNICEF to introduce a similar approach; led by state and local governments but involving civil society. This approach could potentially leverage top-down and social accountability to improve governance for children.

Conclusion

With the SDGs, there is a renewed focus on making cities 'inclusive, safe, resilient and sustainable'—which is an incentive for cities to play a central role in implementing the broader goals of the other SDGs. However, there are concerns that expectations outstrip cities' capacity to plan, implement and track inclusive development. Monitoring SDG progress at the city level presents a particular challenge. Beyond monitoring, inclusive urban development requires local governments that are accountable and responsive to their residents—a work in progress in many places.

This chapter has looked at a system developed by Equity for Children to monitor and improve child wellbeing and inequalities in urban areas. Based on the experience of implementing the approach in Colombia and Argentina, as well as more recent efforts to translate the method to Nigeria, we believe the system provides a useful model for the monitoring of progress at city-level—and lessons for advancing the equity and inclusion goals of the SDGs with local governments.

In Latin America, teams successfully created a battery of indicators to holistically measure child wellbeing. Using national, regional and local survey and administrative data, Equity for Children was able to measure child wellbeing down to the neighborhood level. At the same time, the resulting data was comparable nationally, enabling measurement at scale. Some 30 percent of children in Colombia were covered by the approach. However, the process also revealed remaining gaps in data on urban children. In particular, data on physical environments is still lagging behind the traditional silos of health and education. The experience highlighted the value of adding participatory surveys to administrative data, as a way to improve the monitoring of children's urban environments.

By disaggregating the data, the teams revealed inequities that hitherto had been invisible. The system has shown that Infant Mortality Rates and adolescent pregnancy, among other indicators, can vary dramatically between wealthier and poorer parts of the city. In Colombia, the analysis revealed that 60 percent of child deaths were preventable; a critical information for accelerating SDG progress for children. In Nigeria, an initial scorecard has shown that even in a relatively wealthy state, investment in basic infrastructure and services has been grossly insufficient, with less than one in five children attending a primary school with adequate toilets and water.

Translating visibility and agenda setting into sustained attention to and action on children's disparities has proven more difficult, an experience common to social accountability initiatives. Local civil society plays an important role in facilitating this attention, and local foundations, in particular, have shown a commitment to providing longer-term support to cities than external funders. However, without commensurate attention to how local governments fund and deliver services, efforts to measure and monitor child wellbeing and inequities cannot reach their full potential.

In short, as a way to tackle the challenges of monitoring urban progress towards the SDG targets, Equity for Children has demonstrated that the data exists—and our methodology can help to unlock information on marginalized and excluded populations. Through creative use of existing data, we have further shown that indicators and monitoring of children's wellbeing can potentially be used as a proxy for urban wellbeing as a whole. As a means to implement the urban SDG, and the broader Agenda 2030 in cities, our experience has reaffirmed the value of inclusive governance, but also served as a caution that civil society alone cannot carry the burden. A commitment to child rights and the SDGs within local government is needed as well.

Bibliography

APHRC. (2002). *Population and Health Dynamics in Nairobi's Informal Settlements.* Nairobi: African Population and Health Research Center.

ARUP. (2017). *Cities Alive: Designing for urban childhoods.* London: ARUP. Retrieved from https://www.arup.com/perspectives/publications/research/section/cities-alive-designing-for-urban-childhoods

Bartlett, S. (1999). Children's experience of the physical environments in poor, urban settlements and the implications for policy, planning and practice. *Environment and Urbanization, 11*(2), 63–74.

Bartlett, S. (2008). *Climate Change and Urban Children: Impacts and Implications for Adaptation in Low- and Middle-income Countries.* London: International Institute for Environment and Development. Retrieved from http://pubs.iied.org/10556IIED.html.

Bartlett, S. (2009). *Environments of Poverty and What they Mean for Child Protection.* Sweden: Save the Children. Retrieved from https://cergnyc.org/files/2011/09/Environments-of-poverty-and-child-protection.pdf

Baumgartener, F., & Jones, B. (1993). *Agendas and instability in American politics.* Chicago: University of Chicago Press.

Biron, C. L. (2016, July 8). *The Worldwide Effort to Shape Sustainable Urban Development.* Retrieved from CITYLAB: https://www.citylab.com/environment/2016/07/cities-turn-to-implementing-the-sustainable-development-goals/490490/

Born, D., Colamarco, V., Delamonica, E., & Minujin, A. (2012). *Urban Children in Latin America and the Caribbean: Disparities, Challenges, and Possible Solutions.* United Nations Children's Fund (UNICEF).

Buckley, R., & Kallergis, A. (2014). African urban policy—a platform for growth? In S. Parnell, & S. Oldfield, *The Routledge Handbook on Cities of the Global South* (pp. 173–190). Abingdon: Routedge.

CCCNY. (2015). *Keeping Track of New York City's Children 2015.* New York: Citizens Committee for the Children of New York.

Cohen, M., Simet, L., Orr, B., De la Cruz, M., & Garcia, D. L. (2018). *Monitoring and Assessing Progress at the City Level.* New York: The Global Urban Futures Project, The New School. Retrieved from https://docs.wixstatic.com/ugd/046e21_a88d5b6a993d4eee8e2b38cfc72efc00.pdf

Custer, S., DiLorenzo, M., Masaki, T., Sethi, T., & Wells, J. (2017). *Beyond the Tyranny of Averages: Development Progress from the Bottom Up.* Williamsburg, VA: AidData, College of William and Mary.

Equity for Children. (2015). *Main Report Findings on Early Childhood in 7 Cities in Colombia.* Retrieved from Equity for Children: http://equityforchildren.org/2015/09/monitoring-social-inequities-in-colombia/

Equity for Children. (2017). *Measuring and Monitoring Child Wellbeing and Inequality at the Local Level—Implementation Phases.* Retrieved from Equity for Children: http://equityforchildren.org/wp-content/uploads/2017/05/Equity-for-Children-Civic-Accountability-Model-03.14.18-1.pdf

Evans, A. (2017). Amplifying Accountability by Benchmarking Results at District and National Levels. *Development Policy Review.*

Fatile, J., & Ejalonibu, G. (2015). Decentralization and Local Government Autonomy: Quest for Quality Service Delivery in Nigeria. *British Journal of Economics, Management and Trade, 10*(2), 1–21.

Fotso, J., Ezeh, A., Madise, N., & Ciera, J. (2007). Progress towards the child mortality millennium development goal in urban sub-Saharan Africa: the dynamics of population growth, immunization, and access to clean water. 7: 218. *BMC Public Health, 7*(218). Retrieved from https://bmcpublichealth.biomedcentral.com/track/pdf/10.1186/1471-2458-7-218

Fox, J. (2014). *Social Accountability: What does the evidence really say?* Global Partnership for Social Accountability. Washington D.C.: World Bank.

Fuentes, P., & Niimi, R. (2002). Motivating municipal action for children: the Municipal Seal of Approval in Ceará, Brazil, Environment & Urbanization. *Environment and Urbanization, 14*(2).

Gibbs, W. W. (2016). Bill Gates Views Good Data as Key to Global Health. *Scientific American.*

Glaeser, E., Resseger, M., & Tobio, K. (2009). Inequality in Cities. *Journal of Regional Science, 49*(4), 617–646.

Hodgson, J. (2016, June 2). *Community Philanthropy: it's a thing, and you need to know about it.* Retrieved from From Poverty to Power: https://oxfamblogs.org/fp2p/community-philanthropy-its-a-thing-and-you-need-to-know-about-it/

Lindert, P. (2004). *Growing Public: Social Spending and Economic Growth Since the Eighteenth Century.* New York City: Cambridge University Press.

Lucci, P., & Bhatkal, T. (2014). *Monitoring progress on urban poverty: Are indicators fit for purpose?* London: ODI.

Lucci, P., Bhatkal, T., & Khan, A. (2016). *Are we underestimating urban poverty?* London: Overseas Development Institute (ODI).

Malena, C., Forster, R., & Singh, J. (2004). *Social Accountability: An Introduction to the Concept and Emerging Practice.* Social Development. Washington D.C.: World Bank.

Matthews, Z., Channon, A., Neal, S., Osrin, D., N., M., & Stones, W. (2010). Examining the "Urban Advantage" in Maternal Health Care in Developing Countries. *PLoS Med, 7*(9). Retrieved from https://doi.org/10.1371/journal.pmed.1000327

MEASURE Evaluation. (2017, May). *Using DHIS 2 to Strengthen Health.* Retrieved from MEASURE Evaluation: file:///C:/Users/Heathcliff/Downloads/fs-17-212%20(1).pdf

Minujin, A. (2005). Constructing a definition and measurements of children living in poverty. *Global Policy Section contribution to Innocenti Research Centre meeting on Child Poverty in Central and Eastern Europe/Commonwealth of Independent States*, 24 January. Florence, Italy.

Minujin, A. (2016). Increasing childhood equality in cities: a practical intervention through policy, research and advocacy. In I. I. UNESCO, *World Social Sciences Report* (pp. 291–292). Paris: UNESCO. Retrieved from https://en.unesco.org/wssr2016

Minujin, A., & Delamonica, E. (2012). Multidimensional child poverty in Tanzania: analysis of situation, changes and sensitivity of thresholds. In A. Minujin, & S. Nandy, *Global child poverty and well-being: Measurement, concepts, policy and action* (pp. 263–286). Bristol: Bristol University Press, Policy Press.

Minujin, A., Bagnoli, V., Mejía, A. M., & Quintero, L. F. (2015). *Primera infancia Cómo Vamos: Identificando desigualdades para impulsarla equidad en la infancia colombiana*. Cali: Fundación Corona, Equidad para la Infancia, Red de Ciudades Como Vamos, Pontificia Universidad Javeriana Cali.

Montgomery, M. R. (2009). Urban Poverty and Health in Developing Countries," Population Bulletin 64, no. 2 (2009). *Population Bulletin, 64*(2).

NBS and UNICEF. (2017). *Multiple IndicatorCluster Survey 2016–17, Survey Findings Report*. Abuja, Nigeria: National Bureau of Statistics and United Nations Children's Fund.

Nuestra Cordoba, Fundacion Arcor. (2016). *Indicators for the Assessing Children's Wellbeing in the City of Cordoba*. Cordoba, Argentina: Red Cuidadana Nuestra Cordoba, Fundacion Arcor.

Nuestra Cordoba; Fundacion Arcor. (2016). *Análisis de las inequidades en la infancia urbana: Córdoba, Argentina*. Retrieved from Equidad para l'Infancia: http://equidadparalainfancia.org/2017/07/continuamos-el-analisis-de-las-inequidades-en-la-infancia-urbana-cordoba-argentina/

O'Neill, T., Foresti, M., & Hudson, A. (2007). *Evaluation of Citizens' Voice and Accountability: Review of the Literature and Donor Approaches*. London: DFID.

OECD. (2013). *Strengthening statistical systems to monitor global goals. Elements 5, Paper 1*. Paris: OECD.

Paterson, S., Bustamante, A. S., Hirsh-Pasek, K., & Michnick Golinkoff, R. (2017, August 21). *Brain matter matters: Should we intervene well before preschool?* Retrieved from Brookings Institute: https://www.brookings.edu/blog/education-plus-development/2017/08/21/brain-matter-matters-should-we-intervene-well-before-preschool/

Ragan, D. (2012). *Cities of Youth: Cities of Prosperity*. UN-Habitat.

Riggio, E. (2002). Child friendly cities: good governance inthe best interest of the child. *Environment and Urbanization, 14*(2), 45–58.

Satterthwaite, D. (2015, October 9). *Commentary: The SDGs don't adequately spell out cities' role in implementation*. Retrieved from Citiscope: http://citiscope.org/habitatIII/commentary/2015/10/sdgs-dont-adequately-spell-out-cities-role-implementation

Satterthwaite, D., & Bartlett, S. (2016). *Cities on a Finite Planet*.

Satterthwaite, D., & Bartlett, S. (2017). Editorial: The full spectrum of risk in urban centres: changing perceptions, changing priorities. *Environment and Urbanization, 29*(1), 3–14.

Schragger, I. (2016). *City Power: Urban Governance in a Global Age*. New York City: Oxford University Press.

Simon, D., Arfvidsson, H., Anand, G., Bazaz, A., Fenna, G., Foster, K., ... Wright, C. (2015). Developing and testing the Urban Sustainable Development Goal's targets and indicators—a five-city study. *Environment and Urbanization, 28*(1), 49–63.

Stephens, C. (2011). Revisiting urban health and social inequalities: the devil is in the detail and the solution is in all of us. *Environment and Urbanization, 23*(1), 29–40.

Stren, R. (2008). International assistance for cities in low- and middle-income countries: do we still need it? *Environment and Urbanization, 20*(2), 377–392.

The Guardian. (2014, April 19). *Homegrown philanthropy: the rise of local giving in the south*. Retrieved from Guardian development network: https://www.theguardian.com/global-development/2014/apr/19/homegrown-philanthropy-local-giving-global-south

Tulchin, J. S., Varat, D. H., & Hanley, L. M. (2003). Introduction. In W. W. Scholars, *Youth Explosions in Developing World Cities: Approaches to Reducing Poverty and Conflict in an Urban* Age (pp. 1–6). Washington D.C.: Woodrow Wilson International Center for Scholars.

UNFPA. (2012). *The State of the World Population 2012.* New York: United Nations Population Fund (UNFPA), Earthscan Publications Ltd.

UN-Habitat. (2013). *State of the World's Cities 2012/2013: Cities of Prosperity*. New York: Earthscan/Routledge.

UN-Habitat. (2015). *Financing Sustainable Urban Development: Challenges and Opportunities.* Retrieved from United Nations Department of Economic and Social Affairs: http://www.un.org/esa/ffd/ffd3/wp-content/uploads/sites/2/2015/03/Financing-Urban-Development_UN-Habitat.pdf

UNICEF. (2012). *The State of the Worlds Children: Children in an Urban World.* New York: United Nations Children's Fund.

UNICEF. (2013). *Methodological Guide of the UNICEF Municipal Seal of Approval 2013–2016 Edition.* Brasilia, Brazil: United Nation's Childrens Fund.

UNICEF. (2018). *Advantage or Paradox: The challenge for children or young people of of growing up urban*. New York City, NY: United Nations Childrens Fund.

Walgrave, S., & Van Aelst, P. (2016, August). *Political Agenda Setting and the Mass Media.* Retrieved from Oxford Research Encyclopedia of Politics: http://politics.oxfordre.com/view/10.1093/acrefore/9780190228637.001.0001/acrefore-9780190228637-e-46?print=pdf

WHO and UNICEF. (2008). *World report on child injury prevention.* Geneva: World Health Organization and the United Nations Children's Fund. Retrieved from http://www.who.int/violence_injury_prevention/child/injury/world_report/en/

Wridt, P. (2015). *Global evaluation of a participatory, child rights approach to intergenerational assessment, planning and local development.* New York: Childrens' Environments Research Group, CUNY Graduate Center.

Wridt, P., Atmakur-Javdekar, S., & Hart, R. (2015). Spatializing Children's Rights: A Comparison of Two Case Studies from Urban India. *Children, Youth and Environments, 25*(2), 33–85.

Annex 1—Battery of Child Wellbeing Indicators (Colombia)

Basic set of childhood wellbeing indicators		
Dimension	Component	Indicator
Population	Demographic	Population between 0 and 17 years old by city
Identity	Legal identity	Birth certificate
Material Wellbeing	Poverty	Multidimensional Poverty
	Quality of housing	Access to public utilities
		Structure of housing
Health	Mortality	Mortality Rate in Children
	Nutrition	Prevalence of Chronic Malnutrition *
	Prevention of diseases	Vaccination Coverage DPT3 *
	Sexual Health and Reproductive	Adolescent Fertility Rate
	Health coverage	Percentage of children affiliated according to health regime
Education, Care and Recreation	Care and Initial education	Children cared for in public care and early education programs
	Preschool Education	Gross Coverage Rate in Preschool
	Coverage in basic education and a half	Gross coverage rates
		Repeat Rate
		Adolescents who neither study nor work
	Game Recreation and Culture	M2 available for game and recreation
Familiar Surroundings	Maternal Mortality	Maternal mortality ratio
	Mother and Father situations	Parent Education *
	Children who are not in company with his family	Children in foster care, Institutionalized, etc.
Participation	Means of information	Computers per child
		Internet Connection
MISSING INFO	Death by external causes	Homicide rates
		Rate of deaths due to external causes
	Victims of armed conflict	Victimization rate by case type *
Protection against violence	Violence against NNA	NNYA in street situation
		Child Abuse Rate
		Cases of sexual violence
	Child labor	Child Labor Rate
	Special guarantees of the justice system	Adolescents linked to the criminal responsibility system for adolescents

* not always available
Source: Equity for Children (2017)

Annex 2
Spatial Analysis of Infant Mortality Rates by neighborhood in Bogota (2015)

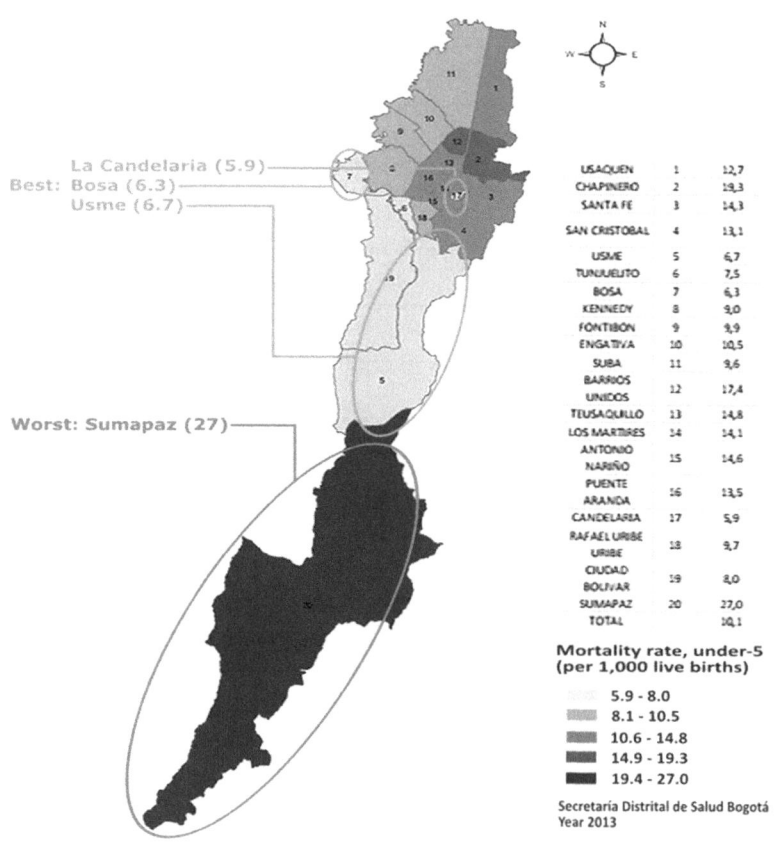

Source: Minujin A. (2016)

Capturing Children Left Behind in Urban Poor Communities: Lessons for Equity-Focused SDG Monitoring From the Bangkok Small Community MICS, Thailand

Tomoo Okubo,[12] Ana Maria Restrepo,[13] Chirawat Poonsab[14] and Christina Popivanova[15]

Background

The growing urban population and the SDGs

Urbanization in Thailand is a defining trend for the future in line with broader regional and global orientations. According to a report by the United Nations, about 54 per cent of the world's population is currently living in urban areas, and the number is expected to rise up to 66 per cent by 2050 (UN DESA, 2014). Coupled with the increase in the total population around the world, this will mean that by the middle of the 21st Century an additional 2.5 billion people will be living in urban areas. 90 per cent of the change is expected to occur in Asia and Africa (ibid). This urbanization trend is being driven by both natural population growth and migration from rural areas to urban areas globally (Baker, 2008).

The global focus on cities and human settlements has been strongly reflected in

> **Box 1: SDG Targets and indicators related to urban slum areas**
>
> **Target 11.1**
> By 2030, ensure access for all to adequate, safe and affordable housing and basic services and upgrade slums
>
> **Indicator 11.1.1**
> Proportion of urban population living in slums, informal settlements or inadequate housing
>
> **Target 11.2**
> By 2030, provide access to safe, affordable, accessible and sustainable transport systems for all, improving road safety, notably by expanding public transport, with special attention to the needs of those in vulnerable situations, women, children, persons with disabilities and older persons
>
> **Indicator 11.2.1**
> Proportion of population that has convenient access to public transport, by sex, age and persons with disabilities

---

12 Social Policy Specialist, UNICEF-Thailand: tokubo@unicef.org
13 Consultant, UNICEF
14 Statistician, National Statistical Office of Thailand
15 Chief, Social Policy, Monitoring and Evaluation, UNICEF-Thailand

the SDGs under Goal 11, 'Making cities and human settlements inclusive, safe, resilient and sustainable'. Other goals are also closely linked with urban issues, such as poverty, food security, water, sanitation, and sustainable energy (SDSN, 2013). The SDGs also explicitly focus on urban slum areas in the targets and indicators presented in Box 1.

Thailand's urban population has also experienced growth over recent decades. Urban areas grew at a rate of 1.4 per cent between 2000 to 2010, while the size of the urban population grew at a rate of 2.3 per cent during the same period (World Bank, 2015). This has led to an increase in the urban population density from 4,000 per square kilometer to 4,300 per square kilometer. The rate of urbanization measured by the percentage of population living in urban areas has been particularly high since 2000 (see Figure 1).

Figure 1. Urban population in Thailand (% of total), 1961–2017

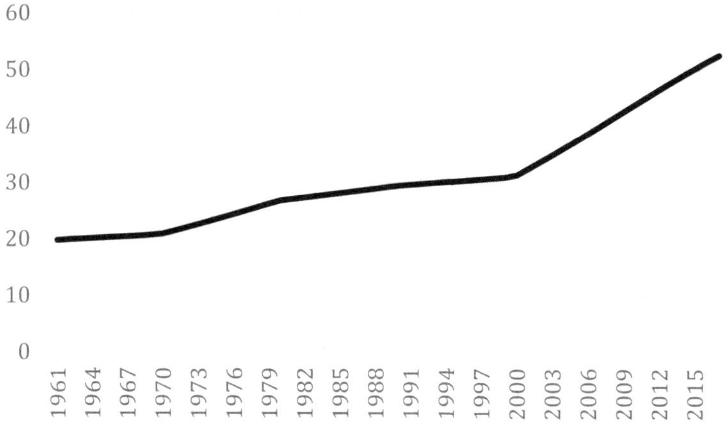

Source: World Development Indicators (2017)

Urbanization in Thailand has been driven by the growing area and population of Bangkok and other cities in Thailand (World Bank, 2015). The rate of urban growth is striking when compared to the size of the population of Bangkok in 1960, which was only 2.1 million, according to the Population and Housing Census carried out by National Statistical Office. Similar to other countries, the population growth in Bangkok is driven more by migration from other provinces to Bangkok than by natural population growth within Bangkok, where it is estimated that around one third of the population are unregistered, mostly composed of rural migrants (Choiejit, 2002; Dhakal & Shrestha, 2016). As the economic center for industrialization in the country, Bangkok attracted many workers from rural areas as Thailand's economy transitioned from an agricultural-based to an industrial economy. While there has been a policy focus on promoting rural area development, the center of economic and social development remains is still in the urban cities across Thailand, especially Bangkok.

The challenge of urbanization

Urbanization is often associated with economic development or improved access to basic services and goods, but managing urban growth can also bring challenges to municipalities (Shummadtayar et al., 2013). Those who migrate from rural areas pursuing greater job or education opportunities may face urban challenges such as overcrowding, congestion, unemployment, lack of community and social networks, inequalities and even violence or crime. These challenges are often the result of unmet resources and capacities in urban areas, inadequate governmental policies, and lack of planning for urban growth and management. Given the continued trend of population growth in urban areas, if planning and policy responses do not meet the increased demands, the problems faced by families in urban areas could worsen over the coming years (Baker, 2008).

Inequity is one of the major concerns for the development of Bangkok, as around 20 per cent of the population in Bangkok live in slum settlements. The term 'Bangkok Small Communities' refers to these urban poor areas, defined by the Bangkok Metropolitan Administration as an 'overcrowded, non-orderly and dilapidated community with unample environment which can be harmful to health and lives and with a minimum of 15 housing units per 1600 square meters' (UN-HABITAT, 2003). In 1985, there were 1,020 slum settlements in Bangkok; whereas by 2016 this number has increased to 2,067. In 2016 the slum population was estimated to be 2.1 million, or 437,433 households, up from 1.96 million in 2009 (BMA, 2009; BMA, 2016).

The urban poor areas of Bangkok are located in various places, including in the vacant spaces owned by public and private entities, some of them lined along the sides of canals, near industrial areas and transport nodes such as Bangkok International Seaport or in the inner and middle area of the central business district (BMA, Department of City Planning, 1999). An established slum community resides in the Klong Toey Slum, an area of a square mile where 100,000 people are estimated to be living (Sapsuwan, 2014; Chandran, 2018). Existing literature points to some of the social problems faced by the urban poor population, including a lack of employment skills, which limits their social mobility, and drug addiction among the youth; local resdients earn, on average, one third of the income earned by an average Bangkok household (Chandran, 2018). However, to the best knowledge of the authors, there has not been a comprehensive survey of the well-being of the population living in urban disadvantaged areas to understand the situation of children and women.

While existing household surveys in Thailand were able to produce disaggregated estimates for the Bangkok area, the estimates cannot be further disaggregated for the more disadvantaged areas due to the low number of households sampled. This has been a challenge not only for Thailand but also for statistics in other countries, as regular household surveys may miss or under-represent the most disadvantaged children. With the SDG's strong focus on leaving no one behind, increased efforts to measure poverty for all children is now more important than ever. The BSC MICS presented in this paper was an attempt led by the National Statistical Office of Thailand, together with UNICEF Thailand, to address this challenge by conducting a survey specifically to capture the situation of the population living in urban poor areas, including those who may be unregistered by municipalities and therefore not captured by administrative data. The rest of the sections and analysis in this paper will describe the methodology in more details, present some of the key findings, and conclude with a discussion on improving data collection instruments for SDG monitoring, using the BSC MICS as an example.

Methodology

The Multiple Indicator Cluster Survey (MICS) is an international household survey that collects a wide range of indicators on child well-being and the situation of women, conducted in more than 110 countries around the world for over 20 years. It is a comprehensive survey that provides more than 80 internationally-agreed indicators related to children and women. Three rounds of MICS have been conducted in Thailand: MICS 3 in 2005–2006, MICS 4 in 2012 and MICS 5 in 2015–2016.

The latest MICS in Thailand, MICS 5, was conducted by the National Statistical Office with technical and financial support from UNICEF and financial support from the National Health Security office. A steering group guided initial planning of the survey while a technical group, composed of representatives from key line ministries and local experts, assisted in customizing and adapting the global MICS 5 tools to the local context. In total, 31,010 households were sampled in all 77 provinces, including 14 of the most vulnerable provinces, where a larger number of households were sampled to allow provincial-level disaggregation along with the BSC MICS.

Four sets of questionnaires were used in the national MICS: (1) to collect basic demographic information on the household and the dwelling; (2) for individual women in each household aged 15–49 years; (3) for individual men in each household aged 15–49 years; and (4) a questionnaire for children under the age of 5, administered to the parents or caretakers of all children under 5 living in the household. In addition to the questionnaires, the enumerators tested the iodine content of salt used for cooking, observed the place for handwashing, and measured the weights and heights of children under 5 years. Details of the questionnaires and sampling methodology can be found in the survey report (NSO, 2016).

The BSC MICS was part of MICS 5 conducted nationally and thus the same questionnaires were used. The critical element of the BSC MICS was its unique sampling frame. In order to ensure that the samples represented the populations of Bangkok's small communities, the sampling framework was designed by the National Statistical Office, in consultation with sampling experts from UNICEF and the Bangkok Metropolitan Administration (BMA).

The primary sampling units (PSUs) at the first stage were enumeration areas (EAs). The 2010 Population and Housing Census (PHC), which had been updated by the National Statistical Office, was used for the selection of the EAs. In order to sample the small communities of Bangkok, the list of small communities, provided by the BMA, was matched with the enumeration area of the NSO. For each EA selected, a new list of households was used as the sampling frame for the selection of households in the second sampling stage. Enumerators listed all dwellings and recorded the number of all households located in sample EAs. A total of 20 households were selected from each EA, where 10 households had more than one child under the age of 5 and the other 10 households did not.

In total, 2,707 households were interviewed for the BSC MICS, resulting in a sample of interviews with 2,843 eligible women, 1,330 mothers/caretakers of children under 5, and 2,664 eligible men. The response rate for households, women, men and children under 5 was 93 per cent or above for all the questionnaires. The average household size of the sampled population was 3.3, and the proportion of the population under 5 years of age and 18 years of age were 5.2 per cent and 20 per cent respectively. Sample weights were calculated and used in the subsequent analyses of the data to adjust for the sampling framework.

Key Findings

The data from the BSC MICS allows us to compare the situation in Small Communities in relation with the overall average for Bangkok, as well as to other provinces and the national average. To allow comparison between different areas, figures presented in this section show the national average, the average for Bangkok (i.e. disaggregated data for Bangkok from the national MICS) and the average for Bangkok small communities. The indicators selected here focus on the areas where the difference between the national average and in Bangkok compared to Bangkok small communities was significant. While the list of selected key indicators can be found in the Annex, the full list of indicators and results are available from the full MICS report.

1. Health

Immunization coverage
Children living in different Bangkok Small Communities have considerably lower vaccination coverage than other children living in Bangkok and in the country. While in Bangkok 75.2 per cent of children are fully vaccinated, in the small communities only 68.7 per cent are completely covered. The coverage for Polio and Hepatitis B is especially low, as the rates do not even reach 80 per cent of children.

Figure 2. Immunization coverage, (12 to 23 months), (%), 2016

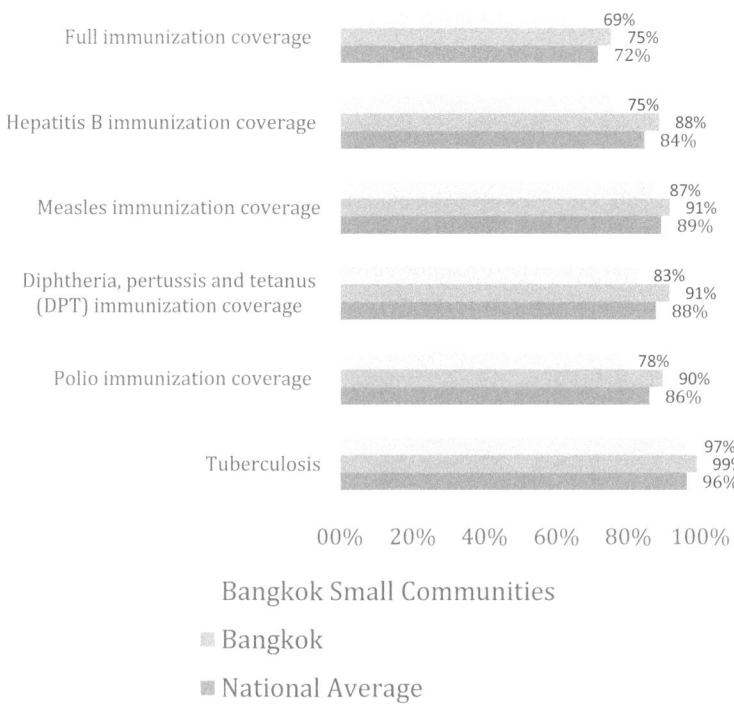

Source: NSO (2016)

Institutional health care

Women living in Bangkok Small Communities have lower coverage of antenatal care (85 per cent) than the national average (91 per cent), and even more compared to Bangkok where 96 per cent of women are covered. Nevertheless, for those with access, the content of the care is complete. In contrast, the national percentage of mothers that had at least three postnatal health checks within 42 days of delivery is only 3 per cent. Although still small, this proportion doubles to 6 per cent for Bangkok Small Communities and reaches 8 per cent in Bangkok, indicating an urban advantage to accessing healthcare services.

Exclusive breastfeeding

Only 1 in 10 children in Bangkok small communities received exclusive breastfeeding in the first 6 months after birth. This percentage is less than half of the national average of 23.1 per cent. The national average of exclusive breastfeeding rate is already quite low in Thailand, falling behind the global target of reaching 50 per cent by 2025. The low breastfeeding rate for Bangkok Small Communities shows that the rate of exclusive breastfeeding is even more concerning in urban poor areas. Further investigation is required to understand the particular challenges facing mothers from urban poor communities, including the impact of the limited duration of maternity leave in Thailand (90 days) and the situation of informal workers who may not be entitled to such protection.

Figure 3. Exclusive breastfeeding for children under 6 months, (%), 2016[16]

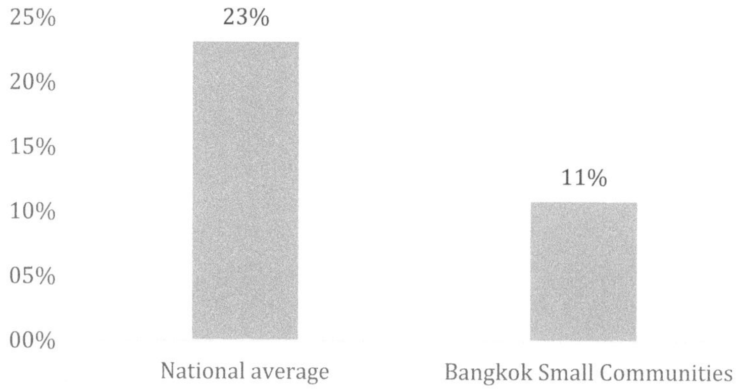

	National average	Bangkok Small Communities
	23%	11%

Source: NSO (2016)

Fertility and adolescent birth rate

Adolescent women living in Bangkok Small Communities have a considerably higher probability of giving birth than their peers in Bangkok and the rest of the country. These poor urban territories have one of the highest adolescent birth rates in the country, with 79 births per 1,000, compared to 51 births per 1,000 in Thailand and 48 per 1,000 in Bangkok. The total fertility rate is similar to the national average (1.6 versus 1.5) but higher than in Bangkok (1.1).

---

16 Figure 3 does not contain data for Bangkok due to the small sample size.

Figure 4. Total fertility rate and adolescent birth rate (per 1,000), 2016

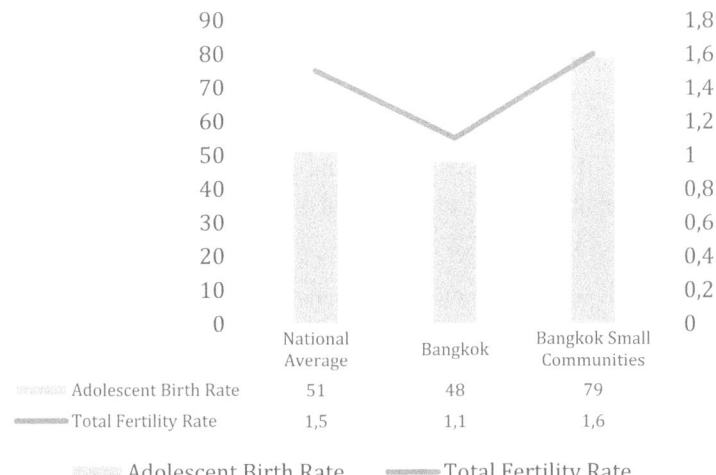

Source: NSO (2016)

Iodized salt consumption

The consumption of adequately iodized salt, defined as salt containing 15 or more parts per million (>15 parts per million), is important to prevent mental retardation and impaired psychomotor development in young children. The percentage of households using adequately iodized salt for cooking in Bangkok's Small Communities is lower than both the Bangkok and national levels (73.3 per cent versus 67.4 per cent), meaning that adequately iodized salt consumption is used in two out of three households in Bangkok Small Communities.

Figure 5. Iodized salt consumption (%), 2016

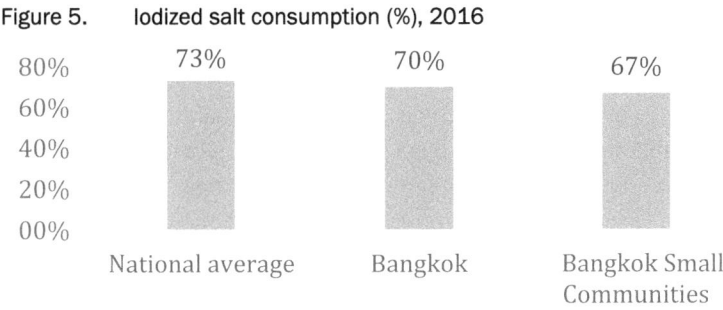

Source: NSO (2016)

2. Child development

Early childhood education and Early Childhood Development (ECD) Index

Children aged 3 to 4 years in Bangkok Small Communities and in Bangkok are less likely to attend to Early Childhood Development programs compared to their peers from the rest of the country. Whereas in Thailand approximately 8 out of 10 children attend ECD services, in Bangkok and in Bangkok Small Communities only 6 out of 10 children are covered (85 per cent versus 63 per cent).

Figure 6. Attendance to Early Childhood Education programme (36–59 months), (%), 2016

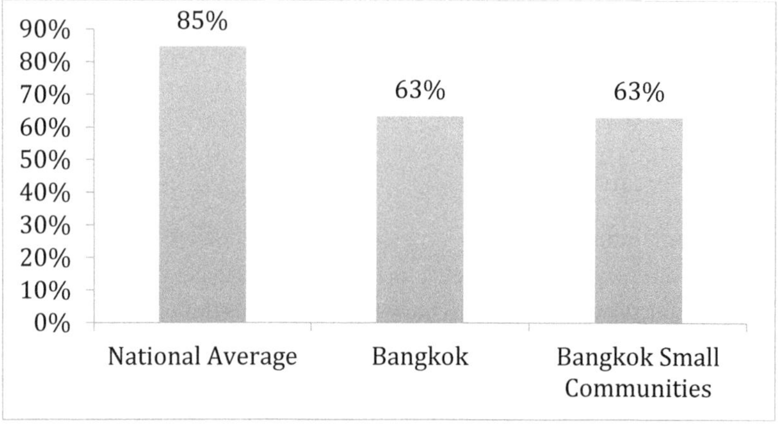

	National Average	Bangkok	Bangkok Small Communities
	85%	63%	63%

Source: NSO (2016)

Interestingly, the lack of attendance is not necessarily reflected in a lower ECD Index for children living in different Bangkok Small Communities, as it records a similar percentage of children developmentally on track compared to the national average (92.1 per cent versus 91.1 per cent) and even higher compared to Bangkok (89.5 per cent). While the reasons for this require further research, one potential explanation from figures 8 and 9 could be that children from Bangkok Small Communities benefit from exposure to other learning opportunities besides organized early childhood learning, such as parental engagement. Following the national pattern, literacy and numeracy is the domain with the least proportion of children developmentally on track. Nevertheless, the average among Bangkok small communities is considerably higher than the national average.

Figure 7. ECD index by ECD domains (36–47 months), (%), 2016

Source: NSO (2016)

Parental involvement in development activities

Considering other relevant practices which benefit the early development of children such as parental involvement in learning, both Bangkok and Bangkok Small Communities report better indicators than the national average. However, the involvement of fathers in the lives of their 3 to 4-year-old children is more limited than engagement by mothers at all levels. Although the percentage of paternal involvement in learning in Bangkok Small Communities is much higher than the national average (44 per cent and 34 per cent, respectively), still less than half of fathers at all levels are involved in development activities with their children.

Figure 8. Maternal support for learning (36–47 months) (%), 2016

- National average: 63%
- Bangkok: 76%
- Bangkok Small Communities: 71%

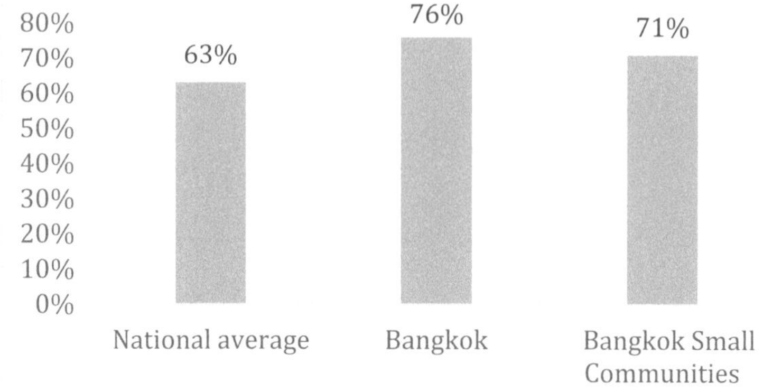

Source: NSO (2016)

Figure 9 Paternal Support for Learning (36–47 months) (%), 2016

- National average: 34%
- Bangkok: 47%
- Bangkok Small Communities: 44%

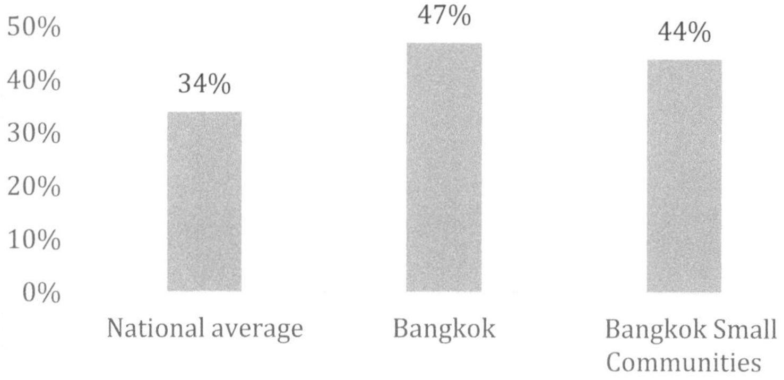

Source: NSO (2016)

3. Education and literacy

School attendance

The school attendance of children living in Bangkok Small Communities at primary and secondary levels shows different patterns in relation to the situation nationally and in Bangkok. While in Bangkok Small Communities primary school attendance is almost universal (96.6 per cent), even slightly higher than in Bangkok (94.7 per cent), the attendance at secondary level drops to 75.5 per cent, which is 10 per cent lower than in Bangkok (85.6 per cent).

Figure 10. Primary and secondary attendance ratio (%), 2016

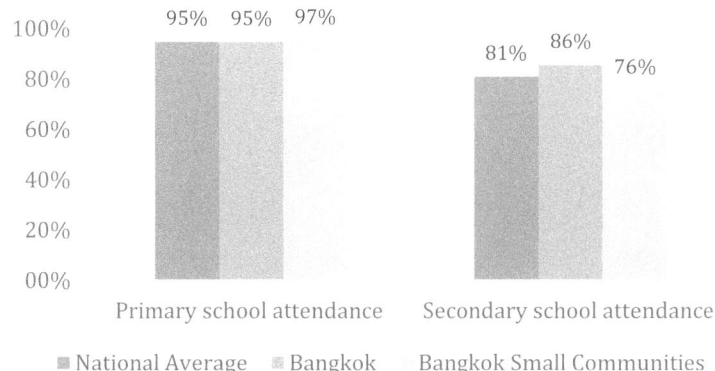

Source: NSO (2016)

Out-of-school children[17]

Aligned with the attendance ratio and following the global trend, out-of-school children in Bangkok Small Communities are mainly boys of secondary school age. However, the gap between boys and girls as well as between children of primary and secondary school age is even more pronounced compared to the national average.

The proportion of out-of-school children of primary school age in Bangkok Small Communities is lower than the national average, especially compared to Bangkok where 6.8 per cent of girls and 3.8 per cent of boys are out of school. Nevertheless, this situation considerably deteriorates for children of secondary school age living in Bangkok Small Communities, as almost 16 per cent of girls and 20 per cent of boys in this age group are out of school.

This means that girls of secondary schools age living in Bangkok Small Communities are twice as likely to be out of school than their peers from Bangkok (16 per cent versus 7 per cent). Although the difference in the proportion of out-of-school boys is not that wide between Bangkok and the national average, the situation for this group in Bangkok Small Communities is even more critical as 1 out of 5 boys (20.3 per cent) of secondary school age are out of school.

---

17 The percentage of out-of-school children of primary school age refers to those not attending school. The percentage of out-of-school children of secondary school age refers to those who are not attending primary, secondary or higher education.

Figure 11. Rate of Out-of-school Children (%), 2016

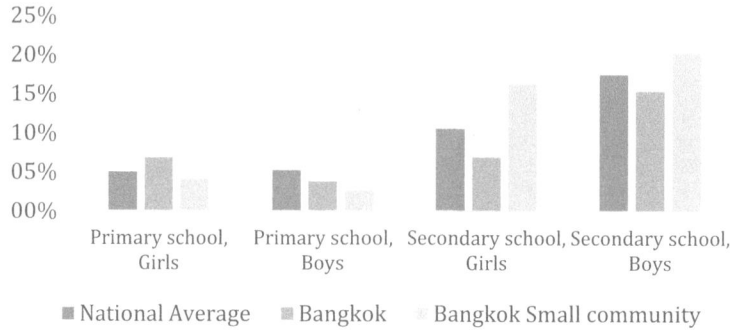

Source: NSO (2016)

4. Child protection

Child living arrangements

Children aged 0–17 years from Bangkok Small Communities are more likely to live with neither biological parent (15.8 per cent) than children in Bangkok (11.2 per cent). Both averages, though, are still lower than the national average of 22.7 per cent.

Figure 12. Child living arrangements (0–17 years), (%), 2016

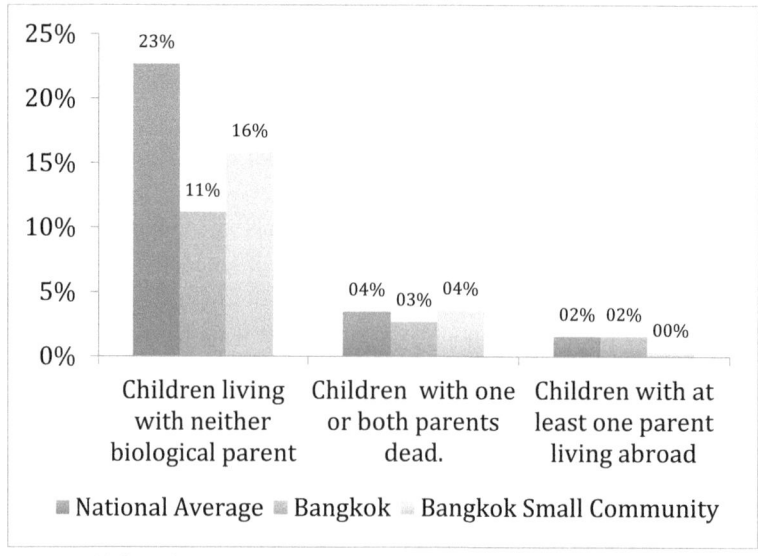

Source: NSO (2016)

Violent discipline

In Thailand, according to survey results, more than 75 per cent of children aged 1–14 years experienced psychological aggression or physical punishment during the previous month. The percentage of households in Bangkok Small Communities using violent discipline methods is quite similar to the national average (73 per cent) compared to 69 per cent at Bangkok level.

Figure 13. Violent discipline (1–14 years), (%), 2016

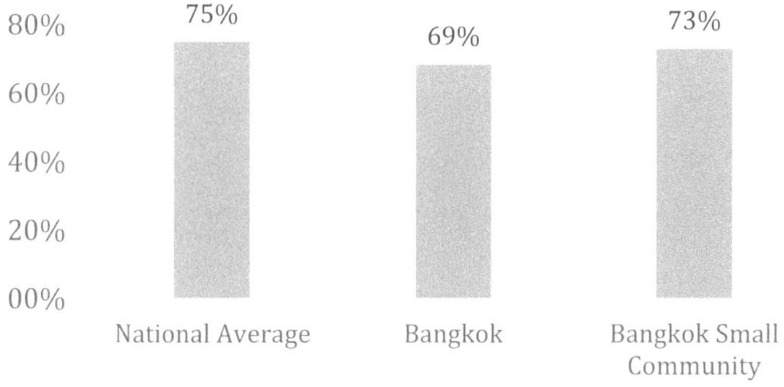

	National Average	Bangkok	Bangkok Small Community
	75%	69%	73%

Source: NSO (2016)

5. HIV/AIDS—knowledge and attitudes of young women and men

Nationally, young women and men demonstrate a similar percentage of knowledge (approximately 45 per cent) on HIV prevention; awareness that a healthy looking person can be HIV positive; and rejection of the two most common misconceptions of HIV/AIDS. However, in Bangkok Small Communities, a lower proportion of men (43.8 per cent) compared to women (51.5 per cent) have comprehensive knowledge.

Worryingly, young women and men living in Bangkok Small Communities are less likely compared the national average to have positive attitudes towards people living with HIV. Nationally, approximately 25 per cent of young people do not discriminate against or stigmatize persons living with HIV, but this proportion drops to around 14 per cent in Bangkok and 11 per cent in Bangkok Small Communities. Although in the country a higher percentage of men have accepting attitudes, in Bangkok small communities the proportions are similar in both sexes.

Figure 14. Comprehensive knowledge and accepting attitudes of HIV/AIDS of young women and men

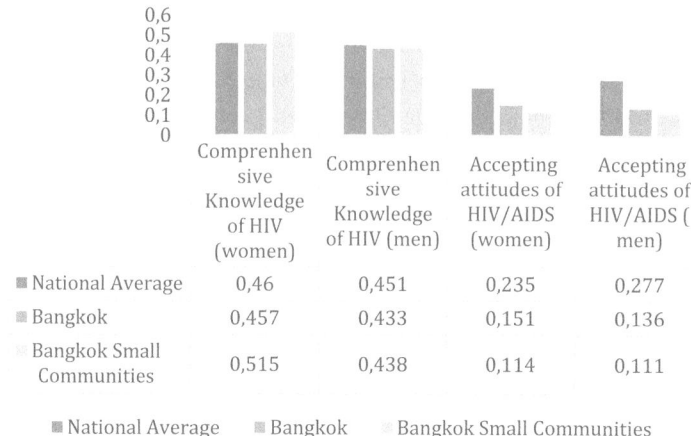

	Comprehensive Knowledge of HIV (women)	Comprehensive Knowledge of HIV (men)	Accepting attitudes of HIV/AIDS (women)	Accepting attitudes of HIV/AIDS (men)
National Average	0,46	0,451	0,235	0,277
Bangkok	0,457	0,433	0,151	0,136
Bangkok Small Communities	0,515	0,438	0,114	0,111

Source: NSO (2016)

6. Living conditions

Across Thailand, almost all households have access to electricity as well as finished roofs and exterior walls. Nationally, the flooring condition is poorer in relation with other housing characteristics, as about 80 per cent of households have a finished floor. Compared to the national average and Bangkok, the percentage of households with a finished floor is lower in Bangkok Small Communities at 72.5 per cent, especially compared with the rate of 87.9 per cent in Bangkok.

Figure 15. Housing characteristics (%), 2016

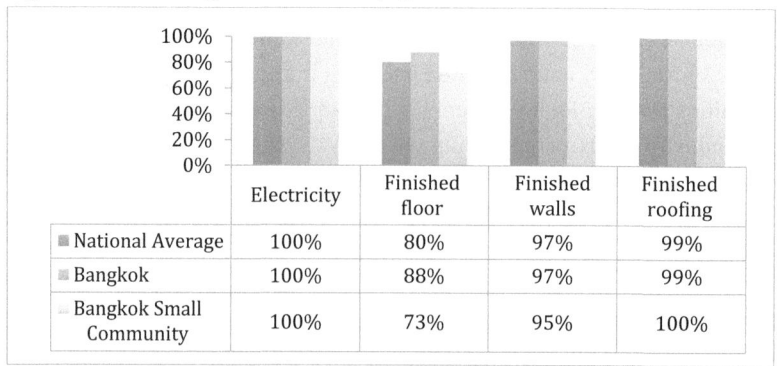

	Electricity	Finished floor	Finished walls	Finished roofing
National Average	100%	80%	97%	99%
Bangkok	100%	88%	97%	99%
Bangkok Small Community	100%	73%	95%	100%

Source: NSO (2016)

7. Water and sanitation

Safe drinking water and improved sanitation are critical dimensions in the living conditions of children, and determinants to prevent diseases and child mortality. In Thailand, including in Bangkok Small Communities, the access to improved drinking water sources is almost universal. The use of improved sanitation in the country overall is slightly lower. However, the percentage of household without access to adequate sanitation in Bangkok Small Communities (10 per cent) is double that of Bangkok, where only 5 per cent do not have access to improved sanitation.

Figure 16. Use of improved drinking water sources and sanitation by household, (%), 2016

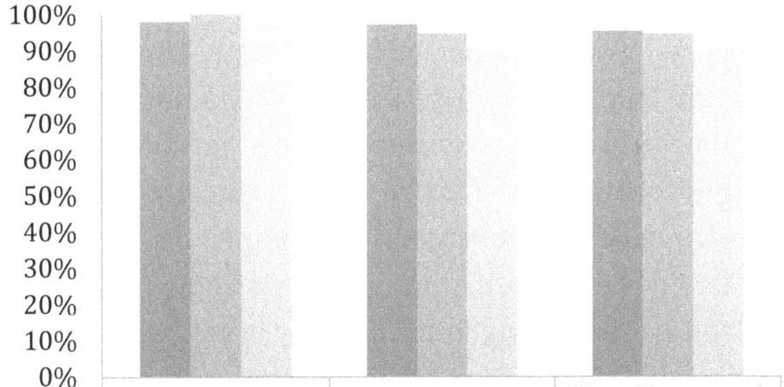

	Use of improved drinking water sources	Use of improved sanitation	Use of improved drinking water sources and sanitation
National Average	98%	97%	95%
Bangkok	100%	95%	95%
Bangkok Small Community	100%	91%	91%

Source: NSO (2016)

Discussion and conclusions

This paper presents the results from the Bangkok Small Community MICS (2015-2016) as a unique approach to capture one of the most disadvantaged groups in Thailand—children and women living in urban poor communities. Even though more than 2 million people live slum settlements in the Bangkok metropolitan area, comprehensive statistics on their well-being and living situation have often been hidden by the average statistics of Bangkok as a whole, as Bangkok almost always performs better than the national average. Therefore, the National Statistical Office of Thailand, with support from UNICEF, conducted the BSC MICS in coordination with the Bangkok Metropolitan Administration to produce reliable and extensive data on the well-being of children and women in urban poor areas of Bangkok.

The analysis compared the results from the national MICS (including the disaggregated figure for Bangkok) with statistics from the BSC MICS. In many indictors across different areas of child well-being—such as the vaccination rate, adolescent fertility rate or access to secondary school—the average performance of Bangkok was higher than the national average. However, when we also compare the Bangkok average with the average rate for Bangkok Small Communities, these areas often performed lower than the national average. The full reasons are difficult to capture from the MICS data alone. While this trend was not observed in all indicators, the results demonstrate that conducting a Bangkok Small Community MICS was effective in capturing urban inequalities and identifying the children left behind, which is a vital step in achieving the SDGs.

While the BSC MICS brings new insights into the situation of children and women living in urban poor areas, we would like to conclude with possible ideas for further exploration to strengthen the data and evidence on children living in poor areas. First, while the MICS data can be used to monitor the situation of children and women, further analysis of the administrative data or qualitative data are necessary if we wish to go further into understanding the reasons behind the data. For example, while the access to early childhood development education services were significantly lower in Bangkok and in Bangkok Small Communities compared to the national average, the reasons remain unclear only from the MICS data. Comparing the results with administrative data, qualitative research and interviews with the parents, or secondary analysis that seeks to understand the correlates, are therefore necessary to identify the drivers of certain areas of concerns and to derive policy recommendations.

Second, there are pros and cons of using the same survey instrument for the national MICS and the BSC MICS. The advantage is straightforward: it allows comparison of the same indicators and highlights issues particular to Bangkok Small Communities. At the same time, it can also be argued that small communities in Bangkok face different types of challenges or issues compared to other households nationwide, therefore some questions or indicators could be added or further customized to understand the situation in Bangkok Small Communities more fully. For instance, violence, lack of community networks or inadequate physical environments could be of particular concern for the families living in urban poor areas, which may require additional data collection and/or sampling approaches.

Finally, the experience of Bangkok Small Communities could also have implications in terms of building a national statistics and data system for SDG monitoring. There is a need for a tailored data system to monitor the SDGs, particularly to capture the population segment that is often hidden from the analytical scope of regular statistics. Capturing invisible populations requires an effective combination of traditional household data, administrative data, along with more customized data collection instruments focused on certain populations. A tailored approach of data collection at country level may also imply possible decentralization of the data function, especially for large independent administrative units such as the municipalities or provinces. Such a decentralized data function could also help boost ownership and improve the monitoring/response to the situation of hidden populations.

As the trend of urbanization continues globally and with the increased focus on urban issues under the SDGs, we believe that the background, methodology and results from the BSC MICS presented in this paper highlight the importance of developing survey instruments to capture inequities in urban areas, which can trigger discussions and actions in other countries and cities.

References

Baker, J. (2008). *Urban Poverty: A Global View*. Washington, DC: The World Bank.

Bangkok Metropolitan Administration. (2016). *Bangkok State of the Environment 2016*. Bangkok: BMA.

Bangkok Metropolitan Authority. (2009). *Statistical Profile of Bangkok Metropolitan Administration 2009*. Bangkok: BMA.

Bangkok Metropolitan Authority, Department of City Planning. (1999). *Bangkok's city planning (first revised.)* Bangkok: BMA.

Chandran, R. (2018, March 7). *'Always a fight' for Bangkok's slum dwellers, says activist of 50 years.* Retrieved from https://www.reuters.com/article/us-thailand-landrights-women/always-a-fight-for-bangkoks-slum-dwellers-says-activist-of-50-years-idUSKCN1GJ194 (Accessed June 2020)

Choiejit, R. (2002). *The relationships between population density and commuting* (Doctoral dissertation). Mahidol University, Thailand.

Choiejit, R., & Teungfung, R. (2005). *Urban Growth And Commuting Patterns Of The Poor In Bangkok.* Retrieved from http://siteresources.worldbank.org/INTURBANDEVELOPMENT/Resources/336387-1269364699096/6892630-1269364758309/choejit.pdf (Accessed June 2020)

Dhakal, S., & Shrestha, A. (2016). Bangkok, Thailand. In S. Bartlett & D. Satterthwaite (Eds.), *Cities on a Finite Planet: Towards Transformative Responses to Climate Change.* New York, NY: Taylor and Francis.

National Statistical Office. (2016). *Multiple Indicator Cluster Survey 2015–2016.* Bangkok: NSO.

Sapsuwan, P. (2014, April 28). *Bangkok's Klong Toey Slum.* Retrieved from https://www.borgenmagazine.com/bangkoks-klong-toey-slum/ (Accessed June 2020)

Sustainable Development Solutions Network (SDSN). (2013). *Why the world needs an urban Sustainable Development Goal.* Retrieved from http://unsdsn.org/wp-content/uploads/2014/02/130918-SDSN-Why-the-World-Needs-an-Urban-SDG-rev-1310291.pdf (Accessed June 2020)

Shummadtayar, U., Hokao, K., & Iamtrakul, P. (2013). Investigating the low-income settlement in an urbanization and urban form a consequences of Bangkok Growing City, Thailand. *Lowland Technology International* (Saga) Vol. 15, No.1, 45–54.

United Nations Department of Economic and Social Affairs (UN DESA). (2014). *World Urbanization Prospects.* Retrieved from https://esa.un.org/unpd/wup/publications/files/wup2014-report.pdf (Accessed June 2020)

UN-HABITAT. (2003). *The Challenge of Slums: Global Report on Human Settlements 2003.* Retrieved from https://www.un.org/ruleoflaw/files/Challenge%20of%20Slums.pdf (Accessed June 2020)

World Bank Group. (2015). *East Asia's Changing Urban Landscape: Measuring a Decade of Spatial Growth.* Washington, DC: The World Bank.

Annex: List of selected indicators and averages for Thailand, Bangkok and Bangkok Small Community

Indicator*	National Average	Bangkok	Bangkok Small Community
NUTRITION			
Exclusive breastfeeding	23.1%	N/A	10.8%
Children with low birth weight (below 2,500 grams)	8.6%	5.9%	8.1%
Median duration of breastfeeding (any breastfeeding)	7.9	6.1	7.0
Use of Iodized Salt (Household)	73.3%	70.2%	67.4%
VACCINATION			
Tuberculosis immunization coverage (Children 12–23 months)	96.2%	99.0%	96.7%
Polio immunization coverage (Children 12–23 months)	85.8%	89.5%	78.2%
Diphtheria, pertussis and tetanus (DPT) immunization coverage (Children 12–23 months)	87.6%	91.3%	82.5%
Measles immunization coverage	89.0%	91.4%	86.9%
Hepatitis B immunization coverage (Children 12–23 months)	84.3%	88.4%	75.3%
Full immunization coverage (Children 12–23 months)	71.6%	75.2%	68.7%
WATER AND SANITATION			
Use of improved drinking water sources (Household)	98.0%	100.0%	99.8%
Use of improved sanitation (Household)	97.2%	94.7%	90.7%
Use of improved drinking water sources and sanitation (Household)	95.3%	94.6%	90.5%
REPRODUCTUVE HEALTH			
Total Fertility Rate	1.5	1.1	1.6
Adolescent Birth Rate (women 15–19)	51.0	48.0	79.0
Antenatal care coverage (at least four times by any provider)—(women 15–49)	90.8%	95.5%	84.8%
Content of antenatal care (women 15–49)	97.0%	99.1%	98.3%
Post-natal health check for mothers (women 15–49). At least three post natal health checks for the mother within 42 days of delivery	3.0%	8.1%	6.1%

CHILD DEVELOPMENT			
Attendance in Early Childhood Education (Children 36–59 months)	84.7%	63.4%	63.0%
Father's Support for learning (Children 24–59 months)	34.0%	47.3%	44.2%
Mother's support for learning (Children 24–59 months)	62.8%	75.7%	71.2%
ECD Index (Children 36–59 months)	91.1%	89.5%	92.1%
Adequate development in literacy-numeracy	69.3%	76.0%	77.8%
Adequate development physical	97.7%	97.6%	97.3%
Adequate development social emotional	79.4%	79.4%	79.0%
Adequate development Learning	97.6%	97.8%	98.5%
EDUCATION			
Primary school attendance (All)	94.8%	94.7%	96.6%
Primary school attendance (Women 15–24)	95.0%	94.7%	97.3%
Children of primary school age Out of school (All)	5.1%	5.3%	3.4%
Out of school girls (Primary)	5.0%	6.8%	4.1%
Out of school boys (Primary)	5.2%	3.8%	2.7%
Secondary school attendance (All)	81.0%	85.6%	75.5%
Children of secondary school age Out of school (All)	14.1%	11.0%	18.4%
Out of school girls (Secondary)	10.5%	6.9%	16.2%
Out of school boys (Secondary)	17.5%	15.3%	20.3%
CHILD PROTECTION			
Violent discipline (Children 1–14)	75.2%	69%	73.1%
Children's living arrangements—living with neither biological parent (0–17 years)	22.7%	11.2%	15.8%
Children with one or both parents dead (0–17 years).	3.5%	2.7%	3.6%
HIV			
Female comprenhensive Knowledge of HIV	48.8%	50.7%	48.0%
Male comprenhensive Knowledgef of HIV	49.0%	52.5%	47.4%
Young women 15–24 comprenhensive Knowledge of HIV	46.0%	45.7%	51.5%
Young men 15–24 comprenhensive Knowledge of HIV	45.1%	43.3%	43.8%
Female Accepting attitudes of HIV/AIDS	31.6%	16.0%	14.3%
Male Accepting attitudes of HIV/AIDS	33.0%	17.3%	13.1%
Accepting attitudes of HIV/AIDS (young women 15–24)	23.5%	15.1%	11.4%
Accepting attitudes of HIV/AIDS (young men 15–24)	27.7%	13.6%	11.1%

A Safe and Inclusive City for Adolescents in Kolkata: Lessons From a Participatory Mapping of an Urban Ward in India

Sudeshna Chatterjee[18]

Introduction

Since 2008 more children are growing up in cities than in villages across the world, including in India, which is one of the most populous countries in the world. India is also the most youthful country, with a median age of its 1.36 billion inhabitants standing at 27 years (Statista, 2019). Further, India is home to the largest adolescent (10–19 years) population in the world, with 253 million adolescents (Census of India, 2011). Despite a relatively slow and steady pace of urbanization (India was 33.6% urbanized in 2019), Indian cities are likely to house 40 percent of India's large population by 2030 (Sankhe et al., 2010). Moreover, India is one of the three countries that will contribute the most to world urbanization by 2050 (United Nations, 2014).

The UN Sustainable Development Goals (SDGs) call for bringing about transformational change to the world's most pressing problems by the year 2030, including the problems in cities. India's cities, similar to those of many developing countries, are considered to be in crisis as urbanization has far outpaced infrastructure development. This resulted in the proliferation of slums, growing urban poverty and crime, as well as pollution and ecological damage (UNICEF, 2012, Ellis & Roberts, 2016). The Census of India 2011 shows that over 65 million people live in informal settlements or slums, which is an increase of 13 million from 2001 figures. Slums, which are a good proxy indicator of urban deprivation, are the default housing options for mostpoor households in Indian cities,

---

18 Founder and CEO, Action for Children's Environments (ACE). Consulting Senior Evaluation Specialist, UNICEF Headquarters, New York. The author would like to thank UNICEF India Country Office and UNICEF State Office for West Bengal for commissioning this work to Action for Children's Environments. The author also thanks all ACE colleagues and in particular Saumya Bahuguna, Shalini Gupta, Partha Pratim Saha, Swarna Dutta and Harisankar Krishnadas for their hard work and active participation in this project.

which have 13.7 million slum households, comprising more than 17% of the total urban households in the country (Census of India, 2011).

The urban advantage typically bypasses the millions of Indians living in slums and threatens to undermine the developmental goals achieved for children and adolescents over the last few decades. A study on child well-being and equity analysis in India shows that for the indicators of nutrition, education and shelter, urban children in the lowest wealth quintile were more deprived than children in the lowest wealth quintile in rural India (Rustagi et al., 2012). Crimes against children too are on the rise in cities in India. According to the National Crime Record Bureau data for 2016, overall crimes against children have increased from previous years with a sharp spike in incidents of rape of children; an increase by over 82% compared to 2015 (National Crime Records Bureau, 2016).

The New Urban Agenda (NUA) offers a roadmap to help implement the Sustainable Development Goals (SDGs) in cities and is committed to leaving no one behind, ensuring urban equity and eradicating poverty by providing equitable access for all to physical and social infrastructure, recognizing and leveraging culture, diversity and safety, while enabling participation and enhancing the livability and quality of life. What does this mean for vulnerable adolescents living in cities, particularly in India, where every fifth person is an adolescent? There is compelling evidence to suggest the need for investing in adolescence to promote healthy growth, develop modern skills while preventing risky behavior (UNICEF, 2011). For poor urban adolescents to enjoy any urban advantage as envisioned in the NUA for groups needing 'particular attention', it is important to develop evidence-based urban programs to reduce risks and vulnerabilities, build resilience, and strengthen the capacity of local governments and civil society to bring about the larger societal transformation needed to deliver on the promise of safe, inclusive, resilient and sustainable cities.

Urban safety, inclusion and the SDGs

The commitments in the SDGs and the NUA recognize the importance of cities to national economies as more than 80% of global GDP is generated in cities (World Bank, 2018). However, as Satterthwaite (2016) points out, economic success in any city does not automatically contribute to a healthier and safer city, or to a more inclusive and sustainable city. This view is shared by the Safe Cities Index, created by the Economist Intelligence Unit (2015), which ranked 50 cities on the basis of digital security, health security, infrastructure safety and personal safety. The living conditions of the vast majority of the urban poor in cities is rendered unsafe typically due to insecurity of tenure and forced evictions, urban crime and violence, weak social support networks, and natural and human-made disasters (UN-Habitat, 2007). These threats to safety are further exacerbated by poverty. Moreover, impoverished urban children simply cannot thrive without resilient urban infrastructure, social protection mechanisms, inclusive urban planning and good governance that will lift them out of extreme poverty or declining conditions (McGranahan & Satterthwaite 2014). For SDG 11, the urban goal, experts believe that success is critically linked to progress on other urban critical goals dealing with poverty, health, inequality, employability, water and sanitation, infrastructure and so on (Rudd et al., 2018).

Discourses on urban safety typically focus on prevention of crime and violence. However, the Habitat III Issue paper on Safer Cities expanded the definition of safety to also include the enhancement of individual rights including the physical, social and psychological integrity of a person (UN Habitat, 2015a). This is very important from an ecological perspective of urban safety and its impact on child development. For example, if we improve safety in schools and on the routes to school, we improve school attendance, retention and performance, which together enhance the right to education of individual children as well as their right to development. A good education in turn contributes to better and more secure incomes, livelihoods and thus ensures the future of entire families.

In the context of safer cities, the New Urban Agenda echoes the widely acknowledged notion that inadequate urban development and poor local governance that inevitably generate social and territorial exclusion patterns encourage crime and violence (UN Habitat, 2015). Local governments are considered to be the form of government closest to children and young people (Bartlett et al., 1999). The 12th schedule of the 74th Constitutional Amendment Act of India defines 18 tasks for Urban Local Bodies (ULB) ranging from planning functions to provision of basic services and amenities such as water, sanitation, garbage management, street lighting, health, and education. It also includes developing and maintaining parks and open spaces, as well as the safeguarding of the interests of the poor and promoting social welfare. The various local area development funds available to Members of Parliament, Members of Legislative Assembly and Local Councillors also support development work in these sectors and beyond. Many of these functions are significant to adolescents in their everyday life, both for their immediate health and well-being and for their longer-term development. In addition, these development initiatives form an important part of adolescents' legally established right to an adequate standard of living.

Relevance of an ecological approach for urban safety and child protection programming

Keeping children and young people safe by preventing and addressing violence, abuse, and exploitation is part of the gobal goals (SDG 16). Reducing risks to children's protection and well-being as is demanded in the SDGs as well as in Indian national law is a profound challenge. While there is agreement among practitioners to develop or strengthen protective factors at multiple levels, such as the family, community, and national levels, conceptualizing such a multi-dimensional model of child protection, particularly in the urban context, requires the adoption of a systems approach, such as the ecological model of child development (Bronfenbrenner, 1979), which places the child at the centre of a nested hierarchy of interconnected influences ranging from the child's genotype to the wider political economy (Bartlett, 2018; Wessells, 2009).

In the mapping reported in this chapter, the interconnectedness of the roles of different actors, in an urban context, in nurturing the development and promoting protection of children, is conceptualized using the frame of the ecological model (see figure 1). As all these ecological levels are interconnected, any pressures on the system at the furthest (macrosystem) level such as through excessive urbanization, climate change, and large non-climatic disasters such as earthquakes, trigger local hazards that impact children at the most immediate (microsystem) levels. Similarly, reduction in household income due to loss of jobs, disruption to education, and loss or sickness of family members, also impact children's well-being. Government actors and institutions, particularly urban local bodies, have crucial roles to play in promoting community safety by providing for personal and family security, maintaining law and order, and developing child-friendly services, regulations and policies that promote children's protection and well-being (Wessells, 2009).

Figure 1:   An ecological model of child development in the urban context*

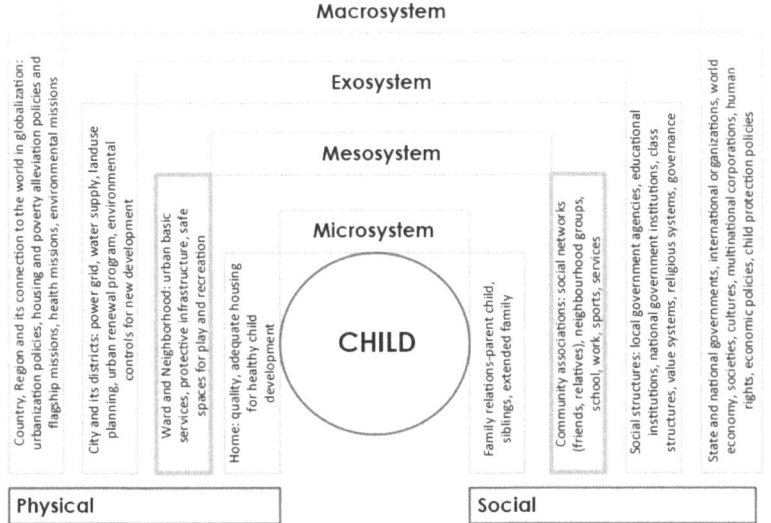

* Adapted from Bronfenbrenner (1979), Wachs and Shpancer (1998) and Chatterjee (2006).

A Safe and Inclusive City for Adolescents in Kolkata

Since 2016 UNICEF and its partners, Action for Children's Environments (ACE), Child Rights and You (CRY), and Sanlaap, have all been engaged in an urban program in Kolkata called 'A Safe and Inclusive City for Adolescents in Kolkata'. The first phase of the program adopts an ecological perspective to map the risk factors threatening safety and protection of urban adolescents as well as assessing the factors contributing to insecurity of vulnerable families living in an urban ward. The mapping heeds the call for high quality, timely, reliable data disaggregated by income, gender, age, migratory status, location among others within the SDGs (target 17.18) as well as in the NUA (160: ... 'the creation, promotion, enhancement of open, user-friendly, and participatory data platforms using technological and social tools').

Before the Kolkata program, UNICEF and its partners were engaged in the 'Promoting Safe Communities' program in two other Indian cities: Bhopal and Mumbai. ACE as the lead technical partner conceptualized the city level projects; designed the battery of indicators and multiple tools for mapping the multi-dimensional safety and protection issues at the household, community and ward level in each city with the participation of all project partners including the community and government representatives. ACE also trained and built capacity of local NGO partners, and provided leadership to the Safe Community model building process in the two cities. Three local NGOs in each city conducted the mapping at the slum level with participation of children, adolescents and the community volunteers. UNICEF and ACE subsequently adapted this program in the context of Kolkata as a convergent model for accelerating outcomes for adolescents in partnership with Kolkata Municipal Corporation (KMC), relevant government departments and local NGO partners.

The Kolkata urban program was designed as a pilot with plans for scaling up to other wards with large vulnerable populations. It was targeted at a ward level because the ward is the lowest unit of decentralization of urban governance in India. The urban local body responsible for urban governance in Kolkata, KMC and its ward office in Ward no. 26 were program partners and were keen to improve living conditions for adolescents.

The Urban Context of Kolkata

Kolkata, erstwhile Calcutta, is the capital of the state of West Bengal and was the former capital of India until 1911. It continues to serve as a primary city in eastern India. The Kolkata Metropolitan Area (KMA), with a population of over 14 million, is the urban agglomeration of Kolkata comprising portions of six districts, including the KMC area, which is a fully urban district in itself. The KMA comprises 4 municipal corporations, 38 municipalities and 527 non-municipal towns and villages (Census of India, 2011). The KMA is one of India's three mega cities, after Mumbai and Delhi.

According to Census of India 2011, over 4 million (4,496,694) people resided in the city (KMC area) and the male and female population was 2,356,766 and 2,139,928 respectively. In 2011 the adolescent population of Kolkata was 707,364, of which 370,051 were males and 337,313 females. About one-third (31.35%) of Kolkata's population lived in slums (Census of India, 2011), which typified over-crowded, unsanitary settlements often without adequate basic services.

Governance structure

The city of Kolkata, with 144 wards, comprises the core of KMA and is governed by the KMC. Kolkata is the only city in India with an empowered mayoral system, the Mayor-in-Council, which is responsible for overall decision-making within the KMC through political consensus. The administrative wards of Kolkata are grouped under 15 boroughs. Each of the wards elects a Councillor to the KMC. Each borough has a committee consisting of the Councillors elected from the respective wards of the boroughs. Through the borough committees, the KMC maintains government-aided schools, hospitals and municipal markets, and participates in urban planning and road maintenance. Local governance is further decentralized at the ward level through the ward committees, which are constituted for each ward and empowered to carry out most of the important functions of an urban local body at the ward level.

Slum development

Starting with the city's Basic Development Plan (1960), many programs have attempted to improve the living conditions of slums in KMA. The Vision 2025 Plan, which is the latest plan guiding the development of the city, outlines a strategy of slum development that includes continuing infrastructure development as in previous programs, but also creating durable housing on the land notified under the Thika Tenancy Act. Historically, most of Calcutta's slums were located on private land, rented by middle men called *Thika* tenants who built hutments to sublet to others. Because of this system, there was little scope for State initiated improvements in the slums in the absence of clear legislation. In 1981 the Kolkata Thika Tenancy (Acquisition and Regulation) Act was passed. This allowed the government to take possession of all the private land on which Thika tenant slums had developed but allowed the Thika tenants to collect the rent from the slum dweller; the Thika tenant kept the house rent and paid the land rent to the government (Ghosh, 1992). The State henceforth legally assumed the role of the universal landlord of slum land in Kolkata (Mitra, 2015). The Vision 2025 Plan further considers the development of social infrastructure related to education, health, economic rehabilitation, and community development in parallel to physical infrastructure development.

Theory of change and program components:

The theory of change for this UNICEF-supported program sought to link change strategies with the delivery of outputs that contribute to higher-level results, including the realization of relevant goals and targets of the Sustainable Development Goals (UNICEF, 2017) and the NUA; plans and policies for children at the national and state level; and the priority areas of UNICEF's Urban Strategic Note (2017) which have the following five pillars of programmatic action and strategy:

1. Reducing equity gaps in urban areas through technical support and partnerships to extend quality social services to marginalized children living in urban settings and protect all children from violence.
2. Promoting a safe and sustainable urban environment for children.
3. Adapting urban planning and budgeting for children living in urban settings, particularly the most disadvantaged.
4. Enhancing the voice and participation of poor children living in urban settings and strengthening partnerships with urban communities and organizations.
5. Strengthening the evidence base on children in urban areas, in data, policy and research.

The three key strategies of the theory of change for the Kolkata program were:

1. **Adolescent and community participation in mapping** to strengthen the evidence base beyond data, to contribute to the body of knowledge related to urban issues affecting slum dwelling children and the community. The specific outputs included identification of risks and vulnerabilities, deprivation and exclusion, child protection challenges, community needs and resources at a ward level and a plan of action for improving neighborhood safety and environmental sustainability.
2. **Building the capacities of select stakeholders** such as adolescents, parents, community and service providers at the neighborhood and ward level to enhance their voice and strengthen partnerships to respond to and prevent abuse, exploitation and

violence against children with the goal of creating a safe and sustainable urban environment for children. Creation of ward level platforms of participation for adolescents, parents, and other stakeholders for demand generation, monitoring and evaluation, and providing feedback to the ward level local government in keeping with the commitments embedded in SDG Target 16.7 ('ensuring responsive, inclusive, participatory and representative decision-making at all levels').

3. **Strengthening the system of response** to reduce equity gaps in urban areas through technical support and partnerships to extend the delivery of quality urban basic and protective services to vulnerable children and communities, and protect all children from violence. Strategic urban cross-sectoral integration and capacity building for service delivery is needed to implement SDG 11 at the local level.

Choice of ward

Several vulnerability criteria were considered for selecting the pilot ward in consultation with the Department of Women and Child Development and Social Welfare (WCD&SW) of the state of West Bengal. These included:

- Female Literacy Rate less than the total Female Literacy Rate of Kolkata (84.06)
- Child Sex Ratio less than Child Sex Ratio of Kolkata Slums (925.78)
- High concentration of Scheduled Caste (SC) & Scheduled Tribe (ST) (more than 2%) as these comprise marginalized populations in Indian society
- Large slum population

Six wards were shortlisted out of which the Department of WCD&SW chose KMC Ward no. 26 for the first pilot as that fulfilled all the above criteria and had a proactive ward office.

The Mapping Process

The mapping was designed to be participatory, involving adolescents and adults residing in the slums and other vulnerable pockets of Kolkata Municipal Corporation Ward no. 26. Mapping indicators were developed based on the ecological model of child development as explained earlier and indicators were framed across three vulnerability domains. The well-known 'assets/vulnerability' framework (Moser et al., 2010) categorizes vulnerability according to physical (external) and social (internal) categories. Social vulnerability was subsequently expanded by Roy et al. (2013) to include politico-legal and socio-economic vulnerability. This expanded categorization was adopted for developing the mapping indicators as it more fully captured the range of the community's physical, economic, social or political susceptibility to risks. The development of indicators was an iterative process starting with the Mumbai and Bhopal programs, where a participatory process was adopted with the involvement of local partner NGOs, children and adolescent representatives from the selected slums, representatives from District Child Protection Units and UNICEF state offices. In these urban programs a conscious effort was made to include data categories that are relevant to urban children's experience such as tenure security, access to safe recreational and play spaces and green public spaces, road safety, platforms for participation of adolescents in local decision-making, among others.

The indicators for Kolkata mapping were based on the same framework as the other two cities but in this case the indicators ranged across nine dimensions and the sub-indices of home, community, ward and city wherever applicable:

- Governance and planning
- Security
- Environment
- Safety
- Protection
- Health
- Education
- Play and recreation
- Participation and empowerment

Due to the large scope of this comprehensive multi-dimensional mapping, it will not be possible to discuss all the findings within the limited scope of a book chapter. The author will discuss the relevant findings from across the mapping dimensions of security, safety, protection, urban infrastructure, play and recreation, as well as participation and empowerment, as they all relate to the wider discussion on inclusion and safety in cities.

Methodology

The mapping used mixed methods, both quantitative and qualitative, to collect data about urban adolescents and their families in Ward 26 in Kolkata. Secondary data was collected from official sources such as the latest Census data, National Family Health Services (NFHS) and District Family Health Services (DFHS) data, National Crime Records Bureau (NCRB) data, and state level education surveys among others. The ACE team visited government departments to collect data relating to health, education, and protection at city and ward level. But this proved to be very time consuming and, in some cases, data was released too late for inclusion in the analysis. Internet based research of accessible government documents provided data on urbanization of Kolkata and its metropolitan area. Secondary data was also collected from local government schools, police stations, health centres, and local NGOs at the ward level. Several mapping tools were used for primary data collection from adults and adolescents living in the ward, such as household surveys (one administered by trained adults to adults in 675 households and one administered by trained adolescents to adolescents in 320 households); observation checklists (for systematically observing the home environment in 320 households, the neighbourhood environment across all 18 vulnerable pockets and safe and unsafe spaces in the ward by adolescents across the entire ward); focus group discussions; transect walks by 166 adolescents; and key informant interviews with 7 different types of stakeholders, ranging across Integrated Child Development Services (ICDS) workers, ULB members, social workers associated with the ward office, teachers, community leaders, local NGO staff and parents.

Scoping study to identify vulnerable pockets in the ward

An initial scoping study, undertaken by ACE, helped to identify the pockets of vulnerability as defined by the three vulnerability domains of physical, socio-economic and politico-legal. Based on data kept at the ward office (not publicly available) and in consultation with social workers attached to the ward office, vulnerable pockets were identified and then verified through field visits. Typically, these included red-light areas, pockets with concentration of poor migrant populations, pockets of extreme poverty and deprivation, and slums. These were geo-referenced and plotted on the ward map to provide an immediate visual understanding of the vulnerable areas of the ward and to create base maps for mapping the risks in the physical environment, safe and unsafe spaces by adolescents and the ACE team. The scoping study and the piloting of the tools in the ward aided in outlining the typical problems and child protection issues within the vulnerable pockets and helped in sharpening the research tools. A purposive representative sampling strategy was adopted to obtain a wide representation of the vulnerable populations in Ward 26 residing in the vulnerable pockets identified in the scoping study.

KMC Ward no. 26

Ward 26 is an administrative ward of the Kolkata Municipal Corporation in Borough No. 4 of North Central Kolkata. It is an old habitation site, very well connected to the rest of the city by roadways and the metro and rail network. The ward has a mixed population with the rich and the poor living side by side in diverse types of housing.

For the purpose of this study, the ward was divided into two parts—east and west of Chittaranjan Avenue, which is a major north-south arterial road running through the city. Eighteen vulnerable pockets were identified on the two sides (see figure 2). While the east side only has a few scattered pockets of vulnerability, the western side, in contrast, has a large dense settlement comprising many vulnerable families. The three lanes of this dense settlement form a small red-light area on the western side of Chittaranjan Avenue. The ward has a population of 25,371 (Census of India, 2011) and the population density is 260 persons/acre. The slum population of the ward is 8,425.

Figure 2:   Map of Ward 26 showing the vulnerable pockets

Key mapping findings related to Inclusion

Inclusiveness is a major aspiration of the 2030 Agenda for Sustainable Development as reflected in its main pledges. In cities, inequality and exclusion often occur at rates greater than the national average driven by not only economic drivers of inequality such as income but also others such as social, legal, spatial, cultural, political and environmental drivers that reinforce deprivation and deepen inequalities (UN-Habitat, 2015b). In this section we will restrict the discussion of the key findings linked to the following SDG targets:

- Target 10.2: By 2030, empower and promote the social, economic and political inclusion of all, irrespective of age, sex, disability, race, ethnicity, origin, religion or economic or other status.
- Target 11.1: By 2030, ensure access for all to adequate, safe and affordable housing and basic services, and upgrade slums

A third of the population in Ward No. 26 (30.11%) lived in slum-like conditions similar to the trend in Kolkata and in other cities in the developing world. Social protection policies around the world target poverty reduction, lack of inclusion and improving living conditions for all. The main goal of social protection is to enhance security in people's lives across many domains. In the context of creating safer more inclusive cities, this mapping focused on three forms of security whose lack deepens vulnerability and exclusion: Income security, social security and housing security.

- *Income security:* The population living in the vulnerable pockets of Ward 26 had limited income security. This can mostly be attributed to inadequate education and a lack of vocational skills training. Based on data from the household surveys, 50% of households were below the poverty line (BPL),[19] with the west side of the ward being more vulnerable (51% BPL households) as compared to the east (42% BPL households). The average monthly income of a male (INR 9,118 or USD 126.95) in Ward 26 was low, as men reported to be self-employed or working as casual labourers (contractual and seasonal). However, their income was found to be 16% higher than that of a female who typically worked as a domestic worker or a casual labourer. The workforce participation of women (39.2%), though found to be much lower than men (69.8%) in the ward, was in fact higher than for the city of Kolkata (23.3%) as recorded in Census of India 2011. Even though each family reported having at least one earning member, the income of the family was close to the total expenditure. Due to the income insecurity linked with self-owned businesses (40% of the men and 22% of the women reported running their own business mostly as hawkers), about 18% reported having taken loans for business purpose.
- *Social security:* The mapping also found many adolescents and their families to be deprived of basic social security cover. More than 30% of the adolescents did not have birth certificates, a crucial document for securing social entitlements. While 50 per cent

---

19   Below Poverty Line is a benchmark used by the government of India to indicate economic disadvantage and to identify individuals and households in need of government assistance. Identified families become eligible for social protection and many other poverty reduction schemes of the government. To benefit from such schemes, families need certification from the local government institutions to confirm their BPL status.

households considered themselves to be below the poverty line (BPL), about 75 per cent of them had no official proof of being a BPL family. 92% of the households possessed a ration card,[20] while 73% of them possessed white cards for people above the poverty line. Despite majority of the households possessing important documents, such as a voter identity card, a PAN card, and Aadhar card,[21] very few households accessed social protection schemes, mainly due to a lack of awareness and adequate outreach. Lack of access to schemes further added to the social exclusion of these groups and in turn perpetuated the cycle of poverty.

- *Housing Security*: In 1989, a socio-economic survey by the Kolkata Metropolitan Development Authority (KMDA) identified a majority of the city's slum dwellers as migrants with first generation migrants representing 60% of the households surveyed (Chakrabarti & Halder, 2004). Kolkata's first planning document, the Basic Development Plan 1966, identified housing in the city as a major issue. Out of the 675 families surveyed in the mapping reported in this chapter, 161 families (23.85%) reported having migrated to the city. 141 of the migrant families (87.58%) lived in the more vulnerable west side of the ward. Around 83% of the households of migrants reported moving to Kolkata for better economic opportunities. 24% of the migrants also reported being development displaced. A survey of the ownership status of homes in 675 households revealed greater housing insecurity among migrants. 50% of the overall households lived in rental housing and only 17% of them possessed rental agreements. In comparison, 74% of the migrant families lived in rental housing with only 24% possessing a proper rental agreement. 43% of the

---

20 Ration cards are official documents issued by state governments in India to eligible poor households to purchase subsidized food grain from the Public Distribution System (under the National Food Security Act).
21 Aadhar is a 12-digit unique identity number that can be obtained by residents of India, based on their biometric and demographic data. The data is collected by the Unique Identification Authority of India (UIDAI), a statutory authority established in January 2009 by the government of India, under the jurisdiction of the Ministry of Electronics and Information Technology, following the provisions of the Aadhaar (Targeted Delivery of Financial and other Subsidies, benefits and services) Act, 2016.

overall households lived in self-owned houses but only 22% of them possessed ownership papers. Only 19% of the migrants lived in self owned houses, with merely 11% of them in possession of ownership papers, a fact indicating greater housing insecurity among migrants. This mapping method found that access to adequate housing continues to be a major vulnerability of migrant families and contributes to their lack of social, economic and political inclusion even in a more established, economically stable ward of Kolkata.

Key mapping findings related to Safety

Earlier in this chapter, the child's environment as a multi-level dynamic system has been discussed. From an ecological perspective, in order to keep urban children safe and end all forms of violence against children (Target 16.2), a safe city must promote community safety by addressing safety in homes, schools, neighbourhoods and at the ward levels while simultaneously enhancing protection and well-being of children through policies, regulation and services. In this mapping initiative, the concept of 'perceived safety' within the ward, had been studied at the following three levels: Home, school and neighbourhood. Analysis of data from the adolescent administered household survey found that majority of adolescent boys and girls living across the home, school and neighbourhood dimensions, to be unsafe.

Safety at home:

Among the younger adolescent age group (10 to 14 years), 86% of the girls and 73% of the boys (n = 66 boys and 64 girls) reported feeling unsafe at home because of physical hazards such as the presence of pests and rodents, naked wires (fear of accidents), no proper doors, houses with fragile structures (fear of collapse and sustaining injuries), and lack of light, among others. Fear of ghosts was also high. Among lesser fears were fear of relatives and sexual harassment. Similarly, among the older adolescent age group (15 to 19 years), 93% of the girls and 70% of the boys (n = 20 boys and 16 girls) perceived their home to be unsafe because of physical hazards such as the presence of pests and rodents, followed by a fear of ghosts and sexual harassment. For boys, the fear of ghosts and darkness was the top reason for considering the home unsafe.

Both younger and older adolescents cite similar reasons for considering the home as unsafe. Even though these are mostly linked to physical hazards, the fear of ghosts was common to both age group. Children often forge links between the exceptional, the supernatural and the ordinary in their minds to justify fear. In a study with slum dwelling children in Delhi (Chatterjee, 2006), adolescent girls frequently cited a fear of ghosts and haunted places as reasons why they did not have access to public places.

During the FGDs, almost half of the girls and boys also reported that their homes did not have proper doors, raising security concerns such as strangers forcibly entering their homes. Girls, particularly older adolescents, cited a heightened fear of relatives at home as well as the fear of experiencing sexual abuse, which makes the home an unsafe space for them. When parents were asked about violence at home in the adult administered survey, 53 per cent adults shared that their own child/children were victims of violence and abuse. Most of this violence and abuse takes place at home (according to 90% of respondents) and take the form of physical, verbal, and psychological abuse, where the perpetrators are parents, older siblings or relatives. This finding is comparable to the findings of the Know Violence in Childhood report (2017). However, the adolescents themselves were reticent about discussing about violence in their own homes, preferring to report experiences of physical violence, verbal abuse, psychological abuse and domestic violence in the context of families other than their own. Only 23 per cent of boys and 13 per cent of girls claimed they had personally faced violence and abuse.

Safety at school:

In the adult household survey, parents reported that adolescents enjoy attending school. 83% of the parents also mentioned that schools provide good guidance to children. The survey also reported that children do not face problems at school, such as discrimination based on gender, class or community. During the focus group discussions with a smaller sub-sample of adolescents it was also revealed that adolescents enjoy going to school because they meet and play with friends and sometimes can use the school playground after school hours.

However, the detailed questioning on school safety in the adolescent administered survey to adolescents in 320 households paint a different picture. It was found that the perception of the school being unsafe is very high among both younger (92% of the girls and 85% of the boys) and older adolescents (87% of the girls and 65% of the boys). The same pattern of fears persists for both groups. The biggest reason why boys consider the school as unsafe is because of the dangers of walking in heavy traffic to school. Unsafe roads comprise a unique everyday vulnerability of urban children with an estimated incidence of road traffic injuries of 880 per 100,000 urban 0–19 year olds, as noted by a South Asian review (Hyder, 2006). Road safety is addressed in SDG Target 11.2. Other reasons of considering the school as unsafe include fear of punishments and complaints to parents, as well as harassment and bullying at school. Girls in the same age group cited fear of punishments and complaints as reasons for feeling unsafe. Adolescents also cited fear of exams and inability to cope academically leading to their disinterest in studies, which in turn leads to more disciplinary action at school and home, as reasons for feeling afraid about going to school.

Adolescents were subject to disturbingly high levels of physical violence at home and psychological abuse at school. However, adolescents did not perceive physical punishment by parents or teachers as violence, but as a disciplinary measure to 'teach appropriate conduct', indicating social acceptance. During focus group discussions, adolescents argued that they did not have any support systems when experiencing violence, other than sharing with their friends, which helps them to cope with the violence and abuse and make them feel less alone.

Safety in the neighbourhood:

94% of the boys and 89% of the girls among the younger adolescents, and 70% of the boys and 94% of the girls among the older adolescents reported feeling unsafe within their neighbourhood. This is mainly due to the presence of a red-light area, desolate pockets, the fear of experiencing public sexual harassment, the presence of alcohol shops, heavy traffic, pockets and open spaces frequented by men and older boys playing cards and/or consuming alcohol. These features limit the independent mobility of children and adolescents, especially girls, triggering insecurity in them and their parents.

As adolescents were directly involved in mapping the physical infrastructure and related services in the ward, they reported issues with water collection from public taps, access to community toilets and streetlights that put them at risk every day. SDG 6 has specific targets for equitable access to safe drinking water (target 6.1) and adequate, equitable sanitation and hygiene (6.2). Both these issues comprise major deprivations in urban slums and threaten inclusion and safety of adolescents as is reflected in the mapping data below. Improving streetlights is an integral part of promoting adequate, safe and affordable housing and basic services, and upgradation of slums (11.1). However, the mere numbers of streetlights in any slum is not an indicator of success. Rather, success must be measured by the rationalization of streetlight coverage across the slum and in particular in relation to critical infrastructure elements such as public toilets, community spaces and perceived unsafe spaces within the slum.

- *Water collection:* More than 50% of the households did not have a piped water supply; hence, water had to be fetched from the common tap in the slum lane mainly by the women in the family (85% of the households). Adolescents were often drawn into the water collection routine and 5% of both boys and girls reported feeling unsafe doing so as frequent quarrels break out. 33% of the adolescents reported that water collection had a negative impact on their daily routine and it caused them to be late for school or even to miss school altogether on many days.
- *Community toilets*: 59% of the households reported using a common toilet due to lack of privacy in the in-house toilets. Unlike most slums, the community toilets in ward no. 26 were used by far fewer number of users (around 30 persons) as these are not public toilets but provided in each slum lane by the KMC if there was space to build one. Girls however reported feeling uncomfortable and unsafe using these community toilets as they lacked cleanliness, adequate lighting and were flooded during the rainy season. A common coping strategy used by girls is never to go alone to use the toilets and get a friend or family member to accompany them.
- *Streetlights*: The mapping showed that the ward had an adequate number of street lights, but they were unevenly distributed. For example, there was an overabundance of street lights within some slum pockets causing extreme glare at night, about which residents in the eastern side of the ward complained. Adoles-

cents however complained about the lack of lights inside the common toilets in some pockets.
- *Safe public spaces*: The SDGs have a specific target (SDG Target 11.7) in the urban goal to promote access to safe, inclusive public spaces for children among other groups. Typically, this is a critical element for granting everyday freedoms to children but little data exists on urban children's access to green public spaces for play and recreation needs. In this mapping, around 166 adolescents in two age groups (10 to 14 years and 15 to 19 years) were asked to mark as safe or unsafe the public spaces on a map of their neighbourhood, and state the reasons for their choices.

What makes places safe?

Typically, the adolescents viewed as safe places where familiar trusted adults and families were present (such as own house, lanes), as well as every day familiar and frequented places (market, neighbourhoods), and places which offer the opportunity to spend time with friends and engage in play (such as parks, local clubs, dance and computer classes. It is interesting to note that dance and computer classes had been perceived as safe, not because of the skills they offered but because these spaces provided adolescents with opportunities for social interaction with peers.

What makes places unsafe?

72% of the adults cited petty theft as the most common form of crime in the ward, corroborated by police records, which showed prevalence of criminal trespass, housebreaking, breaking into commercial spaces, snatching jewellery, mobile phones and wallets in public spaces and in the process causing hurt and wrongful restraint of victims. However, adolescents did not refer to these crimes as reasons for their own consideration of what makes places unsafe. Instead, physical and social hazards shaped their perceptions of unsafe places. Most unsafe places were pockets that either included the red-light area, were in close proximity to the red-light area, or otherwise where women in prostitution solicited customers. Areas and pockets where men occupied open spaces playing cards and/or consuming alcohol, areas where people used profanities and where conflicts occurred, and pockets where adolescent boys and girls had either directly or indirectly experienced public sexual harassment, were also identified as unsafe. During the survey 14% of the adults as well as the adolescents complained about 'eve teasing' or public sexual harassment, though police data showed that this crime was mostly reported as committed against adult victims. It is likely that adolescents did not report sexual harassment for fear of repercussions. In addition, areas and pockets with physical hazards such as the presence of stray animals, heavy traffic, lack of walking space, and spaces that were desolate, were also identified as unsafe.

The safe and unsafe places recommended by adolescents using the three step Observation Checklist-3 tool[22] were subsequently digitized using GIS to produce safe and unsafe place maps of the ward from adolescent's perspectives. Child friendly versions of these maps were created by ACE for use at the ward level by local NGOs working with adolescents (see figures 3 & 4). It is not surprising that among the top three accessible safe public places were two formal parks, one large park in the ward (Rabindra Kanan) and the other just outside the north-eastern boundary of the ward. The park within the ward was perceived as the top safe place as adolescents, typically boys, frequented this park where they were able to spend quality time with their friends. The park was developed as a major recreational centre in the ward. The presence of a security guard and restricted entry timings ensured safety in the park. However, adolescents considered this park to be unsafe at night when men took over the park for drinking and they got in trouble if they got too close.

---

22 A sequential three-step tool was used to gauge the perceptions of safety in the community. First the adolescents aged 10–18 years worked in two age groups to annotate a large community base map of Ward 26 placing green and red dots on safe and unsafe spaces. Facilitators recorded their discussions and the data generated was tabulated to generate a list of safe and unsafe spaces to be visited during the transect walks in step 2. A subsample of adolescents led walks through the community taking photographs of safe and unsafe spaces, which the facilitators later helped them annotate. In step 3, the list of places pointed out during the transect walk as safe and unsafe was compared to the list produced during step 1 through group discussions. The transect walks and focus groups helped validate the data gathered from the safe and unsafe space mapping. ACE then digitized the map data using GIS for further analysis.

Figure 3: Map of Safe Spaces for Adolescents in Ward no. 26

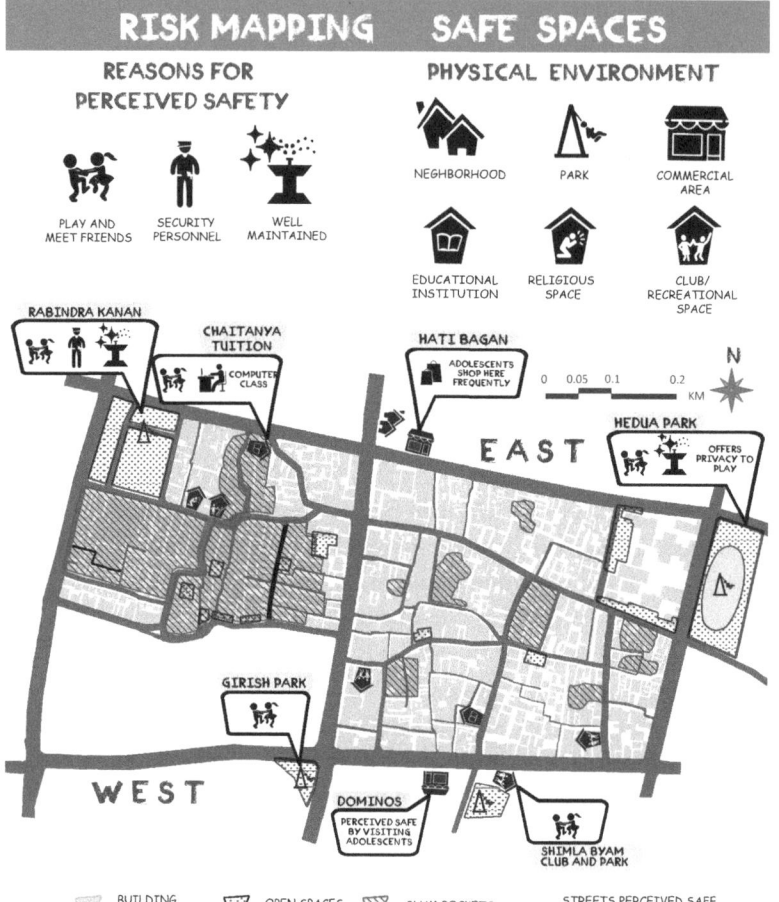

Figure 4: Map of Unsafe Spaces for Adolescents in Ward no. 26

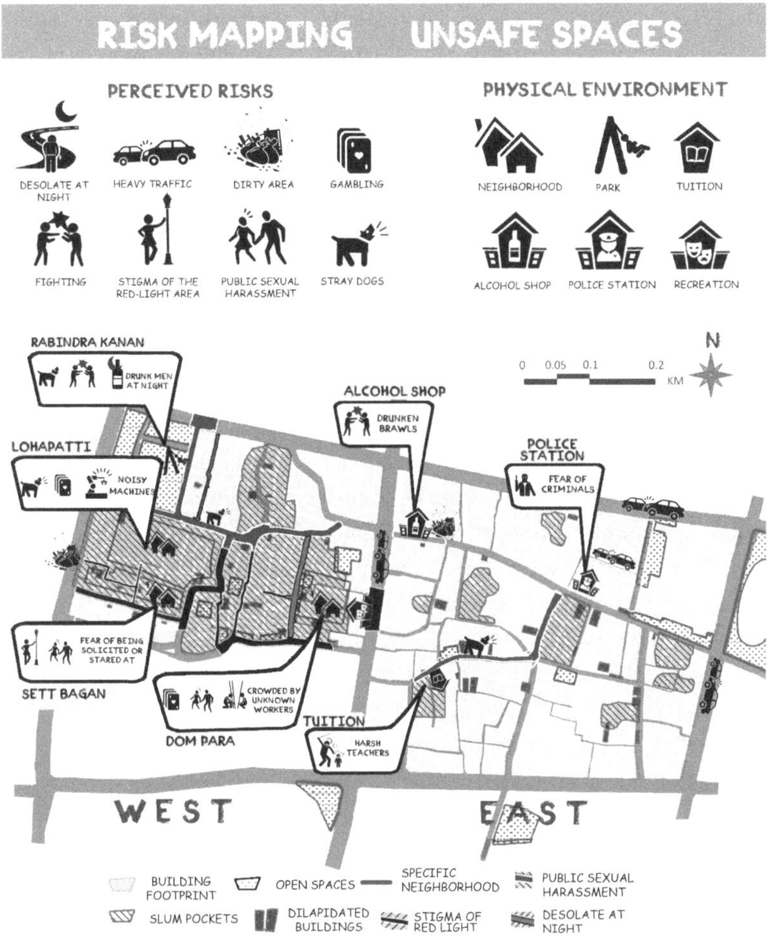

Other than this one park, no organized play and recreational spaces existed for girls and boys of different ages within the ward. The incidental open spaces available in and around the ward were mostly occupied by parked vehicles, which restricted play. Younger children and adolescent girls had no parental permission to walk to Rabindra Kanan Park on their own if they lived far away from it. With no access to play in the incidental spaces near home, younger children and adolescent girls were thus left with no option but to play in the crowded streets and by-lanes near their homes. While some adolescent boys and some girls have recently started accessing the Rabindra Kanan Park for football coaching organized by a local NGO, most children and adolescents across age and gender had to continually compete for play space with young people from other wards who came to play organized sport in the same green space. They had to compete with adults as well to claim space for free play in the park. Consequently, ward no. 26, in spite of having a large green public park (unlike many other inner-city older wards of Kolkata) and many other incidental green spaces, did not actually provide universal access to those spaces to all children as mandated in SDG 11.7.

Building the capacities of select stakeholders

Alongside the mapping process, the local partners CRY and Sanlaap started working with children, adolescents and parents to increase their capacity to participate in all the existing forums in the ward in keeping with the commitments of capacity for participation in creation of sustainable human settlements as codified in Target 11.3 and for responsive, inclusive, participatory and representative decision-making at all levels (Target 16.7). They created adolescent and parent groups among the vulnerable populations and organized regular meetings to generate awareness about social problems such as child marriage, child labour, dropping out from education, health and hygiene, and security, among others. Rallies and cultural events were organized to generate awareness about these issues. Local residents participated in these events and shared the responsibility of organizing them. Such events were supported by the ward office, sometimes financially, and sometimes by providing space. However, these events were not yet initiated and led only by the community at large until late 2018.

The newly formed Ward Level Child Protection Committee (WLCPC) as a result of this project provides a platform for adolescents and adults to enjoy a space for dialogue on issues faced by the adolescents, and work towards addressing the problems. This is an example of an 'invented space' of citizenship where new spaces are opened for excluded groups to drive solutions in the hope of larger societal change (as envisaged in the SDGs) as opposed to an 'invited' space, which promotes inclusion of the grassroots and their allied non-governmental organizations within existing structures typically to provide the poor with coping mechanisms and propositions (top down) to support survival (Miraftab, 2004). Community participation in various cultural and play events is also increasing, as coaching in football (including for adolescent girls), cricket, dance, drama and art are offered by different organizations. A few mothers groups set up by NGOs are quite active in the field of education and also provide support for sports and skill-building, especially for girls. Through these efforts, the level of girls' social participation has increased, as they have started playing sports in Rabindra Kanan Park, once an almost exclusive territory of boys and men.

Some of these ground level efforts are beginning to collectivize the community on issues important to them as was envisaged in the theory of change used by the program. A few of the groups are working as vigilance committees for the community. In particular, they help changing the mind-sets of mothers by encouraging them to allow adolescent girls to use public places for recreational purposes, addressing cases of abuse with the help of the WLCPC, encouraging adolescent girls to continue their studies and refuse early marriage, and checking the usage of mobile phones to ensure online safety. These initiatives are changing attitudes and behaviour in the community, and although initiated by NGOs/CBOs, they are not entirely dependent on them.

Lessons learned from the participatory mapping in Kolkata

The mapping analysis of Ward 26 has revealed much social exclusion across different sectors, which are detrimental to the well-being of adolescents. It also showed considerable gaps in safety and protection of adolescents within their community. The lessons drawn from the mapping exercise helped ACE to create a set of indicators for a Safe and Inclusive City for Adolescents that address three levels of deprivation that are adolescent-specific, family/household specific and community/neighbourhood specific. These indicators take into consideration the urban critical SDGs, particularly SDG 11 and the planning and urban spatial development objectives in the New Urban Agenda. Using these evidence-based indicators, Ward 26 and other wards in the future could create contextually relevant plans of action to achieve the goal of creating a Safe Inclusive City for Adolescents ward by ward, while finding solutions to the problems and plugging the gaps in service delivery and quality. Adolescents play an important role in implementing this plan of action based on the SDGs at the local level.

The first goal in the theory of change employed by this project was community based multi-dimensional participatory mapping, some aspects of which have been discussed in detail in this chapter from the perspective of inclusion and safety. But such a mapping exercise is not without challenges. First and foremost, it is a lengthy, time consuming process especially if several diverse stakeholders are to be involved from the inception phase, including in the development of indicators and tools. This was the situation in the case of the slum-level mapping in Bhopal and Mumbai for the 'Promoting Safe Communities' program that preceded and informed the Kolkata program. Reaching consensus and securing stakeholder buy-in were important for the program and the mapping in those two cities took double the time of the Kolkata mapping. The Kolkata mapping targeting adolescents and at the level of an urban ward instead of slums used the indicators and tools developed in the other two cities; and then revised them based on expert reviews by a small reference group. This helped to speed up the process instead of reinventing the wheel. This is the first lesson for future mapping exercises seeking to address vulnerabilities of urban children: Review and adapt existing indicators from similar projects with the help of an expert group instead of going back to communities to develop indicators and tools from scratch.

Second, the adults and youth who helped in the mapping were mostly community volunteers. Consequently, attrition levels were high and required frequent retraining of field researchers, particularly for the lengthy household surveys. Budgeting for a dedicated research team for local data collection is an excellent investment for future mapping and may expedite the process.

Third, the respondents were predominantly working-class residents and were unable to devote much time to interviews and surveys, or participate in focus group discussions. The community also cited research fatigue as there were many development organizations working in the ward, sometimes with overlapping agendas, who regularly visited the community for data. Moreover, when the residents realized that participating in the surveys would not provide any direct material benefits, many lost interest. It is important to keep the surveys short and inform people about how that data is going to be used and the platforms they could join at the ward level to improve safety, security and protection of their families. Moreover, a ward level database under the Ward Office is a good idea for storing and sharing the data collected by different organizations to rationalize future studies involving primary data collection from the community.

The fourth lesson is the importance of the recruitment of local political support to a program of this nature. The members of the urban local body (ULB) associated with the Ward Office, who are responsible for the welfare of the local community through their outreach work, played an active role in introducing the research teams to families and children. Along with the local councillor, they explained the purpose of this mapping to the community. This process helped the community develop trust in the program and allowed their children to take a part in it.

The fifth lesson is the challenge of overcoming difficulties in working with adolescents on sensitive issues. In 2016, the programme was still very new and the field partner did not have a long-established field presence in Ward 26. Considering the sensitivity of issues relating to adolescents' experience of growing up in slums or other vulnerable living environments, the local research team included experienced staff capable of providing psychosocial support. The local teams were also aware of referral services in the area in case of disclosure of abuse or other significant concerns during the mapping.

This multi-dimensional participatory mapping was able to fulfil the first two goals in the theory of change used by this program to a large extent. The third goal of strengthening the system of response to reduce equity gaps in service delivery—including for the protection of children and youth—is an ongoing process at the ward level. But the stage has been set for its continuity by the program and the robust mapping provides an excellent entry point for understanding how service delivery could be adapted to meet the needs of disadvantaged children. The participatory mapping for the Safe and Inclusive City for Adolescents in Kolkata presents a good case study of low-tech, low-cost ways of engaging children in spatial mapping for local area development. The program also shows how invented platforms developed for engaging the community and young people for the purpose of advocacy and demand generation work, and to what extent these spaces have the potential for influencing broader policy discussions with local governments in implementing SDG 11 and other urban critical SDGs for vulnerable populations.

References

Bartlett, Sheridan (2018). *Children and the Geography of Violence: Why space and place matter.* Oxon and New York: Routledge.

Bartlett, Sheridan, Roger Hart, David Satterthwaite, Ximena De La Barra, and Alfredo Missair (1999). *Cities for Children: Children's Rights, Poverty and Urban Management.* London: Earthscan.

Bronfenbrenner, Urie (1979). *The ecology of human development.* Cambridge: Harvard University Press

Chakrabarti, Asok M. and Halder, Animesh. (2004). "Slum Dwellers of Calcutta, Socio-Economic Profile—1989–90, March 1991". In Calcutta Metropolitan Development Authority. Socio-Economic Planning Unit (ed) *Metropolitan Kolkata: An Anthology of Socio-Economic Studies and Survey Reports of KMDA 1970–2004,* Volume IV, 134–178. Kolkata: Socio-Economic Planning Unit, Directorate of Planning and Development, KMDA.

Chatterjee, Sudeshna (2006). *Children's Friendship with Places: An Exploration of Environmental Child Friendliness of Children's Environments in Cities.* PhD Dissertation. North Carolina State University: Raleigh.

Census of India, 2011. [Online] Available at: http://www.census2011.co.in/census/city/302-bhopal.html (Accessed June 2020)

Economist Intelligence Unit (2015). *The Safe Cities Index 2015.* Available online: https://safecities.economist.com/the-safe-cities-index-2015/ (Accessed June 2020).

Ellis, Peter and Roberts, Mark (2016). *Leveraging Urbanization in South Asia: Managing Spatial Transformation for Prosperity and Livability.* Washington, DC: World Bank.

Ghosh, Swati (1992). Thika Tenancy in Bustees of Calcutta: A Study. *Discussion Paper No. 6,* Centre for Urban Economic Studies, University of Calcutta.

Hyder, Adnan Ali; Amach, Omar Hussein; Garg, Nitin and Labinjo, Mariam Temitope. (2006). Estimating the burden of road traffic injuries among children and adolescents in urban South Asia, *Health Policy,* 77 (2): 129–139.

Know Violence in Childhood (2017). *Ending Violence in Childhood: Global Report 2017.* New Delhi: Know Violence in Childhood.

McGranahan, Gordon and David Satterthwaite (2014). "Urbanisation concepts and trends", IIED working paper, available at http://pubs.iied.org/10709IIED.html. (Accessed June 2020)

Miraftab, Faranak. (2004). Invited and Invented Spaces of Participation: Neoliberal Citizenship and Feminists' Expanded Notion of Politics. *Wagadu.* 1: 1–7.

Mitra, Iman Kumar (2015). Urban Planning, Settlement Practices, and Issues of Justice in Contemporary Kolkata. *Policies and Practices* 72, 16–31.

Moser, Caroline; Norton, Andrew; Stein, Alfredo & Georgieva, Sophia (2010). *Pro-Poor adaptation to climate change in urban centers: Case studies of vulnerability and resilience in Kenya and Nicaragua* (Washington DC: The World Bank).

National Crime Records Bureau (2016). *Crime in India 2016*. Ministry of Home Affairs. Retrieved from http://ncrb.gov.in/StatPublications/CII/CII2016/pdfs/NEWPDFs/Crime%20in%20India%20-%202016%20Complete%20PDF%20291117.pdf (Accessed June 2020)

Roy, Manoj; Hulme, David & Jahan, Ferdous (2013). "Contrasting adaptation responses by squatters and low-income tenants in Khulna, Bangladesh". *Environment & Urbanization*, 25(1): 157–176.

Rudd, Andrew, Simon, David, Cardama, Maruxa, Birch, Eugene L., & Revi, Aromar. (2018). The UN, the Urban Sustainable Development Goal, and the New Urban Agenda. In (eds.)

Thomas Elmqvist, Xuemei Bai, Niki Frantzeskaki, Corrie Griffith, David Maddox, Timon McPhearson, Susan Parnell, Patricia Romero-Lankao, David Simon, Mark Watkins, *Urban Planet: Knowledge towards Sustainable Cities*. Cambridge University Press. Pp. 180–196.

Rustagi, Preet; Kapoor Mehta, Soumya;, Mishra, Sunil Kumar; Mehta, Balwant. S. & Subrahmanian, Ramya. (2012). *Beyond averages: Child well-being through an equity analysis.* New Delhi: UNICEF & Institute for Human Development.

Sankhe, Shirish; Vittal, Ireena; Dobbs, Richard; Mohan, Ajit; Gulati, Ankur; Ablett, Jonthan; Gupta, Shishir; Kim, Alex; Paul, Sudipto; Sanghvi, Aditya and Sethy, Gurpreet. (2010): *India's urban awakening: Building inclusive cities, sustaining economic growth*. London: McKinsey Global Institute

Satterthwaite, David. (2016, December). *Commonwealth Journal of Local Governance.* Retrieved from UTS ePress: https://epress.lib.uts.edu.au/journals/index.php/cjlg/article/view/5446/5901(Accessed June 2020)

Statista. (2019). *Age distribution in India 2007–2017*. Retrieved from www.statista.com: https://www.statista.com/statistics/271315/age-distribution-in-india/ (Accessed June 2020)

Wachs, Theodore. D. and Shpancer, Noam. (1998) A Contextualist Perspective on Child Environment Relations. In (eds.) Gorlitz, H. J. H. D., Mey, G., and Valsiner, J. (Ed.). *Children, Cities, and Psychological Theories: Developing Relationships.* Berlin and New York: Walter de Gruyter. p. 164–192.

Wessells, Michael. (2009). What Are We Learning About Protecting Children in the Community? An inter-agency review of the evidence on community-based child protection mechanisms in humanitarian and development settings. Available at http://www.unicef.org/wcaro/What_We_Are_Learning_About_Protecting_Children_in_the_Community_Full_Report.pdf (Accessed: September 4, 2015)

The World Bank. (2018, October 5). *Urban Development Overview.* Retrieved from World Bank Group-International Development, Poverty & Sustainability: https://www.worldbank.org/en/topic/urbandevelopment/overview

UNICEF. (2017, July 18). Theory of Change Paper, UNICEF Strategic Plan 2018–2021 Realizing the rights of every child, especially the most disadvantaged. Retrieved from https://www.unicef.org/about/execboard/files/2017-EB11-Theory_of_Change-2017.07.19-EN.pdf

UNICEF (2012). *The State of the World's Children 2012: Children in an Urban World*. New York: United Nations Children's Fund (UNICEF).

UNICEF (2011). *The State of the World's Children 2011: Adolescence: An Age of Opportunity*. New York: United Nations Children's Fund (UNICEF).

UNICEF (2008). Summary of Highlights from: *Global Child Protection Systems Mapping Workshop*, Bucharest, Romania. Retrieved from http://www.unicef.org/video audio/PDFs/global_child_protection_workshop.pdf

UN Habitat (2016). *The Slum Almanac*, 2015–2016. Retrieved from https://unhabitat.org/slum-almanac-2015-2016/

United Nations Habitat (2015a). *HABITAT III Issue Papers 3—SAFER CITIES*. New York: UN Habitat.

United Nations Habitat (2015b). *HABITAT III Issue Papers 1—INCLUSIVE CITIES*. New York: UN Habitat.

United Nations. (2014). World Urbanization Prospects: The 2014 Revision, United Nations Department of Economic and Social Affairs, Population Division. New York, NY, USA, 2014.

PART II

MAKING INVISIBLE CHILDREN AND YOUTH VISIBLE

Exploring and Addressing the Exclusion of "Invisible" Youth: Applying a Relational Framework to SDG 10.2

Katie Hodgkinson,[23] Nicky Pouw[24] and Marielle L.J. Le Mat[25]

1. Introduction

Youth in institutional care organisations and leaving care are an invisible group, largely missing from governmental and institutional statistics and agendas. This is despite evidence that these young people are particularly vulnerable and consistently have poorer outcomes in education, employment, housing and social integration (Berkman, 2007; Stein, 2006). The Sustainable Development Goals (SDGs) call to 'leave no one behind' makes the visibility and inclusion of youth from care a pertinent issue. This paper addresses target 10.2 of the SDGs. The paper is based on a two-year research project that sought to answer the question 'how are young people from care affected by social, economic and political exclusion in terms of their human wellbeing, employability and social acceptance?' The mixed-methods research took place in low, middle and higher income countries: Côte D'Ivoire, Guatemala, Indonesia, Kenya, Malawi and the Netherlands. This paper draws on findings from all six of these countries, highlighting that despite widely different contexts, similarities can be seen in the relational experience of exclusion amongst youth from care.

In order to both understand and assess both the social inclusion and exclusion of vulnerable youth, this paper presents a relational framework that reveals the multiple transitions that young people experience in care. It highlights the dynamic interactions between relational movements and identity formation, and the complex processes of social and self-exclusion within the multifaceted context of social, cultural, economic and political drivers of exclusion. Whilst social-cultural and political-economic contexts, policies and practices regarding young care leavers are crucial, the

---

23 MSc in International Development Studies, Post-Graduate Researcher in the School of Languages, Cultures and Societies at the University of Leeds. Email: mlkah@leeds.ac.uk
24 PhD in Economics of Development, Associate Professor in Governance and Inclusive Development at the University of Amsterdam
25 PhD in Education and International Development, SRHR Researcher/Advisor at the Dutch Royal Tropical Institute (KIT)

research also brings global similarities to light. One of these is the fact that young care leavers struggle to integrate in society to embark upon a positive process of independence. As a result, independence is postponed, leading to a situation of 'waithood'.

The remainder of this paper is organized as follows. Section 2 reviews the literature on drivers and outcomes of social exclusion of young people from care. This is followed by section 3, which presents a relational framework to guide the analysis of the social exclusion of youth from care. Section 4 presents the research methodology and research locations. The main research findings are discussed in section 5, in terms of connectivity of youth from care, the multiple transitions they go through, the role of relational images, the drivers of social exclusion and institutional care policies. Section 6 discusses the key findings and makes recommendations, followed by the concluding section 7.

2. The social exclusion of young people from care

SDG 10.2 calls for the 'social, economic and political inclusion of all irrespective of age, sex, disability, race, ethnicity, origin, religion or economic or other status' (United Nations, 2015). This goal will not be met unless 'invisible' social groups are taken into account. One such group is young people in care organisations and young people leaving these organisations; 'care-leavers'. Despite growing academic and programmatic interest in this group of young people, understandings of their experiences of both inclusion and exclusion remain limited, not least because it is practically difficult to collect and analyse data on this topic due to large numbers of children in unregistered care organisations (Pinkerton, 2011). Moreover, in many developing countries, care institutions seem to operate within an institutional void with limited control and regulation. As a result, there is little attention as to what happens to young people by the time they have to leave these care institutions. Many 'disappear' in informality and fail to integrate in society on mutually beneficial terms. The available academic literature is primarily focused on developed countries, which limits the possibility of a global perspective on the topic and possibilities for international action and networks of exchange (Pinkerton, 2011). This limitation is particularly important in a world of increasingly globalised social and economic relations, where the outcomes of vulnerable groups are no longer just shaped by national policy and advocacy, but increasingly by global policy debates and alliances (Mendes & Moselhuddin, 2006; Pinkerton, 2011).

Young people in care, and care-leavers in particular, can be considered one of the most vulnerable groups in society, with difficulty accessing essential services and provisions and consistently poorer outcomes in education, employment, housing and crime (Mendes & Moselhuddin, 2006; Stein & Verwijen-Slamenscu, 2012; Frimpong Manso, 2012; Jackson & Cameron, 2012). A substantial body of literature explains that these poorer outcomes are largely a result of the shorter and quicker transitions care-leavers must make to independence and adulthood (Frimpong Manso, 2012; Stein, 2006). Transitions for all groups of youth are becoming extended and less progressively linear, due to declines in the youth labour market, shortages in affordable housing and the growth of education and training. Such extended transitions involve greater discontinuity, risk and movement back and forth (Wade & Dixon, 2006) and can leave many young people in a phase of 'waithood', where they are unable to reach the traditional markers of adulthood in their societies (Honwana, 2014). However, there is a noticeable difference between extended and accelerated transitions—the latter, which involve young people finishing school prematurely to seek work and living independently early, leave young people even more vulnerable; and it is these accelerated transitions that the majority of young people from care are forced to make (Wade & Dixon, 2006). Added to this is the fact that these accelerated transitions for care-leavers are made without the support of family and without a fall-back position, meaning that young people from care are at a greater risk of being disadvantaged and excluded, and the consequences of this are more severe (Höjer & Sjöblom, 2011; HM Government, 2013).

In order to socially, politically, and economically accommodate the integration of young people into society after care, it is essential to understand what drives their exclusion. Social exclusion is a multi-dimensional and dynamic concept, which can be understood as '[...] a process and a state that prevents individuals or groups from full participation in social, economic and political life and from asserting their rights' (Beall & Piron, 2005, p. 9). Social exclusion is usually structural in nature (Alston & Kent, 2009; Beall & Piron, 2005; Thompson, 2011) and those who are socially excluded often share similar social, economic and political barriers and lack security, justice and economic opportunities in life (HM Government,

2013; Alston & Kent, 2009; Berkman, 2007). Importantly, young people do not always recognise the structural factors that are driving their exclusion, and blame themselves for their exclusion. Indeed, the embedded 'myth of meritocracy' encourages young people to believe that their exclusion is due to their own short-comings, and not a result of wider societal and structural issues (Alston & Kent, 2009). This can lead to feelings of shame and result in youth self-excluding from participating in different domains of society. In anticipation of stereotyping and rejection, they opt-out of social interactions with people and institutions they are not familiar with.

The scholarly literature often draws an analytical distinction between the 'drivers' and the 'outcomes' of social exclusion. Yet it is important to note that these are closely interconnected and mutually reinforcing; with 'outcomes' of exclusion, often becoming 'drivers' of deeper exclusion. Highlighted amongst the many drivers of the social exclusion of vulnerable youth are: (i) childhood drivers, such as ill health, neglect, abuse, lack of education; (ii) family drivers, such as family breakdown, instability, low aspirations (often due to previous experiences of exclusion); (iii) socio-cultural drivers, such as class, discrimination based on race/ethnicity/religion/gender; (iv) economic drivers, such as poverty, lack of employment, poor living conditions; and (v) political drivers such as a lack of rights, inequality embedded in institutions, lack of decision-making power (AIHW, 2012; Alston & Kent, 2009; Bynner, 2001; Bynner & Parsons, 2002; Gaetz, 2004; Morrow, 2001; Susinos, 2008; Thompson, 2011; Partos, 2015).

The outcomes of social exclusion of youth from care include the delay or disruption of the transition from childhood to traditional markers of adulthood; self-exclusion from key elements of society; improvised livelihoods, which can blur the line between legal and illegal and include homelessness and work in the informal sector; turning to crime in order to survive, to fit in (for example stealing clothes in order to feel like others), or to gain social status where the normal routes to this are not available; and turning to substance abuse as a coping mechanism (Frimpong Manso, 2012; Honwana, 2014; Hook & Courtney, 2010; HM Government, 2013; Stein, 2006; Alston & Kent, 2009; Paolini, 2013; Berkman, 2007; Sommers, 2010; Savelsberg & Martin-Giles, 2008). These outcomes often lead to further social exclusion, demonstrating the vicious circle of exclusion and the negative feelings associated with this process that have a psychological impact too.

3. A Relational Framework to Explore the Social Exclusion of Youth from Care

Based upon the above literature review and in light of the complex interactions between youth moving through care institutions and their social and institutional environments, we have adopted (and adapted after multiple fieldwork trips) a relational framework to guide this research (see Figure 1). The relational framework considers that individuals experience relational movements throughout their lives. A relational movement is 'the process of moving through connections; through disconnections; and back into new ... connections with others' (Comstock et al., 2008, p. 282). This research extends the approach to consider the importance not only of connections to other individuals, but connections to the broader society and the institutions that shape and impact an individual's life. When individuals are in a phase of connection with others and with society, they have a greater sense of worth and are able to act more constructively in the world. When they are in a phase of disconnection, the ability to act constructively is limited (Comstock et al., 2008). Acute phases of disconnection are continually present in life, but when addressed can actually lead to the strengthened connectivity of a person, as the individual learns that they are relationally effective and that they can express their feelings in a way that leads to positive outcomes. On the other hand, if phases of disconnection are not addressed, this can lead to self-blame, disconnection and even the alteration of an individual's understanding of reality, as they begin to feel ineffectual in relationships and helpless at shaping them. This in turn leads to chronic disconnection, where a person moves into isolation, self-blame and immobilisation (Jordan, 2001).

Relational images are an important aspect of the relational approach. 'Self-images' are individual expectations of how you will be treated based on previous experiences. Here, relational images can cause an individual to experience disconnection in anticipation of perceived negative outcomes. For example, young people who have experienced parental neglect might believe they will not experience love (Comstock et al., 2008). Relational images are also the prejudicial images that others hold of an individual that can affect their treatment of that individual, for example teachers and potential employers might expect a young person from care to be troublesome, and automatically treat them as if this is the case. This also happens at the societal level, where the more powerful hold prejudice and apply bias over individuals or groups, forcing them into inauthentic connection and often silencing them; resulting in chronic disconnection and marginalisation (Jordan, 2001).

Utilising this theoretical approach allows for an exploration of the lived realities of youth, their experiences of inclusion and exclusion, and their outcomes in life, with a specific focus on their connection to other individuals, groups and institutions, and the positive and negative effect these (dis)connections have on youth from care.

Figure 2   Relational Framework to Analyse the Social Exclusion of Youth from Care

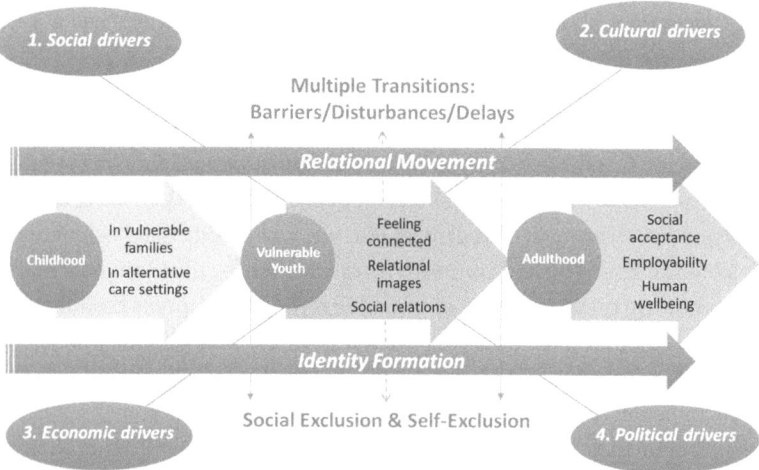

Source: Pouw & Hodgkinson, 2016; Pouw, Hodgkinson, Le Mat & Van Dam, 2017.

During the transition from childhood to independence/adulthood, youth can experience barriers, disturbances or delays, due to social, cultural, economic and political drivers, which may lead to social exclusion and/or self-exclusion because of negative relational movements. Negative relational movements consist of increased levels of disconnectedness, negative self-images and prejudicial images held by others, and the breakdown or loss of social relations. Positive relational movements may help young people from care to overcome experiences and feelings of social and self-exclusion, and develop counter strategies. Our research shows that these experiences affect young people's identity formation over time, and ultimately, will affect their level of social acceptance, employability and human wellbeing. Social acceptance is defined as the acceptance of a person (or group of persons) into a group or society as a whole. Employability is defined as 'A set of achievements—skills, understandings and personal attributes—that make graduates more likely to gain employment and be successful in their chosen occupations, which benefits themselves, the workforce, the community and the economy' (Yorke & Knight, 2006, p. 3). Human wellbeing is defined as feeling satisfied with what one can have, be and achieve in life; broken down for this research into social-relational wellbeing, material wellbeing and subjective wellbeing.

4. Research Methodology and Locations

The research underlying this paper used a mixed-methods approach. Qualitative and quantitative methods were combined to collect data with 347 young people from care and 105 stakeholders including caregivers, teachers, employers, government workers and health workers (see Table 1). The research took place in 6 countries spanning lower, middle and higher income: Côte d'Ivoire, Guatemala, Indonesia, Kenya, Malawi and the Netherlands. The young participants in the research were part of, or had transitioned out of family based care programs or family strengthening programs provided by SOS Children's Villages and in each country one or two external care organisations. This was different in the Netherlands, where SOS Children's Villages doesn't currently run a program. Here, youth participants were from foster care, assisted living and a refugee care program. A systematic comparative analysis of the different types of care organisations is not within the scope of this study, especially given the wide variance in the type of care organisations included. Much of the differences in experience of the young people included in the research depended on the policies and practices within organisations—these varied considerably even within the same type of care. Future comparative research into the impact of different policies, as well as different types of organisation, would be very valuable.

Table 1   Research Locations and Sample Sizes

Country	Number of youth participants	Number of care organisations	Number of stakeholders interviewed
Côte d'Ivoire	57	2	13
Guatemala	71	3	21
Indonesia	50	3	15
Kenya	70	2	25
Malawi	66	3	17
Netherlands	33	1	14
Total	**347**	**14**	**105**

A structured survey, containing both open and closed questions, was conducted with 246 young people, exploring youth's perceptions and experiences of inclusion and exclusion, connections, preparations for leaving care, experiences of independent living, employment and their aspirations. 70 youth (many of whom were also surveyed) took part in individual life history interviews, which included social-relational mapping exercises, to unpack the nature and scope of their social relations and connections and how these change throughout their transition to independence. Finally, 32 focus group discussions (FGDs) were held with male and female youth separately (with the exception of Kenya, where one out of five FGDs was held with a mixed-sex group of young people). The FGDs explored questions on exclusion and discrimination, with country-specific vignettes developed to aid the discussion of more sensitive issues, such as experiences of independence and engagement in gang activities. Stakeholders were engaged through semi-structured interviews, which varied according to their position and relation to young people in care, but asked questions about young people's relations, inclusion, experiences, education, health and employment.

In Côte d'Ivoire, the research took place primarily in Aboisso, but care-leavers who had moved to the nearby city of Abidjan were also included. In Guatemala the research took place in Quetzaltenango; in Indonesia, Bandung and Lembang; in Kenya, Nairobi; in Malawi, Lilongwe; and in the Netherlands, Amsterdam. The care organisations were situated in or near major cities. These locations were selected by the in-country SOS Children's Villages offices. The research was designed and fieldwork coordinated by the authors and further researchers at the University of Amsterdam, while the majority of data collection was conducted by in-country researchers, who spoke the local language(s). The study touches upon many sensitive issues of young people from care, and so careful consideration was paid to the ethics of the study, from the creation of research tools to the presentation of results. Ethical approval for the study was granted by the Ethics Committee at the University of Amsterdam.

While there is a significant lack of data on the number of youth in care in most countries that were part of this study, Table 2 summarises the statistics and estimates that are known.

Table 2   Number of vulnerable youth and youth in residential care per country

Country	Number of Orphans or Vulnerable Children (0–18 yrs) (percentage of total population)	Number of children (0–18 yrs) in residential care (percentage of total population)
Côte d'Ivoire	1.3 million (>14%)	unknown
Guatemala	Unknown	5,500 (<1%)
Indonesia	Unknown	unknown
Kenya	3.6 million (almost 8%)	40,000–42,000 (1%)
Malawi	1.2 million (almost 15%)	10,000 (<1%)
The Netherlands	No statistics for orphans of vulnerable youth; 350,000 youth (0–22yrs) in care (10.3%)	40,000 (0–22 yrs) (1,2%)

Data based on: UNICEF Côte d'Ivoire, 2013; UNICEF Guatemala, 2014; Government of the Republic of Kenya, 2012; UNICEF Kenya, 2014; UNICEF Malawi, 2011, 2018; CBS, 2015

5. Research Findings

The connectivity of youth in and leaving care

Young people's relational networks

A key finding from this research is that young people from care homes have a strikingly limited relational network; at the personal, societal and institutional level. This applies both to when young people are within care, and when they have transitioned to independent living. Young people generally form very strong connections with their care-givers and peers whilst in care, and this network often remains important to them throughout their youth and early adulthood. They also generally feel socially accepted by their (biological) families and friends and the majority of youth wish to maintain in contact with their families. However, this is not always possible due to family problems, financial constraints on the part of the family (which restricts the possibility for visits) and rules and regulations within some care organisations. When this is the case, it amplifies young peoples' feeling of disconnection and can result in youth questioning their identity. A number of the young people in care in the lower to middle income countries were there for financial reasons, as their families could not afford to care for them, or believed they would be better off in care as they would have greater access to education and resources. Indeed, many young people said they felt thankful for the opportunities afforded to them as a result of being in care. However, the disconnection from their families was still a significant issue for many young people:

> 'I love my parents. I am thankful for them sending me here. I can go to school. I can live independent at young age. But deep down inside my heart, I wanted to live and grow up with my parents like any other children who lived with their parents.' (Male care-leaver in Indonesia)

In Guatemala, young people in care brought up the topic of 'love', describing it as something they were missing and seeking in life, and sometimes using it to explain behaviour such as engaging in relationships and having children at a young age. Indeed, it has been highlighted by care staff that young people in care, especially in overcrowded institutions, are generally not emotionally satisfied. In Guatemala, a striking 27.8% of young people from one care organisation said they (would) have no one to turn to should they need support after leaving care. This lack of support and connectivity is especially pronounced for young men. In the other care organisations in Guatemala 23.1% of males also reported having no one to turn to, whereas no females felt this would be the case. Across all six countries, only 6.1% of youth say they (would) have no one to turn to in case they needed help, but 80% of these youth were male. This is a striking finding and the gender dynamics related to this high number of young men who think they would have no one to turn to should be further explored in future research. The young men who offered some reflection on this feeling of having no one to turn to, explained that they felt that it was not expected of young men to depend on others, which might have increased their feelings of lack of support and lack of connectivity.

For migrant youth, who are in special care in the Netherlands, waiting for a decision about possible family unification, their anger and anxiety about this can stand in the way of positive social interactions.

> 'I would very much like family unification, via [care organisation]. I am always angry. After school I return straight home and sit by myself. I don't talk to anyone, which is really difficult.' (Male in the Netherlands)

The 'outside world'
Perhaps most indicative of the lack of connections young people have is that they frequently refer to society beyond their care organisation as the 'outside world', which they know relatively little about. In Indonesia, for example, young females in care discussed having very little, if any, contact with other youth in their community. This makes transitioning to independence an especially nerve-wracking time for youth, who can struggle to adapt to their new and unfamiliar surroundings. In Kenya, some young people from institutional care reported that they pretended to come from a different place to explain to their new community why they were so unfamiliar with how things worked.

> 'We have been brought up like bread and butter, and trying to adapt to that [outside] life is very difficult' (Male care-leaver in Kenya)

> 'I haven't been outside or I haven't spent much of the time there, I have been here [in care organisation] for a long time so that makes me nervous and to separate from the people I have been with.' (Female in Guatemala)

Connectedness after care
After leaving care, some youth return to their biological families in their home communities. This can have a positive effect on their connectedness, as young people experience a renewed sense of belonging. On the other hand, some youth also report this enhances feelings of disconnection, or produces negative connections. This is especially the case when young people have grown up in a care environment that has different customs, or even a different religion, as was found to be the case in Côte d'Ivoire, and if young people have lost the ability to speak the same language as their family, having grown up in care with a different language. In these cases, young people can be left feeling like they do not 'fit in' at home. In Kenya, Malawi and Côte d'Ivoire, some young people also found that expectations were put on them by their biological family that they were unable to manage leaving them to feel disconnected, for example, expectations that they will be able to support the family income.

> 'I have the feeling of not being loved because they [biological family] are only concerned about the money I receive at the end of the month; they do not care about my daily life.' (Female care-leaver in Côte d'Ivoire)

Research findings indicate that there are three key aspects of young people's lives that affect their connectedness (or in/exclusion). These are the multiple transitions youth experience through care; relational images; and policies.

Multiple transitions

Young people make many transitions through-out their time in care; not only into care and out of care, but also within the care system itself. These transitions, unsurprisingly, mark new phases in the relational movements of young people into connection and disconnection with their institutional environment, caregivers and other peers in care—which can affect their overall connectivity and in- or exclusion.

Transitions into care

Poverty, the illness, death or disappearance of one or both parents, migration, crime, abuse and neglect are some of the key reasons why the participants of this study were taken into care, although a number of young people recalled that it was not always clear to them why they were taken away from their families and for how long they would be staying. Entering into care is clearly a phase of disconnection for children and young people, especially those who enter care at an older age; moving away from their family, friends and often their hometown. Young people discuss finding it difficult to get used to new customs, rules and caregivers. Those who came from minority or indigenous backgrounds tended to find the transition harder as they often had to adapt to a different culture and experienced a language barrier in communicating with both caregivers and peers in care. Nevertheless, young people in the lower and middle income countries often discussed feeling lucky to be in care, due to the opportunities it afforded them, especially in terms of access to better quality education, and not having to work at the same time, or instead of their studies. The two quotes below highlight the two sides of this story:

> 'To leave my family ... because they were the people with whom I spent my time. And by leaving them things were not going to be the same. Things got difficult ... it's unexplainable. But yes that year was difficult for me.' (Male care-leaver in Guatemala)

> 'In [my hometown], children around my age already worked [...] They did not finish their school. How lucky I am to be taken into [care organisation], live in a family and finish my school with the course I am interested in.' (Female care-leaver in Indonesia)

Young people in the Netherlands experienced this transition differently, as many were forcibly removed from their parents. Yet, despite the difficulties and problems at home, they remain very loyal towards their parents and family and stay concerned and involved in family affairs. This can divert their attention from other social engagement and schoolwork.

> 'Especially, when families are under pressure, [young people] are loyal to their own parents and they pay attention to their parents. In that case, they turn their back, in a way (sub-consciously), against other social circumstance.' (Expert Youth Care in the Netherlands)

Transitions within care

Within care, young people experience transitions between care organisations and within care organisations, where many of the participants of this study moved to a youth house run by their care organisation as part of their preparation for independent living. For organisations where youth houses were present,[26] this resulted in youth moving away from their caregivers into a shared-house, with one supervisor. The age that this takes place varies by organisation, with young men usually moving to youth houses earlier, around the age of 14–16, and young women around the age of 18. Staff argue that this is done in order to avoid relationships developing between young men and women living together. This transition is associated with disconnection from youths' caregivers and care families, which some young people found very emotionally difficult, as one male care-leaver in Guatemala highlighted:

> 'I could not express my feelings living far from [primary caregiver]. The situation was different. I found it difficult to adjust with the new environment' (Male care-leaver in Guatemala).

---

26 In SOS children's village settings, all family-based care youth would move into youth houses. In other care programmes, youth houses were not part of the care arrangements. In the Netherlands, whether a young person moves to a youth house is decided based on the individual needs and circumstances of the young person (for more information see Pouw et al., 2017).

For males in Côte d'Ivoire and Kenya, the move is connected with negative relational movements through developing 'negative friendships', substance abuse and school truancy:

> 'This transition changed my life negatively. I was brilliant at school, but when I got to the youth house, my academic performance declined. I started drinking alcohol, smoking cigarettes.' (Male care-leaver Côte d'Ivoire).

For other youth, however, the move is associated with the ability to develop deeper connections with their friends and family as they have more freedom over their time and relationships. Often, this transition is experienced as both positive *and* negative and youth's experiences largely depend on the policies of different care organisations and on the individual's needs and experiences. For example, young people who had a positive relationship with their primary caregiver and enjoyed the family set-up, found the disconnection much more difficult than those who had a more negative or volatile relationship with their caregiver. Furthermore, some youth houses remain in the same vicinity as the care organisation compared to others which are based outside or further away. Some young people enjoy the closeness to their previous primary caregiver that being in the vicinity allows, whereas others find that they are still not free enough to come and go as they please and manage their own schedule. For others still, as the Côte d'Ivoire example highlights, the freedom of being further away can be coupled with a sense of a loss of structure or control.

Transitions out of care
Young people's transition out of care to independent living represents a major relational movement in their lives. There are several positive aspects to this move; notably that young people have less regimented daily lives and more freedom, which for some means they can spend more time with their family and friends. For those who experience stigma as a result of being in care (see below) it is also a chance for them to break free from this, as one young female in Malawi stated: 'I want to be excused from the verbal abuse and taunts I suffer from the public here because of my homelessness [associated to the care organisation].' However, for many young people, the transition to independence represents a time of significant disconnection and loneliness, as well as concern of how they will look after themselves. Young people speak of the sadness they feel moving away from their caregiver and peers, into a life on their own. Many youth strug-

gle to cope with the move financially, meaning they have to spend a great deal of time at work to manage their financial independence, especially if they are studying. This means that often youth lack the financial resources to travel to visit their friends, family or former care-givers:

> 'The priorities change, because when one was at the youth house, there was time to do other things. To hang out with my friends or to do other things. But being by myself, things change. Work becomes a priority, and also the studies if one studies. So the time that is left [to socialise] is not that much. Because if the work is full time there is not much time to spend' (male care-leaver from Guatemala).

Youth's perception of society beyond care as the 'outside world' proves especially problematic here, as young people lack the connections in society that could help them cope with independence on a practical and emotional level. This transition is made further difficult by the fact that support ends very abruptly for young people, sometimes with them having little warning that their care and support is going to finish.

Relational images: prejudice and self-exclusion

Relational images are a key element of the relational approach, affecting the connectedness of an individual. This research finds that young people from care experience being labelled with prejudicial images. Young people not only experience this as a form of exclusion in itself, but prejudicial images also often result in young people forming negative self-images and withdrawing from different parts of society. This demonstrates the cyclic effect of social exclusion and self-exclusion, as well as highlighting that supporting youth from care must go beyond addressing the economic needs of youth. Teachers and employers were indicated as being the key groups who demonstrated holding prejudicial images against young people from care. In Indonesia and Guatemala, youth and care staff highlighted that teachers, and sometimes fellow students, assumed young people from care were naughty and untrustworthy, and were automatically blamed for trouble in the classroom. In Kenya, it was discussed that employers expect young people from care to steal from them, and pay them lower wages because they believe they are 'doing youth a favour'. In the Netherlands, the stereotyping of youth from care as having a lower education causes youth from care to feel insecure and not good enough.

At the broader societal level, the label of 'orphan' or 'youth from care' can result in young people experiencing discrimination and exclusion, with assumptions made about the character and behaviour of this group of young people, including that they would not want to socialise. As care staff in Guatemala highlight: 'So they have made a generalisation out of a few. All these things damage their social environment and this affects them negatively in the society.' In Malawi, girls highlighted that people assumed they were 'promiscuous' due to being from care: 'Some people think that just because I live at this care centre, I am promiscuous. They think that I make sexual relationship with men so that I meet my personal needs, which is not the case' (Female in Malawi). Also in Malawi, young people stated that the public would assume they were HIV positive due to their care status. The negative association of these labels also affects young people's personal relationships. In Indonesia, care staff highlighted that being from care can mean for young women that their partner's parents will not accept her, and so the relationship is ended. In Kenya and Malawi, young men highlighted that that girls do not want to date them, because they are considered an 'orphan' and 'less of a man'.

Many youth themselves discuss how these experiences of exclusion and prejudicial images result in them questioning their identity and withdrawing from different parts of society or their social life, as well as describing themselves as having 'low self-esteem'. In Indonesia, a young careleaver highlighted that it '[...] affected my relationship in which I only have few friends and I do not know much about my society.' and in Malawi a young person described how: 'The social exclusion that I experienced made me to withdraw and live a very secluded life'. In Kenya and Malawi, young people alluded to the impact prejudicial images and experiences of exclusion had on their self-images, discussing the difficulties they have in developing trust with others, who they assume will not understand them, or being cautious in developing friendships for fear of being bullied for coming from care. The prejudice that some in society hold against young people from care therefore not only constitutes exclusion in itself, but can also result in young people from care excluding *themselves* from certain parts of society in response to, and in anticipation of, negative treatment—simultaneously limiting the number of connections that young people have.

Care policies

The policies of care organisations and (local) government bodies can also affect the connectedness of young people from care in different ways. Care organisations are of course highly focused on the safety and wellbeing of the young people they care for, however a key policy young people frequently highlighted is that they have very restricted schedules in care, which limits their ability to maintain friendships outside of their organisation. For example, young people discuss being allocated specific time slots in the day for completing their homework, carrying out chores and engaging in group activities, which prevent them from having friends from outside care around to visit, or from visiting these friends. Indeed, some policies prevent young people from spending time after school outside of the organisation, which can make it difficult for young people to develop and maintain friendships. This results in disconnection with young peoples' peers, and also appears to be one of the reasons for young people viewing the broader society as the 'outside world'.

At a wider governmental level, strikingly little is done for young people as they transition out of care and into independence, with virtually no support for care-leavers across the countries beyond that offered by specific care organisations. Indeed, 59.8% of young people believe that the government is not helpful during the transition out of care. Care organisations themselves often do not have the capacity to provide this support or to monitor youth, meaning that care-leavers are very abruptly left without support when they leave care. Moreover, governments do not keep track of what happens to young people after leaving care and care organisations themselves often are not able to fulfil this role (not least due to a lack of resources for this). This means that young care-leavers often become 'invisible' to organisations that should and could provide support and the possibility of developing protective and supportive policies for care-leavers is significantly restricted.

Social-cultural, economic and political drivers of exclusion

Social drivers of exclusion

The lack of connections of young people from care can be considered a form of social exclusion in itself; however, it also impacts and reinforces the social, economic and political exclusion experienced by youth. Of the young people surveyed, 27.6% said that they felt socially excluded because of their care background—these results varied significantly by country, as Table 3 demonstrates. Only 8.4% of young people in Côte d'Ivoire felt their care background resulted in social exclusion, compared to 68.2% in Malawi. These differences are most likely due to societal perceptions about what it means to be a young person in care, and the relational images and treatment of youth that follow. In Kenya and Malawi, where youth were most likely to feel socially excluded because of being from care, youth also reported having negative relationships with their caregivers. Qualitative data shows that this exclusion based on care background is primarily felt in reference to people in the society beyond their care organisation, with youth outside of Kenya and Malawi generally feeling very accepted by their caregivers and peers within care, and also often their peers in school.

Table 3   Youth feeling socially excluded because of care background (N=246)

Country	Feeling socially excluded* because of care background (%)
Côte d'Ivoire	8.4
Guatemala	13.0
Indonesia	11.4
Kenya	40.9
Malawi	68.2
Netherlands	33.4
Total Average	27.6

*Feeling 'somewhat' or 'largely' affected by their care background.

As we have seen above, experiencing exclusion and prejudicial images can lead to young people withdrawing from certain parts of society, which further limits their connections and deepens their exclusion. In Côte d'Ivoire and Guatemala, young people also said that young men are particularly susceptible to becoming involved in gangs when they experience disconnection, as a way of finding belonging in society. As young men in an FGD in Guatemala described, a young man may join a gang '[…] because he has been threatened, he has no job. It is the easiest thing to do. Because he feels discriminated or excluded.' As well as the violence and danger that gang members experience, youth highlight that after joining a gang, young people face deeper societal discrimination and lose their existing social and support network as their previous connections disassociate from them.

Economic drivers of exclusion

Importantly, the social exclusion and lack of connections that young people in care experience can also go on to affect their economic exclusion. Young people highlight that having connections is considered crucial for care-leavers finding accommodation and employment, especially in the low and middle income countries which have high levels of youth unemployment. This is of course an issue for the majority of young people in these countries, with Table 4 demonstrating the most recent data on levels of youth not in employment, education or training in the study countries. However, young people from care reported feeling especially vulnerable in this this regard, as they saw their peers getting access to work and accommodation through their family connections and ties, which many young people from care did not have access to. It can therefore be seen that the lack of connections young people have when transitioning out of care creates an additional barrier to overcome in accessing the labour market and finding a place to live. Indeed, despite many of the young people who were part of this study having, and being very grateful for, better access to education—and often the more advanced levels of education[27]—a number still believed they were disadvantaged in gaining employment due to being from care. This intersects with difficulties that they highlight all young people experience in the labour market, such as a lack of adequate opportunities and discrimination based on age. The young people who do have access to employment highlight working very long hours and a lack of stability in their work, including a lack of contract. Young women in the three African countries were also susceptible to abuse and sexual exploitation by their employers. Across the countries, young people say that they are not able to earn a sufficient income to sustain themselves. As one young male care-leaver in Indonesia stated: 'To be honest, the money I gain is not enough to provide my daily needs'. It is likely that these experiences also hold true for young people who have not been in care, but it should be highlighted that young people from care lack a fall-back position when they find themselves in financial difficulty or in

---

27 This finding differs from some of the findings reported in the literature review, where it is stated that young people from care have lower levels of education(al attainment). This is likely to be the case due to the fact that this study focuses on lower and middle income countries as opposed to the higher income country focus of much literature. Indeed, youth in the Netherlands often opt for 'lower' levels of education, as discussed.

periods of unemployment; with no one to turn to for financial assistance or to provide temporary accommodation and a lack of connections to help them find (temporary) employment.

Table 4   Youth not in employment, education or training (NEET) in study countries

Country	Youth NEET rate levels (%)
Côte d'Ivoire	36
Guatemala	27.3
Indonesia	21.5
Kenya	32.4
Malawi	32.9
Netherlands	4

Data from ILO STAT, 2019.

This employment and economic exclusion, feeds back into youth's social exclusion, with young people from care finding it difficult to continue their education after finishing in care, due to the need to balance their studies with the immediate need to earn enough money for their accommodation and food. This can lead to young people giving up on leisure activities with friends or dropping out of education. In the Netherlands, where access to better quality education is more widespread, young people from care opt for 'lower' levels of education, which both costs less and lasts for a shorter period of time—meaning that youth are able to start earning an income to support themselves at an earlier age. However young people face prejudice in society as a result of their educational level, and have difficulties accessing the type of jobs that they aspire to.

Furthermore, young people discuss that not being able to find work results in low self-confidence, desperation, questioning of themselves and ultimately 'giving up' and isolating themselves from society. In Kenya it was highlighted that being unemployed or from a poor background leads to an individual being classified as a second class citizen who is 'failing', resulting in prejudice and exclusion from their society and their family. In Guatemala, young people and stakeholders discussed that youth unemployment and a lack of money resulted in 'socially deviant' behaviour, such as involvement in gangs or stealing clothes or technology in order to 'fit in' with their peers. Indeed, across the countries young people highlight feeling excluded because they are unable to buy the latest fashion or gadgets and unable to participate in social activities with their friends due to a lack of finances.

Political drivers of exclusion

The economic exclusion that young people experience is closely linked to their political exclusion. In the low and middle income countries, young people felt there was a lack of political attention given to job opportunities for young people. Indeed, interviews with youth and with local government officials highlight that, due to high levels of youth unemployment, young people are encouraged or pushed towards engaging in informal business or entrepreneurship. This appears to be especially problematic for young people from care who not only lack the financial capital to start up their own business, but also lack a fall-back position in case they face economic set-backs in their business. Entrepreneurship very much involves taking risks and often provides an unstable income, resulting in precariousness that young people from care cannot afford. Furthermore, young people who have developed their own (informal) business highlight that it does not provide them with enough money for a stable livelihood. This approach therefore overlooks the necessity of a stable income for young people, and the capital needed to start up a business.

More broadly at the political level, the majority of the participants in this research felt strongly disconnected from politics and policies and generally believe that their voices are not heard by politicians who do very little in their favour. Interviews with local government workers in the low and middle income countries depicted poor implementation of legal frameworks and protection policies, where they existed. They demonstrated a lack of responsibility at government level for the wellbeing of young people in and leaving care, with responsibility for the care and protection of youth left in the hands of care organisations, which are generally not monitored or registered. Young people in care in the Netherlands are monitored by the local government, but here the focus, especially for refugee youth, is on ensuring that youth obtain their *startkwalificatie* (the basic level of education needed to enter the labour market), with the broader social and emotional barriers to their social inclusion being overlooked. This lack of government attention limits the representation and voice of young people from care who have no, or very little, leverage on local and national political agendas, making them more vulnerable to exclusion. The lack of meaningful political attention afforded to the issues affecting young people from care reinforces the disconnection they experience and can result in young people feeling they do not have control over their own futures. As one young man in Indonesia stated about politics: 'Youth critical thoughts are often being ignored'. It is highly likely that young people more generally experience similar political disconnection, meaning that young people's vulnerabilities are being overlooked. This is especially true for young people from care, who are not considered as a key target group in local and national politics, meaning their needs and rights are overlooked, despite the very specific vulnerabilities that they face as a group.

6. Discussion and recommendations

By utilising a relational approach it is possible to understand and explore the social exclusion of young people from care not as an independent phenomenon, but as a dynamic process that both affects and is affected by youth's relations to other individuals, to society and to institutions. Importantly, it also allows for a dynamic understanding of how experiences of social exclusion can lead to a spiral of deeper exclusion. With young people from care, we see that youth's economic exclusion combined with a lack of support, means that they do not have the financial stability or support to make investments that may benefit their future, in terms of education, for example. This can result in further financial instability into adulthood, which perpetuates care-leavers exclusion. Indeed, it seems that young people from care frequently have to make choices between their aspirations and meeting their basic needs. Young care-leavers are therefore often found to be in a period of waithood, where they are unable to meet the traditional adult markers of society such as finding a job and owning a home (Honwana, 2014).

Furthermore, we see that the onus of responsibility can be placed on young people for their own exclusion, especially from the job market where young people are encouraged to develop their own employment, rather than there being a stronger focus on addressing the structural causes of youth unemployment. Worryingly, when discussing why access to employment was so difficult, many youths explained that it was because young people were 'lazy'. This echoes the comments of some stakeholders who stated that young people just need to work harder. The comments, however, did not reflect the considerable time and concern that young people were investing in their education and employment. This could be sign of negative self-images and young people blaming themselves for their exclusion from the labour market and not recognising the wider societal factors at play (See Alston & Kent, 2009). As we have seen, both negative self-images and economic exclusion can result in young people self-excluding, and/or experiencing deeper exclusion.

The relational approach also allows us to consider how different (dis)connections combine to shape and influence young people's inclusion and their lives more broadly. A combination of young people's social, political and economic disconnection and exclusion means that youth from care are often confined to informal spaces, especially in the economy. Within these restricted spaces, perpetuated by political disconnection, young people find it difficult to access their rights and have their voices heard. Young people from care therefore often remain invisible to the organisations and institutions that should be supporting them; their rights are often not protected by their governments and they have no leverage on local and national political agendas. This results in deeper disconnection and exclusion, especially from the politics and policies that influence a young person's lives. The fact that young people often actively avoid participation is telling; they do not feel represented or treated as equals and are not being harnessed by society as a potential positive force for future change.

Based on the findings and analysis developed through the relational approach, it is possible to see how recommendations can be drawn to address the social exclusion of 'invisible' youth, thus working towards addressing SDG10.2. Firstly, it is essential to develop systems to monitor and gather information on young people from care, and especially care-leavers. Information is lacking on this group of young people, which is contributing to their invisibility and resulting in a shortage of policies that address their specific needs. More specifically, from this research, what is especially notable with regards to the young participant's relational movements is that there seems to be few attempts to allow and encourage young people to socialise outside of their care environments. While of course there can be safety and protection issues involved here, this has serious implications for the connectedness and inclusion of care-leavers, and the ability of youth to integrate into the community when they leave care. Activities that encourage safe community integration should thus be encouraged. As well as improving the connectedness, inclusion and integration of youth both during their time in care and after care, this could also work to overcoming negative relational images, and the resulting exclusion, as the community develops better awareness of what it does and does not mean to be a young person from care. In addition, findings of our study have at multiple points revealed the gendered differences in experiences of exclusion. These gender differences should be explored more in future research; studies should, for instance, collect disaggregated data or make use of gender theories in explaining why young men develop fewer connections compared to young women from care. At the level of practice, care programmes should be tailored to possibly varying individual needs, which could be influenced by similar gender dynamics.

Similarly, young peoples' feeling of acceptance amongst their family, care givers and often at school may provide constructive entry points for extending their limited social networks. Importantly, connections within the employment market and with organisations and institutions that can support young people and enhance their voice need to be found whilst young people are still in care.

7. Conclusion

This paper has demonstrated that young people from care experience multiple transitions throughout their time in care, including an accelerated transition to independence (Wade & Dixon, 2006). During these transitions, young people can lose their relationships with key individuals and institutions in their life, and experience moments or extended periods of disconnection. Young people from care are also subject to prejudicial images; being labelled as naughty, untrustworthy, uneducated and un-masculine. These labels result in young people experiencing exclusion from society, including from schools and employment. They also result in young people questioning their own identity and excluding themselves from personal relationships and engagement in society in response to, and in anticipation of, negative treatment—further limiting young people's connections. Care policies themselves also play a role in limiting youth's networks, with what young people believe to be overly-restrictive schedules and rules limiting their ability to socialise beyond their care organisation, resulting in the wider society being considered the 'outside world'. Furthermore, strikingly little is done at the wider governmental level to support and monitor young people as they transition out of care and try to integrate into society.

Applying a relational approach allows for an exploration and understanding of how issues such as those mentioned above affect the experiences of inclusion and exclusion of young person from care overtime. It is particularly useful in developing an understanding of how (dis)connection with people and institutions in a young person's life impacts these experiences. With young people from care, this relational research demonstrates that young peoples limited connections and prejudicial images can affect their social exclusion and economic exclusion: Youth struggle to access the job market and find independent accommodation after leaving care, which in turn limits their ability to continue with their education and socialise with their peers, further deepening their experiences of exclusion. Youth also experience disconnection from politics, with very little political attention paid to protecting and enhancing the lives of young people from care and youth feeling ostracised and ignored.

Acknowledgements

We thank SOS Children's Villages Netherlands for funding this research, as well as facilitating the field research. We also wish to express our thanks to our research colleagues Christian Aboua, Lucy Adoyo, Averil Daly, Karel van Dam, Miranda Evans, Juan Ramón Fuentes, Deogracias Kalima, Cécile Kofi Victoire, Sanita Lielbarde, Sofni Lubis and Ibtissam Ouaali for their contributions to the project.

References

AIHW. (2012). *Children and young people at risk of social exclusion: links between homelessness, child protection and juvenile justice.* Canberra: Australian Institute of Health and Welfare.

Alston, M., & Kent, J. (2009). Generation X-pendable: The social exclusion of rural and remote young people. *Journal of Sociology, 45*(1), 89–107.

Beall, J., & Piron, L. H. (2005). DFID social exclusion review. *London: Overseas Development Institute.*

Berkman, H. (2007). Social exclusion and violence in Latin America and the Caribbean. Working paper. *Inter-American Development Bank, Research Department, 61.*

Bynner, J. (2001). Childhood risks and protective factors in social exclusion. *Children & Society, 15*(5), 285–301.

Bynner, J., & Parsons, S. (2002). Social exclusion and the transition from school to work: The case of young people not in education, employment, or training (NEET). *Journal of vocational behavior, 60*(2), 289–309.

CBS. (2015). Jeugdhulp 2015. *Den Haag, Nederland: CBS*

Comstock, D. L., Hammer, T. R., Strentzsch, J., Cannon, K., Parsons, J., & Salazar II, G. (2008). Relational-cultural theory: A framework for bridging relational, multicultural, and social justice competencies. *Journal of Counseling & Development, 86*(3), 279–287.

Frimpong Manso, K. A. (2012). Preparation for young people leaving care: The case of SOS Children's Village, Ghana. *Child Care in Practice, 18*(4), 341–356.

Gaetz, S. (2004). Safe streets for whom? Homeless youth, social exclusion, and criminal victimization. *Canadian Journal of Criminology and Criminal Justice, 46*(4), 423–456.

Government of the Republic of Kenya. (2012). Kenya Social Protection Sector Review. *Nairobi, Kenya: Ministry of State for Planning, National Development and Vision 2030.*

HM Government. (2013). Care Leaver Strategy. A cross-departmental strategy for young people leaving care. *London: UK Government.*

Höjer, I., & Sjöblom, Y. (2011). Procedures when young people leave care—Views of 111 Swedish social services managers. *Children and youth services review, 33*(12), 2452–2460.

Honwana, A. (2014). Waithood, Restricted Futures and Youth Protests in Africa. Presentation at: *Symposium on Youth Research and Development.* The Hague, Netherlands. 10 April 2014.

Hook, J. L., & Courtney, M. E. (2010). Employment of former foster youth as young adults: Evidence from the Midwest Study. *Chicago: Chapin Hall at the University of Chicago.*

International Labour Organisation (ILO) STAT. Youth NEET rate. Accessed on 17 April 2019. Available at: https://www.ilo.org/ilostat/faces/oracle/webcenter/portalapp/pagehierarchy/Page3.jspx?MBI_ID=20&_afrLoop=2609982354719436&_afrWindowMode=0&_afrWindowId=null#!%40%40%3F_afrWindowId%3Dnull%26_afrLoop%3D2609982354719436%26MBI_ID%3D20%26_afrWindowMode%3D0%26_adf.ctrl-state%3Dnf55niefx_57. (Accessed June 2020)

Jackson, S. & Cameron, C. (2012) Leaving care: Looking ahead and aiming higher. *Children and Youth Services Review, 34*(6), 1107–1114.

Mendes, P., & Moslehuddin, B. (2006). From dependence to interdependence: Towards better outcomes for young people leaving state care. *Child Abuse Review: Journal of the British Association for the Study and Prevention of Child Abuse and Neglect, 15*(2), 110–126.

Morrow, V. (2001). Young people's explanations and experiences of social exclusion: retrieving Bourdieu's concept of social capital. *International journal of sociology and social policy, 21*(4/5/6), 37–63.

Paolini, G. (2013). Youth social exclusion and lessons from youth work. *Brussels: EACEA/European Commission.* Available at: http://eacea.ec.europa.eu/youth/tools/documents/social_exclusion_and_youth_work. (Accessed June 2020)

Partos. (2015). *Leave no one behind! Inspirational guide on the inclusion of ultra-poor and marginalised people in economic development*. *Leiden, the Netherlands: Partos*.

Pinkerton, J. (2011). Constructing a global understanding of the social ecology of leaving out of home care. *Children and Youth Services Review*, *33*(12), 2412–2416.

Pouw, N. & Hodgkinson, K.A. (2016). Research Design Social Exclusion of Vulnerable Youth. *Amsterdam, the Netherlands: University of Amsterdam. Available at: https://www.researchgate.net/publication/301285875_Research_Design_Social_Exclusion_of_Vulnerable_Youth*. (Accessed June 2020)

Pouw, N., Hodgkinson, K.A., Le Mat, M.L.J., and Van Dam, K. (2017). The Social Exclusion of Vulnerable Youth Synthesis Report *Amsterdam, the Netherlands: University of Amsterdam. Available at: https://www.researchgate.net/publication/321082214_The_Social_Exclusion_of_Vulnerable_Youth_Synthesis_Report*. (Accessed June 2020)

Sommers, M. (2010). Urban youth in Africa. *Environment and urbanization*, *22*(2), 317–332.

Stein, M. (2006). Research review: Young people leaving care. *Child & family social work*, *11*(3), 273–279.

Stein, M., & Verweijen-Slamnescu, R. (2012). When care ends: Lessons from peer research insights from young people on leaving care in Albania, The Czech Republic, Finland and Poland. *Innsbruck: SOS Children's Villages International*.

Susinos, T. (2007). 'Tell me in your own words': Disabling barriers and social exclusion in young persons. *Disability & Society*, *22*(2), 117–127.

Thompson, R. (2011). Individualisation and social exclusion: the case of young people not in education, employment or training. *Oxford Review of Education*, *37*(6), 785–802.

UNICEF Côte d'Ivoire. (2013). Côte d'Ivoire statistics. *Available at: https://www.unicef.org/infobycountry/cotedivoire_statistics.html* (Accessed June 2020)

UNICEF Guatemala. (2014). Guatemala Country programme document 2015–2019 (E/ICEF/2014/P/L.14). *Available at: https://www.unicef.org/about/execboard/files/2014-PL14-Guatemala_CPD-Final_approved-EN.pdf* (Accessed June 2020)

UNICEF Kenya. (2014). Situation Analysis of Children and Adolescents in Kenya: Our Children, Our Future. *Kenya: UNICEF*.

UNICEF Malawi. (2011). Malawi Child Protection Strategy 2012–2016. *Malawi: UNICEF*.

UNICEF Malawi. (2018). Child Protection Statistics in Malawi 2018. *Malawi: UNICEF*.

United Nations. (2015). Transforming our world: the 2030 Agenda for Sustainable Development. *New York: United Nations*.

Wade, J., & Dixon, J. (2006). Making a home, finding a job: investigating early housing and employment outcomes for young people leaving care. *Child & family social work*, *11*(3), 199–208.

Yorke, M., & Knight, P. T. (2006). Embedding employability into the curriculum. Learning and Employability Series 1. *York: The Higher Education Academy*.

Finding the Hard to Reach: A Mixed Methods Approach to Including Adolescents with Disabilities in Survey Research

Jennifer Seager,[28] Sarah Baird,[29] Joan Hamory Hicks,[30] Sabina Faiz Rashid,[31] Maheen Sultan,[32] Workneh Yadete,[33] and Nicola Jones[34]

1. Introduction

Adolescents with disabilities are among the most marginalised and poorest of the world's young people. They consequently experience widespread violations of their rights and entrenched social exclusion (UNICEF, 2013; Kuper et al., 2014; Jones et al., 2018). They are excluded from education, particularly vulnerable to violence and abuse, and face significant barriers to accessing health care (Bhatta et al., 2018; Banks and Zuurmond, 2015; Groce and Kett, 2014). Maxey and Beckert (2017: 59) argue that 'societal and cultural views of disability can take on additional meaning during the adolescent years' when young people become increasingly aware of individual differences and young people with disabilities are forced to directly confront and balance their needs for autonomy and support.[35] The World Health Organization (WHO) and World Bank (2011), drawing on the 2002–2004 World Health Survey and the Global Burden of Disease study, estimated that there are between 93 million and 150 million children and adolescents under the age of 18 with disabilities, most living in low- and middle-income countries (LMICs), and particularly concentrated in sub-Saharan Africa. However, the evidence on how

---

28 Assistant Professor of Global Health and Economics at George Washington University
29 Associate Professor of Global Health and Economics at George Washington University
30 Assistant Professor of Economics at the University of Oklahoma
31 Dean and Professor at BRAC James P Grant School of Public Health, BRAC University
32 Visiting Fellow and the Head of the Gender Studies Cluster and the Coordinator of the Centre for Gender and Social Transformation at BRAC Institute of Governance and Development, BRAC University
33 Independent researcher, Ethiopia
34 Director of the DFID-funded nine-year global mixed-methods Gender and Adolescence: Global Evidence research programme
35 The introduction draws heavily from a recent report by the Gender and Adolescence: Global Evidence (GAGE) team titled 'Adolescents with disabilities: Enhancing resilience and delivering inclusive development' (Jones et al. 2018).

disability shapes adolescents' daily lives is limited (Engelbrecht et al., 2017; Groce and Kett, 2014).

The 2030 Agenda for Sustainable Development, with its commitment to 'empower and promote the social, economic and political inclusion of all, irrespective of ... disability ... or other status' in SDG 10.2 and the Convention on the Rights of Persons with Disabilities (CRPD) have contributed to a greater focus on persons with disabilities. Adolescents with disabilities, however, are rarely visible within international development research, policy, and practice. Too often, they are subsumed under the categories of 'children with disabilities' or 'youth with disabilities', leaving their unique age-related needs and vulnerabilities (e.g., puberty and sexuality education, growing independence, and risk-taking) all but overlooked (Jones et al., 2018). There are not only significant data gaps, which hinder evidence-informed programming (Bickenbach, 2011), but adolescents also often fall between the cracks of services for children with disabilities and adults with disabilities. Moreover, they are rarely mainstreamed into programming for young people (Groce and Kett, 2014; WHO and World Bank, 2011, Aguilar, 2017; Shandra and Hogan, 2009; Wilbur et al., 2018).

The Gender and Adolescence: Global Evidence (GAGE) programme[36] is a nine-year (2015–2024) mixed-methods longitudinal research and evaluation programme funded by UK aid focused on the development of young people's capabilities during adolescence (10–19 years).[37] Focusing on the rights of the most marginalised adolescents, GAGE is committed to fully integrating disability issues across all its work. This includes ensuring that adolescents with disabilities comprise 5% of its sample of over 18,000 adolescents. GAGE focuses on two cohorts of adolescents: a young cohort aged 10–12 and an old cohort aged 15–17. These age ranges were selected to span adolescence and to focus on a group of adolescents for which there is relatively sparse evidence (10–12 year olds) and a group of the poorest adolescents that will go through many key transitions during the nine-year GAGE study (15–17 year olds), such as leaving education, working in the informal sector, leaving the household, marriage, and beginning child-bearing. Moreover, two concentrated age ranges were se-

---

36 For more on GAGE see: https://www.gage.odi.org/
37 The World Health Organization (WHO) defines adolescents as individuals aged 10–19 years old.

lected in order to accommodate the need for having a large enough sample within age groups to disaggregate by gender, disability, and other characteristics of interest.

The focus of this paper is on the mixed-methods GAGE work in Bangladesh and Ethiopia. In both countries, GAGE implemented an innovative sampling approach to identify adolescents with disabilities, combining census-style door-to-door listing with the help of key stakeholders involved in providing services for people with disabilities locally. This process highlights the challenges of finding adolescents with diverse impairments—visual, hearing or mobility—as part of a typical sampling process, even when that process is designed to be inclusive.

After describing the sampling approach, we use our rich mixed-methods data to describe the challenges faced by adolescents with disabilities in Bangladesh and Ethiopia. We highlight outcomes across the six GAGE capability areas: education and learning; bodily integrity and freedom from violence; health, nutrition and sexual and reproductive health; psychosocial well-being; voice and agency; and economic empowerment. The data on adolescent girls and boys, their caregivers, and communities provides a comprehensive insight into the life of an adolescent living with disabilities in poorly resourced communities within an LMIC.

2. Sampling to include adolescents with disabilities

In order to meet GAGE's commitment to include the perspectives of adolescents with disabilities in its work, strategies were incorporated at all stages of the data-collection process. These strategies included adding a screening question on disability to the household census form prior to selecting the survey sample, identifying adolescents with disabilities during fieldwork through knowledgeable persons in the community, and including a set of questions intended to identify disability that is endorsed by the Washington Group in the quantitative survey questionnaire.

The research team targeted adolescents with physical, hearing and visual impairments. As GAGE aims to understand the lives of adolescents and observe what works to support the development of their capabilities, it is critical that research participants are able to comprehend and respond to the research tools directly. Therefore, the GAGE team did not specifically target adolescents with intellectual impairments.[38] However, we did not exclude them either, depending on the severity of their impairment, and it was sometimes the case that adolescents in our sample had multiple disabilities, including intellectual impairments.

In all interactions with potential research participants, GAGE abides by the ethical principles of avoiding harm, protecting the rights of the individuals and groups with whom we interact, ensuring that participation in research and evaluation is voluntary and based on informed consent, and ensuring confidentiality of any information provided. As most of the adolescents included in the study are under 18 years, GAGE obtains both informed assent of the adolescent and informed consent of the parent or guardian. In addition, GAGE has a referral mechanism in place for adolescents who are identified as being at risk. Institutional Review Board (IRB) clearance was obtained by each partner institution, including in the country of research.[39]

This analysis focuses on experiences from mixed-methods research in urban areas of Ethiopia and Bangladesh. In Ethiopia, data collection took place in Debre Tabor City in Amhara Regional State, Batu City in Oromia Regional State, and Dire Dawa City Administration in two phases. Phase I was conducted during October through December 2017, and Phase II was conducted during August and September 2018. In Bangladesh, data collection took place in three locations around Dhaka from November 2017 to January 2018. In both countries, there were three stages of data collection in each study area: (1) a household census stage, (2) a baseline survey stage, and (3) a qualitative research stage.

2.1 Identification through quantitative survey tools

In the first stage of data collection, a household census was conducted to identify the population of potential respondents, from which survey re-

---

38 While we are aware of research tools that have been adapted to engage with young people with intellectual and learning impairments (e.g. Nind, 2008), we did not have the resources to incorporate these at baseline, but may consider piloting approaches in the qualitative sample going forward.
39 The GAGE research programme was approved by the George Washington University Committee on Human Research, Institutional Review Board (071721), the ODI Research Ethics Committee (02438), the Ethiopian Development Research Institute (EDRI/DP/00689/10), the Addis Ababa University College of Health Sciences Institutional Review Board (113/17/Ext), and the Human Subjects Committee for Innovations for Poverty Action IRB-USA (14160).

spondents were randomly selected. The household census served two purposes: (1) it provided a complete listing of adolescents aged 10–12 and 15–17 in the study areas; and (2) it identified households that had adolescents with disabilities.

In Ethiopia, the household listing survey included the following question to identify adolescents with disabilities:

- D1. Does [NAME] have difficulty seeing, hearing, walking or climbing stairs?

During data collection in Ethiopia, households sometimes mistakenly identified adolescents as having a disability due to difficulties that were related to a short-term injury (e.g., broken bone). It was also found that knowing the type of disability improved the field team's ability to accommodate adolescents with more severe disabilities, especially for those requiring sign language support. Therefore, the following questions were added to the Bangladesh listing form:

- D2. Which of these does [NAME] have difficulty doing?
- D3. Are any of these difficulties permanent?
- D4. If this person were selected for interview, would any special services be needed for the interview to be conducted?
- D5. What special services would be needed?

As will be discussed in more detail in the following section, in spite of adding these questions, the survey team still listed some adolescents with short-term disabilities. Once the household census was complete, adolescents with disabilities were both included in the random sample for inclusion in the survey, as well as purposely sampled to ensure that adolescents with disabilities comprised 5% of the survey sample.[40] In Dhaka, the household listing identified 54 adolescents with disabilities, 34 of whom were included in the final quantitative sample (17 randomly sampled, 17 purposely sampled). Overall, 780 adolescents were surveyed in Dhaka. In urban Ethiopia, the household listing identified 76 adolescents with disabilities, 75 of whom were included in the final quantitative sample (73

---

40   Detailed information on data collection and respondent selection is in the GAGE Baseline Report (forthcoming).

randomly sampled, two purposely sampled). Overall, 2,189 adolescents were surveyed in urban Ethiopia.

In the second stage of quantitative data collection, researchers administered a baseline survey, which included a set of questions to identify additional adolescents with disabilities. Two versions of these question sets, a short form and a long form, were adapted from the Census Questions on Disability Endorsed by the Washington Group (Washington Group, 2016). All adolescents responded to the short form, and adolescents with disabilities who were identified during listing answered the long form. The inclusion of these questions in the baseline survey provides an alternative to the household listing to identify adolescents with disabilities.

2.2 Identification through qualitative fieldwork

The GAGE research teams sought to include adolescents with both moderate and severe disabilities in their research in order to shed light on the range of experiences adolescents with impairments of different sorts and severity face. The initial qualitative sample of adolescents with disabilities comprised those adolescents for whom the household provided an affirmative response to question D1 during the household listing. However, in general, the household listing questionnaire was more likely to identify mild-to-moderate disabilities and miss adolescents with more severe impairments. This was partly because young people with severe disabilities were more likely to be hidden away by their families, to live in adolescent-headed households that were less likely to be identified through the household-focused listing exercises, or, in cases of adolescents with hearing and visual impairments, to live away from home (e.g. to attend special needs education in urban areas). Therefore, in some communities it was necessary to start with a snowballing approach, beginning with either special needs education teachers or health extension workers, and undertaking the in-depth qualitative interview with the adolescent and his or her caregiver first in order to build up trust, before proceeding with the quantitative survey.

2.3 Challenges in surveying adolescents with disabilities

The quantitative listing did not always correctly identify adolescents with disabilities, particularly severe disabilities, and sometimes identified short-term ailments as permanent disabilities. For example, one adolescent boy selected by the qualitative team for interview was identified as being unable to walk during the listing exercise. However, when the team visited to survey him, they found that he had been injured in the street a week before the household listing survey and had since recovered. In another case, an adolescent girl who was listed as being deaf was not deaf but had recurrent issues with fluid in her ear that sometimes affected her hearing. These cases highlight the importance of incorporating ways to validate the presence of permanent impairments, such as asking probing questions, before conducting the interview, including when targeting for programming purposes. For GAGE, this included contacting the young person's family to confirm the nature of his or her impairment prior to visiting, conducting home visits, or adding supplementary questions to any listing survey, as was done between the data collection in Ethiopia and Bangladesh.

There were also some cases where the respondent's disability was so severe that it was not possible to interview him or her due to ethical concerns or a lack of qualified specialists to assist. Where possible, we worked with sign-language interpreters in the case of adolescents with hearing impairments, and/or adapted the research tools to involve more visual approaches, as this is a medium of expression that school-going children often enjoy and in which they are relatively competent. However, for cases where young people lacked any specialist schooling, this was less effective, highlighting the challenge of having the necessary support when working with adolescents with disabilities, especially in areas where adolescents have not had access to services such as learning sign language or other ways of communicating.

While we followed standard ethical guidelines for working with adolescents, some additional ethical concerns specific to researching adolescents with disabilities emerged. First, for in-school adolescents, we consulted with special needs teachers who, in the case of Ethiopia, sometimes assume guardianship rights on behalf of parents, as adolescents are often compelled to live apart from their families in district towns in order to access special needs education. Second, when the respondent or their parent(s) sought to hide or deny the disability, it was not always possible to focus specifically on the adolescent's impairment and its implications in their life. In Bangladesh, for example, in two cases, qualitative interviews with adolescents with disabilities had to be undertaken in the presence of their mothers, which limited the scope of the interviews because the families did not want to acknowledge the disability. In particular, adolescents with disabilities may not have been as forthcoming about discrimination, stigma, and any hurt faced in the presence of a parent, particularly if they faced discrimination from within the family. This also affected quantitative interviews, where parents of adolescents with disabilities were more likely to check in on the adolescent during the survey, making it difficult to ensure privacy around sensitive questions. Third, we also adjusted our standard research instruments depending on the adolescent's impairment. For adolescents who are deaf, we both worked to ensure sign-language interpreters were present and relied more heavily on visual tools; in the case of adolescents who are blind, we used more vignette exercises and discussion-based tools instead of the visual community and body mapping exercises.

The field teams adopted several strategies to try to maintain privacy for the adolescents who participated, given these additional challenges. One strategy that worked well was finding spaces to conduct the surveys that were away from the adolescent's home, such as in an open room at a school, at the workplace of the adolescent, or at premises belonging to a local non-government organisation (NGO). In Ethiopia, field teams also provided door-to-door transport for adolescents with visual and physical impairments to facilitate their participation.

The additional challenges in surveying adolescents with disabilities are a reflection of some of the myriad challenges faced by adolescents with disabilities day-by-day. The accommodations made by the research teams to overcome these challenges also demonstrate how these difficulties can be lessened with adequate advance planning and flexibility.

3. GAGE capability domains and methods

3.1 GAGE capability domains

GAGE employs a conceptual framework informed by a capabilities approach, which explores the multidimensional assets (economic, human, political, emotional and social) that expand the capacity of individuals—including the most marginalised, such as adolescent mothers or adolescents with disabilities—to achieve valued ways of 'doing and being' (Sen, 2004; Nussbaum, 2011; Kabeer, 2003). We categorise the core capabilities that adolescents require to make successful transitions into adulthood into six capability domains: education and learning; health, nutrition, and sexual and reproductive health, bodily integrity, psychosocial well-being, voice and agency, and economic empowerment. These capability areas span the goal areas of the SDGs, including goals 3 (Good Health and Well-being), 4 (Quality Education), 8 (Decent work and Economic Growth). In turn, we explore the ways in which adolescent capabilities are shaped by micro- (e.g. household/family), meso- (e.g. community, including urban versus rural settings, and organised civil society), and macro-level context factors (including national governance, legal rights, social and economic policy frameworks, and international donor aid). Within these contextual factors, we focus on gender equality (SDG 5) and reducing inequities among marginalized groups (SDG 10), such as adolescents with disabilities, as is the focus here. We pay particular attention to the mediating effects of programme interventions—whether explicitly adolescent-targeted or part of broader efforts to reduce poverty and promote well-being (see Figure 1).

3.2 Quantitative methods

The quantitative analysis focuses on 776 urban adolescents in Bangladesh and 2,189 urban adolescents in Ethiopia. We first identify adolescents with disabilities using the listing data and two definitions for disability based on responses to the Washington Group questions. The first definition is whether the adolescent has a functional difficulty in seeing, hearing, walking, remembering, care or communicating. The second uses the first definition, but also adds people who utilise an assistance device that overcomes the functional difficulty.

Based on the latter two definitions, we explore differences in the means of a set of outcomes of interest across the six capability domains between adolescents with disabilities and those without. We also explore differences within four cohorts: young cohort females, young cohort males, old cohort females and old cohort males, where the young cohort consists of 10–12 year olds and the old cohort 15–17 year olds. All means are weighted to make results representative of the study area. All quantitative analyses were performed using the STATA statistical software.

154 Seager et al.

Figure 1: GAGE conceptual framework

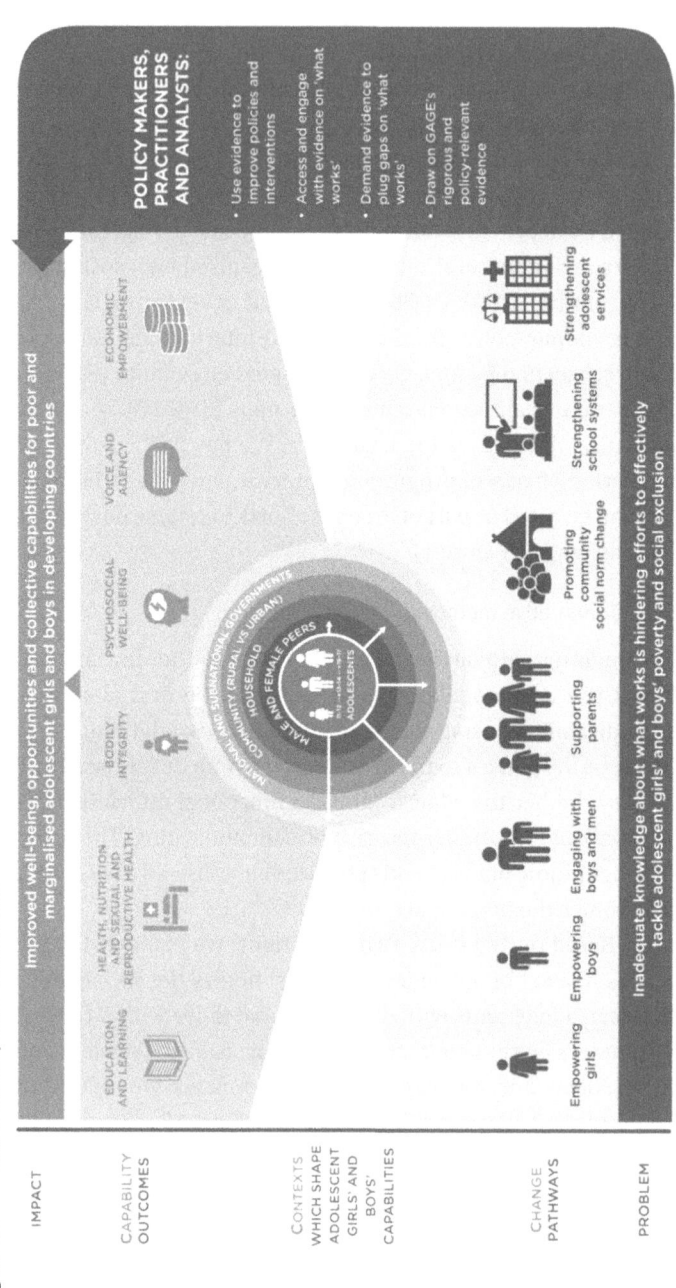

Source: GAGE Consortium, 2017

We chose indicators that capture the breadth of experience of adolescents across the six capability domains identified by GAGE. Under education and learning, we construct three measures: an indicator for whether the adolescent was in school at the time of the survey, the highest grade attended by the adolescent, and an indicator for whether the adolescent feels comfortable speaking up in class (defined for adolescents in school). Under bodily integrity and freedom from violence, we first create a scale of peer violence that assesses the adolescent's experience of peer victimisation in the past 12 months. Questions span four domains (general, direct verbal, indirect verbal, indirect verbal/relational, and physical) and include items such as being left out of games, being called names, being hit or kicked, and having someone close to the adolescent threatened. The scale takes on a value from 0–6, with higher values indicating greater experience of peer violence. Our measure is adapted from the Trends in International Mathematics and Science Study (TIMMS) 2015 Grade 4 Student Questionnaire and Mynard and Joseph (2000). We also construct indicators for experiencing or witnessing violence at home (e.g., an adult in the household calling others names, withholding food, or hitting or beating another member of the household) and for experiencing corporal punishment at school (defined for the in-school sample). The latter includes being or seeing others hit, whipped, or caned by a teacher or being punished some other way, such as kneeling. Under health, nutrition and sexual and reproductive health, we construct four indicator variables that take on a value of 1 if: (a) the adolescent's self-reported health is good or very good; (b) the adolescent has had a serious illness or injury in the past 12 months; (c) the adolescent has experienced hunger because of not having enough food; and (d) the adolescent has a source of information on puberty.

We construct three outcomes to capture psychosocial well-being. The first is the General Health Questionnaire-12 (GHQ-12) developed by Goldberg and Blackwell (1970) as a screening instrument to detect individuals who have common mental health problems (Jackson, 2007). Each item is rated on a 4-point scale with summed scores ranging from 0–12 and higher scores indicating increased psychological distress. Second, we construct the Self Efficacy Scale developed by Schwarzer and Jerusalem (1995), which ranges from 10–40, with higher values indicating higher degrees of self-efficacy. Third, we create an indicator for whether the adolescent self-reports having friends they trust. Under voice and agency, we construct an index of whether the adolescent has a say in the household across six of topics (e.g. when to marry, which level of education to achieve) that takes on a value from 0–6, where 0 indicates 'no say' and 6 indicates 'say' across all items. We also construct indicators for whether the adolescent leaves the village at least once per week and whether the adolescent needs permission to go to places. Under economic empowerment, we create indicators for whether the adolescent has money under his or her control and whether they have participated in paid work in the past 12 months.

3.3 Qualitative methods

For the qualitative research sample, we sought to include a balance of adolescents by gender, age, and type and severity of impairment, as well as adolescents who were in and out of education. In total, the sample includes 27 adolescents with disabilities: nine adolescents with disabilities in Dhaka (out of a total qualitative sample of 40 adolescents in urban Bangladesh sites), and 18 adolescents with disabilities from Batu, Debre Tabor and Dire Dawa City (out of a total qualitative sample of 90 adolescents in urban sites in Ethiopia).

We started the in-depth individual interviews with an interactive in-depth interview tool called 'A Few of My Favourite Things', which explores adolescents' multidimensional capabilities through objects that are personally meaningful to them. For example, objects chosen by the Bangladesh respondents included a cell phone, a television, a cricket bat given to the boy by his brother, a spinning top, a dress bought by the adolescent girl's sister, and a music system bought for a boy by his brother. These were used as the entry point to a free-flowing discussion where the interviewer sought to bring in all of the capability areas. This tool was complemented with a social support network exercise, which looks at the key people with whom adolescents interact (including family members, peers and service providers) and the quality of those interactions. For the younger adolescents, we also interviewed their parents using a life-history timeline to contextualize a more in-depth discussion about their approach to parenting, and, in particular, parenting an adolescent with disabilities and the extent to which they receive support in this role. In Ethiopia, we interviewed teachers at a special needs school to understand the accessibility and quality of classes for in-school adolescents with disabilities, and in Bangladesh we interviewed an NGO manager whose organization has programmes for adolescents with disabilities. Following data collection, the interviews were transcribed and translated, and then coded thematically using the qualitative data software package MAXqda.

4. Summary of findings

Table 1 presents summary statistics of disability rates overall and for each of the four age-gender cohorts for Bangladesh and Ethiopia. The table first shows disability rates according to the two Washington Group (WG) definitions of disability, which include adolescents who have a functional difficulty in seeing, hearing, walking, remembering, care or communicating (definition 1), and then adds adolescents who utilise assistance devices that overcome the disability (definition 2). The table then shows disability rates according to the household listing exercise.

In both countries, disability rates based on the household listing are lower than the rates based on the WG definitions, indicating under-reporting of disabilities through direct questioning during the listing. This is consistent with the qualitative findings that adolescents try to hide their disabilities (or families try to hide having family members with disabilities) because of the associated shame. This is especially true in Bangladesh, where the household listing suggests a disability rate of 3.2% and the WG definitions indicate disability rates of 15 to 20%. Interestingly, while disability rates according to the household listing are similar across both countries (3.2% in Bangladesh and 4% in Ethiopia), disability rates based on the WG definitions are significantly higher in Bangladesh, at 15%, compared to 3.8% in Ethiopia (definition number 1). Disability rates are consistent across subgroups in both countries. Among adolescents with disabilities in Bangladesh, using WG definition number 2, the most common difficulties are with self-care (48%), followed by communicating (39%) and walking (38%). In Ethiopia, the most common difficulties are with hearing (39%) and seeing (34%), followed by walking (21%) and difficulty remembering or concentrating (14%).[41]

---

41 Note that adolescents can have multiple disabilities so these percentages will not add up to 100.

The following subsections compare outcomes of interest between adolescents with and without disabilities, highlighting key findings. There is one table for each capability area, which summarises the outcome for the whole sample and compares across disability status. The discussion of results includes a deeper look at the differences in outcomes across disability status by looking at differences within the four GAGE cohorts.[42] Under each capability domain, we complement the quantitative findings with qualitative data findings.

4.1 Education and learning

SDG 4.5 calls for equal access to all levels of education and vocational training for vulnerable groups, including persons with disabilities. Although improving, adolescents with disabilities face considerable challenges in accessing appropriate and affordable education. Not only are adolescents less likely to be enrolled in school, they are also more likely to drop out, so are disproportionately represented among out-of-school children (Saebones et al., 2015). Our findings highlight that adolescents with disabilities are indeed disadvantaged in terms of realising their right to education, but that the picture is somewhat complex in middle- and low-income settings. Table 2.1 presents evidence that adolescents with and without disabilities have different schooling experiences. Interestingly, these differences are not consistent across Bangladesh and Ethiopia. While panel A of Table 2.1 presents evidence that adolescents with disabilities attain more education in Bangladesh (7 years compared to 6 years), panel B indicates that the opposite is true of adolescents with disabilities in Ethiopia (6.6 years compared to 8 years). In both cases, these differences are driven by older cohort males.

In Bangladesh, older cohort males with disabilities are about 40% more likely to be enrolled in school and have accumulated two additional years of schooling than males without disabilities. Qualitative interviews found that adolescents with disabilities sometimes receive support to access schooling, such as reduced fees, potentially explaining this gap. One interview also revealed that there is a school for children with disabilities located in one of the study areas, indicating progress toward SDG 4.A, which calls for upgraded educational facilities that are child, disability,

---

42 Tables available upon request.

and gender sensitive. The availability of this school may also contribute to high enrolment rates among adolescents with disabilities in this population compared to other slum settlement areas.

In Ethiopia, older cohort males with disabilities are about 14% less likely to be enrolled in school. Qualitative interviews revealed that this gap was driven by a lack of investment in special needs education, insufficient training for teachers, and lack of transportation to the schools. Highlighting the low investment in special needs education, one teacher from Debre Tabor noted:

> "There is no material supply for this year [...] the blind students are learning with the material we bring during the summer season from the college. All the required materials are available in the *woreda* office, but when we requested them they are not providing us." (SNE teacher, Debre Tabor, Amhara, Ethiopia)

Another driver of differential enrolment status of adolescents with disabilities between Bangladesh and Ethiopia could be the different composition of disability types. Whereas the largest share of adolescents with disabilities in Ethiopia have difficulties seeing and hearing, the largest share in Bangladesh have difficulties with self-care. It is likely that difficulty seeing has a greater impact on learning outcomes and the ability to attend school.

4.2 Bodily integrity and freedom from violence

The literature highlights that people with disabilities face heightened risks of physical, emotional, sexual, and gender-based violence (Hasan et al., 2014; Burns and Oswald, 2015). In this capability area, quantitative and qualitative data provide different perspectives on the experience of adolescents with disabilities. While quantitative analysis shows very little evidence of adolescents with disabilities experiencing more violence than those without disabilities (over 80% report experiencing violence in Bangladesh and over 60% report the same in Ethiopia), qualitative interviews suggest that adolescents with disabilities are significantly more likely to be teased or bullied by peers and community members. Such reports are less likely to emerge in a survey setting. In a vignette discussion, one adolescent from Rupnagar Mirpur in Bangladesh explained their community's treatment of a young boy who had cognitive difficulties:

> "When people see him, they beat him, scold him." (Focus group discussion, adolescent girls—17–19 years, Rupnagar Mirpur, Dhaka, Bangladesh.)

Likewise, in Ethiopia, qualitative interviews elicited reports of verbal and physical violence against adolescents with disabilities. One student in Debre Tabor noted:

> "The other children whip us and beat us, and so especially in the beginning I was afraid to come to school." (12-year-old girl with a hearing impairment, Debre Tabor, Amhara, Ethiopia.)

An adolescent boy who is blind highlighted that repeated bullying led to his dropping out of school:

> "I was frequently facing such incidents in the school. I was insulted and harassed by both female and male students and mostly male students who were my own classmates and from other classes." (Adolescent boy, Dire Dawa City, Ethiopia.)

The experience of violence by adolescents with disabilities is also heavily gendered, with females facing greater risks of sexual and gender-based violence. In Ebenat district in South Gondar, adolescent girls with hearing impairments participating in a focus group discussion underscored that their fear of sexual harassment and sexual assault is ever-present, especially when they are on their way to school and when they walk back to their family's rural villages on the weekends in the absence of affordable transport. In urban Bangladesh, adolescents reported in the vignette exercises that, like other girls, adolescent girls with disabilities are more likely to face sexual harassment than boys.

While our measures of peer violence and corporal punishment among adolescents contributes to the development of indicators to measure the proportion of victims of physical or sexual harassment, a key indicator for SDG 11.7, our findings also highlight the difficulty of operationalizing such measures, particularly among marginalized groups, such as adolescents with disabilities. The discrepancy in reporting of violence between the quantitative and qualitative surveys may suggest that adolescents with disabilities find it difficult to report abuse and seek justice, both because of the sense of shame and both internalised and social stigma associated with disability and because less attention is given to cases reported by adolescents with disabilities. As such, it is necessary not only to create a mechanism for measuring instances of violence, but to also provide environments within which victims are comfortable reporting.

4.3 Health, nutrition and sexual and reproductive health

Adolescents' access to general and specialised disability-related health care is overall poorer than that of their peers without disabilities (WHO and World Bank, 2011). Our findings similarly find a pattern of disadvantage. Table 2.3 provides evidence that adolescents with disabilities are less likely to report that their health is good or very good (70% compared to 84% in Bangladesh and 51% compared to 88% in Ethiopia) and much more likely to report a serious illness/injury in the last 12 months (30% compared to about 20% in both countries). Our qualitative findings suggest that this is, in part, because of access issues. Adolescents with disabilities emphasized that they only went to health facilities as a last resort because health professionals often lack training about how to respond to adolescents with disabilities' unique needs, and, in the case of adolescents with hearing impairments when sign interpreters are absent, it was especially challenging to explain their health concerns. As one 17-year-old adolescent from Ebenat, South Gondar (Ethiopia) explained: "I try to bring my sister with me when I visit the doctor, but without sign language it is very hard for me to convey the pain that I'm feeling and for the doctor to give a proper diagnosis." In another case, a boy in Dhaka, Bangladesh with a physical disability was 'treated' by standing with his legs submerged in water for long periods, along with other traditional health practices that were painful and traumatic, even though such practices have no scientific base.

The higher rates of injury and self-reports of worse health are more alarming when taking into consideration that the qualitative research found that, for some families, expenditure on health care or rehabilitation of adolescents with disabilities is a low priority. One parent in Ethiopia explained:

> "I didn't try any medical help and support for my daughter's problem. It was Allah who created her as she is." (Mother of a 13-year-old girl with a hearing impairment and an intellectual impairment, Dire Dawa City, Ethiopia.)

Similarly, a disability-focused NGO key informant in Ershadnagar, Dhaka, Bangladesh, noted that parents were reluctant to spend money for treatment of children with disabilities, even at subsidised costs as provided by his institution, considering them a burden. "What is the benefit of investing in a disabled child? I have to take care of his eating, taking him to the bathroom, everything. If he would die, then it will be better for me."

In terms of nutrition, adolescents with disabilities also face heightened vulnerabilities due to a correlation between poverty and disability, and the intra-family discrimination that young people with disabilities sometimes face within their family (see discussion above). While our survey findings suggest that adolescents with disabilities are no more likely to report being hungry in the last four weeks in Bangladesh, adolescents with disabilities in Ethiopia were substantially more likely to report this (38% compared to 18%). Our qualitative research in Ethiopia found that adolescents reported that they had to limit their dietary diversity in an effort to make ends meet. Findings suggest that this is because adolescents with disabilities are often having to live off very limited social protection stipends and frequently do not receive additional parental support.

4.4 Psychosocial well-being

Overall, evidence on mental health among adolescents with disabilities is relatively scarce. The little evidence that does exist suggests that adolescents with disabilities are more susceptible to substance abuse and depression (Groce and Kett 2014; UNICEF Innocenti 2007). In Bangladesh, quantitative analysis uncovered no significant differences in mental health across disability status among adolescents, with the exception of evidence of lower self-efficacy among older cohort females. In Ethiopia, on the other hand, adolescents with disabilities are more likely to exhibit mental distress (Table 2.4, panel B) and have lower self-efficacy. These differences are driven by older cohort adolescents and are in line with the broader literature, which argues that girls with disabilities are particularly likely to be isolated and lack psychosocial support. They also tend to have lower self-esteem and happiness levels than boys with disabilities (Coe, 2013; Plan, 2014; 2017; UNDESA, 2012; Save the Children, 2008; Mehrotra, 2006), as this quote from a 16-year-old Ethiopian adolescent girl from Debre Tabor who is blind highlights:

> "You know how people in the rural areas are. Once you are sick, nobody loves you. Losing part of your body means you are dead and buried. They see me as a dead person. They don't see me getting an education, with a job, married and having a life of my own." (16-year-old girl, Debre Tabor, Amhara, Ethiopia.)

While quantitative data does not find evidence of adolescents with disabilities being less likely to have a friend in whom they trust in either country, a main finding of the qualitative analysis across both countries is that adolescents with disabilities face higher levels of social isolation, which compounds issues related to lower self-esteem and happiness.

4.5 Voice and agency

The broader literature highlights that adolescents with disabilities face significant restrictions to their mobility due to inappropriate infrastructure and transportation, unaffordable assistive devices, persistent discriminatory attitudes and parental safety concerns, which hamper their opportunities for participation. They also frequently have little awareness of their rights and limited say over their lives, and despite their wish to actively participate, they are often excluded from family, school and community activities (Lansdown, 2005; Groce and Kett, 2014).

The quantitative survey found that adolescents with disabilities in Bangladesh are 9% more likely to need permission to go places than their peers without disabilities (Table 2.5, panel A), indicating less freedom of movement. There is also some evidence, using the first definition of disability, that adolescents with disabilities are less likely to leave their communities at least once a week. Both of these differences are driven by differences across disability status among younger cohort males. In the qualitative sample, adolescents with disabilities who are working or school-going are mobile enough to reach their school or place of work.

The survey data from Ethiopia also suggests that adolescents with disabilities have less freedom of movement. There is also suggestive evidence that they are more likely to report having a say in household decisions than adolescents without disabilities (Table 2.5, panel B). In Ethiopia, this may be in part because we found a high proportion of adolescents with disabilities were living away from their families and were often living alone or in adolescent-headed households. This said, girls tend to face greater restrictions than their male peers.

> "I am not a member of any clubs. All the activities are done outside the class and in an office area. I don't like to go there and here. I didn't feel ashamed of my physical disability. The only factor that hinders me is my tiredness to go here and there." (Girl with a physical impairment, 17 years, Debre Tabor, Amhara, Ethiopia.)

Qualitative interviews in both Bangladesh and Ethiopia also suggest that, aside from mobility restrictions, adolescents with hearing and speaking difficulties face great challenges in communicating with their parents and peers. In the case of adolescents with hearing impairments, family members in Ethiopia reported that they had neither the opportunity nor, in some cases, the motivation to learn sign language to improve communication. This was also the case in Bangladesh in areas where there no specialised institutions to teach children with hearing disabilities. Limited support for adequate communication with key adults in adolescents' lives in turn hinders the realisation of inclusive, participatory and representative decision-making championed in SDG 16.7.

4.6 Economic empowerment

Although there is a fair amount of evidence on youth employment and on employment among adults with disabilities, adolescents and youth with disabilities tend to receive less attention (Engelbrecht et al., 2017). The evidence that does exist suggests that people with disabilities experience greater difficulty accessing and sustaining economic activity, and older adolescent girls and young women with disabilities face the highest rates of economic exclusion (Tripney et al., 2017; UN Women, 2018).

Table 2.6 summarises differences in economic empowerment using the quantitative data, measured by control over income and participation in paid work across disability status. In Bangladesh, there is evidence that adolescents with disabilities are less likely to be involved in paid work (16.7% compared to 25.7%, Table 2.6, panel A). This finding is driven primarily by differences between older cohort boys. This complements the finding in section 4.1 that adolescents with disabilities in Bangladesh are more likely to be enrolled in school. Qualitative interviews found that adolescents with disabilities may be less likely to engage in paid work in Bangladesh because they are eligible to get a card to receive a government allowance, which pays 10,000–15,000 taka every six months. There were no gender difference in the qualitative sample of out-of-school adolescents with disabilities in the involvement in paid work. Older girls with disabilities who were in school were also doing part-time work such as sewing.

While there are no significant differences across disability status over the whole sample in Ethiopia, breaking the sample down into sub-groups reveals varied experiences in paid work across age and gender. Younger cohort females with disabilities are less likely to have money under their control and to participate in paid work. This is in keeping with the broader literature, which highlights that adolescent girls with disabilities are especially likely to face limited opportunities to develop market-relevant skills and to engage in decent and productive employment due to discriminatory gender norms (ILO, 2017). Qualitative interviews in Ethiopia also found that adolescents with disabilities have few opportunities for skills training, and that social protection is very limited. For example, one special needs teacher reported:

> "We advise and recommend to facilitate vocational education for the deaf. They are good and capable to train. However, the government facilitated the vocational training only for those who completed grade 10 and above, but there should be similar training that fits their level of understanding for them." (Special needs teacher, Batu, Oromia, Ethiopia.)

Special needs education teachers also explained that they seek to find students suitable part-time work as the social protection stipend provided by the Ministry of Education to young people with disabilities to attend education is inadequate to meet their basic needs, and there is a risk that they will be compelled to resort to begging to cover their living expenditure.

Despite more limited access to skills training and employment opportunities, job aspirations among adolescents with disabilities remain similar to those without disabilities. Among all adolescents, the most commonly cited job aspiration was to work as a professional, such as a lawyer, doctor or civil engineer. In the words of one adolescent girl in Debre Tabor:

> "I want to be civil servant employed in government offices because I want to live by myself; because I am no different from or inferior to others. ... I want to do what others do. I want to make a living just like others." (Adolescent girl, 16 years, Debre Tabor, Amhara, Ethiopia.)

5. Conclusions

This paper presents the sampling strategies used by the GAGE programme to identify adolescents with disabilities in urban Bangladesh and Ethiopia and presents novel findings on the heterogeneous experiences of adolescents with disabilities in these contexts. Our work found differing perceptions and reports on who is disabled among the researchers, communities, and the individuals themselves. This finding highlights the importance of using multiple approaches in identifying adolescents with disabilities to validate self-reports of disability, especially in cases where this could affect how inclusive programming is targeted. Although including adolescents with disabilities in research poses additional fieldwork challenges, the findings from our baseline surveys and qualitative interviews in Ethiopia and Bangladesh highlight the value of doing so, as it enables us to gain a more complete understanding of their daily lives.

Our baseline findings provide novel data on the distinct experiences of adolescents with disabilities compared to those without. They also highlight areas where disparities persist and where policy and programming actors should pay additional attention in order to be accountable to the realisation of SDG 17, in particular, and to the global 2030 agenda more generally. In particular, GAGE data underscores that adolescents with disabilities fare worse in terms of educational attainment and mental health in Ethiopia and in terms physical health across both countries. Programme interventions need to be informed by this diversity if they are to effectively support adolescents' multidimensional capability development and broader well-being.

6. References

Aguilar, C. (2017). Social protection and persons with disabilities. *International Social Security Review* 70(4), 45–65.

Banks, L.M. & Zuurmond, M. (2015). *Barriers and enablers to inclusion in education for children with disabilities in Malawi*. Oslo: Norwegian Association of Disabled.

Bhatta, C.R., Bhujel, S., Dhakal, S., Gyawali, N., Shah, M.K., Shrestha, S., Sigdel, A., Sunar, M., Bernays, S., Hameed, S., Kayastha, S., Lamsal, P., Panthee, M. & Zuurmond, M. (2018). *Strengthening the voices of adolescents with disabilities in Nepal*. London: International Centre for Evidence in Disability (ICED) at London School of Hygiene & Tropical Medicine (LSHTM), CBM Nepal and Plan International Nepal.

Bickenbach, J. (2011). Monitoring the United Nation's Convention on the Rights of Persons with Disabilities: data and the international classification of functioning, disability and health. *BMC Public Health* 11(4): S8. Published online.

Burns, D. & Oswald, K. (2015). *'We can also make change': Piloting participatory research with persons with disabilities and older people in Bangladesh*. Institute of Development Studies, Sightsavers, HelpAge International, ADD International, and Alzheimer's Disease International. Published online.

Coe, S. (2013). *Outside the Circle: A research initiative by Plan International into the rights of children with disabilities to education and protection in West Africa*. Dakar: Plan West Africa.

Engelbrecht, M., Shaw, L. & van Niekerk, L. (2017). A literature review on the work transitioning of youth with disabilities into competitive employment. *African Journal of Disability* 6, a298. Published Online.

GAGE Consortium (forthcoming). *Baseline Report*. London: Gender and Adolescence: Global Evidence.

GAGE Consortium (2017). *Gender and adolescence: why understanding adolescent capabilities, change strategies and contexts matters*. London: Gender and Adolescence: Global Evidence.

Goldberg, D. P. & Blackwell, B. (1970). Psychiatric illness in general practice: a detailed study using a new method of case identification" in *British Medical Journal* 1, 439–443.

Groce, N. & Kett, M. (2014) *Youth with disabilities*. Working Paper 23. London: Leonard Cheshire Disability and Inclusive Development Centre, University College London.

Hasan, T., Muhaddes, T., Camellia, S., Selim, N., & Rashid, S.F (2014). Prevalence and experiences of intimate partner violence against women with disabilities in Bangladesh: Results of an explanatory sequential mixed-method study. *Journal of interpersonal violence*, 29(17), 3105–3126.

ILO (2011) *Disability Inclusion in Practice*, ILO.

Jackson, C. (2007). The General Health Questionnaire. *Occupational Medicine* 57, 79.

Jones, N., Presler-Marshall, E., & Stavropoulou, M. (2018). *Adolescents with disabilities: enhancing resilience and delivering inclusive development*. London: ODI/GAGE.

Kabeer, N. (2003). *Making rights work for the poor: Nijera Kori and the construction of 'collective capabilities' in rural Bangladesh. Working Paper 200*. Brighton: Institute of Development Studies.

Kuper, H., Monteath-van Dok, A., Wing, K., Danquah, L., Evans, J., Zuurmond, M., & Gallinetti, J. (2014). The impact of disability on the lives of children: cross-sectional data including 8,900 children with disabilities and 898,834 children without disabilities across 30 countries. *PLoS ONE* 9(9), e107300.

Lansdown, G. (2005). *The evolving capacities of the child*. Innocenti Insight. Florence, Italy: UNICEF Innocenti.

Maxey, M. & Beckert, T. (2017). Adolescents with disabilities. *Adolescent Research Review* 2, 59–75.

Mehrotra, N. (2006). Negotiating Gender and Disability in Rural Haryana. *Sociological Bulletin* 55(3).

Mynard, H. & Joseph, S. (2000). Development of the multidimensional peer-victimization scale. *Aggressive Behavior* 26(2), 169–178.

Nind, M. (2008). *Conducting qualitative research with people with learning, communication and other disabilities: methodological challenges*. National Centre for Research Methods NCRM/012, Economic & Social Research Council, <http://eprints.ncrm.ac.uk/491/1/MethodsReviewPaperNCRM-012.pdf>. (Accessed June 2020)

Nussbaum, M. (2011). *Creating capabilities: the human development approach.* Cambridge, MA: Harvard University Press.

Plan International (2017). *Uncovered Realities. Exploring experiences of child marriage among children with disabilities.* Kathmandu: Plan International Norway.

Plan International (2014). *Include us in Education. A qualitative research study on barriers and enablers to education for children with disabilities in Nepal.* Woking: Plan International.

Saebones, A.M., Bieler, R.B., Baboo, N., Banham, L., Singal, N., Howgego, C., McClain-Nhlapo, C.V., Riis-Hansen, T.C., & Dansie, G.A. (2015). *Towards a disability inclusive education.* Background paper for the Oslo Summit on Education for Development. http://unesdoc.unesco.org/images/0023/002338/233897e.pdf. Accessed June 2020.

Save the Children et al (2008) *A Study on Violence against Girls in Primary Schools and Its Impacts on Girls' Education in Ethiopia.* Addis Ababa: Save the Children Denmark Ministry of Education Ministry of Women's Affairs.

Schwarzer, R., & Jerusalem, M. (1995). Generalized Self-Efficacy scale. In J. Weinman, S. Wright, & M. Johnston (Eds.), *Measures in health psychology: A user's portfolio. Causal and control beliefs* (35–37). Windsor, UK: NFER-NELSON, pp. 35–37.

Sen, A.K. (2004). Capabilities, lists, and public reason: continuing the conversation. *Feminist Economics* 10(3), 77–80.

Shandra, C. & Hogan, D. (2009). The educational attainment process among adolescents with disabilities and children of parents with disabilities. *International Journal of Disability Development and Education* 56(4), 363–379.

StataCorp (2017). Stata Statistical Software: Release 15. College Station, TX: StataCorp LLC.

UN Women (2018). *Turning Promises into Action: Gender Equality in the 2030 Agenda for Sustainable Development.* New York: UN Women.

UNDESA (2012). *Building a Better Tomorrow: The Voices of young people with disabilities.* New York: UNDESA.

UNICEF Innocenti (2007). *Promoting the rights of children with disabilities.* Innocenti Digest No. 13. Florence: New York.

UNICEF (2013). *State of the World's Children 2013: Children with Disabilities.* New York: UNICEF.

VERBI Software (2016). MAXQDA Analytics Pro. Berlin: Germany: VERBI.

Washington Group (2016). Short and Extended Set of Disability Questions. Washington Group on Disability Statistics. http://www.washingtongroup-disability.com/washington-group-question-sets/.

Wilbur, J., Kayastha, S., Sigdel, A., Gyawali, A., Mahon, T., Torondel, B., & Kuper, H. (2018). *Disabling menstrual barriers: identifying and addressing the barriers to menstrual hygiene that adolescents and young people with disabilities face in Nepal.* London: LSHTM.

WHO and World Bank (2011). *World Report on Disability.* Geneva: WHO.

Tables

Table 1. Disability Rates

	Bangladesh						Ethiopia					
	Overall	Young Cohort		Old Cohort			Overall	Young Cohort		Old Cohort		
		Female	Male	Female	Male			Female	Male	Female	Male
Sample Size	776	197	196	193	190		2189	425	425	687	652
Disability Definition 1												
=1 if has a functional difficulty	0.152	0.127	0.143	0.193	0.166		0.038	0.035	0.032	0.041	0.041
Disability Definition 2												
=1 if has a functional difficulty, or uses an assistance device	0.192	0.164	0.166	0.266	0.207		0.073	0.055	0.062	0.082	0.079
HH Reported Physical Disability												
=1 if identified as having a disability during listing	0.032	0.033	0.025	0.04	0.032		0.040	0.024	0.028	0.056	0.037

Notes: This table summarizes information from GAGE baseline data collection in Urban Bangladesh and Ethiopia (2017–2018). Means are weighted to make results representative of the study areas. Disability is defined using questions from the Washington Group and includes difficulty in six core functional domains (seeing; hearing; walking; self-care; cognition; communication). Sub-categories are not mutually exclusive, so the percentages should not add up to 100.

Table 2.1 Education and Learning

	Obs	Overall Mean	Min, Max	Definition #1 No Dis.	Definition #1 Dis.	Sig Dif?	Definition #2 No Dis.	Definition #2 Dis.	Sig Dif?
A. Bangladesh									
=1 if Enrolled in School	780	0.746	0, 1	0.746	0.770		0.743	0.777	
Highest Schooling Attained	772	6.216	0, 13	6.096	7.028	X	6.011	7.200	X
=1 if Feels Comfortable Speaking Up in Class	544	0.939	0, 1	0.934	0.968		0.932	0.966	
B. Ethiopia									
=1 if Enrolled in School	2187	0.916	0, 1	0.920	0.818	X	0.922	0.844	X
Highest Schooling Attained	2187	7.949	0, 15	8.007	6.635	X	7.971	7.753	
=1 if Feels Comfortable Speaking Up in Class	2009	0.838	0, 1	0.842	0.723	X	0.841	0.786	

Table 2.2 Bodily Integrity and Freedom from Violence

	Obs	Overall Mean	Min, Max	Definition #1 No Dis.	Definition #1 Dis.	Sig Dif?	Definition #2 No Dis.	Definition #2 Dis.	Sig Dif?
A. Bangladesh									
Peer Violence Scale (0–6)	752	1.560	0, 6	1.571	1.519		1.569	1.537	
=1 if Exper./Witnessed Violence at Home	778	0.871	0, 1	0.873	0.869		0.875	0.861	
=1 if Experienced Corporal Punishment at School	544	0.818	0, 1	0.813	0.860		0.818	0.829	
B. Ethiopia									
Peer Violence Scale (0–6)	2168	1.015	0, 6	1.015	0.994		1.020	0.938	
=1 if Exper./Witnessed Violence at Home	2177	0.632	0, 1	0.613	0.609		0.615	0.593	
=1 if Experienced Corporal Punishment at School	2010	0.664	0, 1	0.667	0.564	O	0.673	0.540	X

Notes: X indicates statistical significance at the 5% level and O indicates 10%.

Table 2.3   Physical and Reproductive Health and Nutrition

	Obs	Overall Mean	Min, Max	Definition #1 No Dis.	Definition #1 Dis.	Sig Dif?	Definition #2 No Dis.	Definition #2 Dis.	Sig Dif?
A. Bangladesh									
=1 if Self-Reported Health (Very) Good	780	0.819	0, 1	0.840	0.709	X	0.838	0.739	X
=1 if Serious Illness/ Injury in Past 12 Months	779	0.204	0, 1	0.182	0.329	X	0.175	0.328	X
=1 if Experienced Hunger Because Not Enough Food	780	0.162	0, 1	0.156	0.181		0.158	0.170	
B. Ethiopia									
=1 if Self-Reported Health (Very) Good	2187	0.873	0, 1	0.887	0.510	X	0.890	0.652	X
=1 if Serious Illness/ Injury in Past 12 Months	2184	0.228	0, 1	0.223	0.323	X	0.224	0.262	
=1 if Experienced Hunger Because Not Enough Food	2185	0.193	0, 1	0.185	0.382	X	0.188	0.258	X

Table 2.4   Psychosocial Well-being

	Obs	Overall Mean	Min, Max	Definition #1 No Dis.	Definition #1 Dis.	Sig Dif?	Definition #2 No Dis.	Definition #2 Dis.	Sig Dif?
A. Bangladesh									
GHQ-12 (0–12, higher is more mental distress)	761	1.888	0, 9	1.866	1.984		1.875	1.924	
Self-Efficacy (10–40)	378	30.37	20,40	30.47	29.87		30.51	29.90	
=1 if Has Friends Can Trust	780	0.845	0, 1	0.843	0.846		0.841	0.855	
B. Ethiopia									
GHQ-12 (0–12, higher is more mental distress)	2167	1.441	0, 12	1.424	1.933	X	1.415	1.804	X
Self-Efficacy (10–40)	1328	29.70	11,40	29.80	26.99	X	29.74	29.21	
=1 if Has Friends Can Trust	2187	0.797	0, 1	0.798	0.776		0.797	0.795	

Notes: X indicates statistical significance at the 5% level and O indicates 10%.

Table 2.5 Voice and Agency

	Overall			Definition #1			Definition #2		
	Obs	Mean	Min, Max	No Dis.	Dis.	Sig Dif?	No Dis.	Dis.	Sig Dif?
A. Bangladesh									
Index of Say in Household Decisions (0–6)	693	2.484	0, 6	2.478	2.533		2.459	2.596	
=1 if Leaves Village at Least Once Per Week	780	0.273	0, 1	0.281	0.212	O	0.279	0.234	
=1 if Needs Permission to Go Places	779	0.799	0, 1	0.787	0.865	X	0.781	0.874	
B. Ethiopia									
Index of Say in Household Decisions (0–6)	2079	3.063	0, 6	3.050	3.395		3.047	3.268	
=1 if Leaves Village at Least Once Per Week	2178	0.274	0, 1	0.276	0.249		0.272	0.313	
=1 if Needs Permission to Go Places	2178	0.852	0, 1	0.857	0.728	X	0.857	0.783	X

Table 2.6 Economic Empowerment

	Overall			Definition #1			Definition #2		
	Obs	Mean	Min, Max	No Dis.	Dis.	Sig Dif?	No Dis.	Dis.	Sig Dif?
A. Bangladesh									
=1 if Has Money Under Own Control	779	0.442	0, 1	0.426	0.546	X	0.429	0.507	
=1 if Has Paid Work	780	0.242	0, 1	0.257	0.167	X	0.259	0.175	X
B. Ethiopia									
=1 if Has Money Under Own Control	2186	0.228	0, 1	0.227	0.262		0.224	0.283	
=1 if Has Paid Work	2186	0.148	0, 1	0.148	0.141		0.148	0.145	

Notes: X indicates statistical significance at the 5% level and O indicates 10%.

The Role of Context in Social Exclusion of Children: Lessons From Children's Homes in Ghana

Ernest Darkwah (PhD)[43] and Marguerite Daniel (PhD)[44]

> "People are excluded by institutions and behaviour that reflect, enforce and reproduce prevailing social attitudes and values, particularly those of powerful groups in society."
>
> (Department of International Development, United Kingdom, 2005: 3)

Introduction

The concept of social exclusion has received research and policy attention in the global community for decades. Social exclusion involves 'a state in which individuals are unable to participate fully in economic, social, political and cultural life, as well as the process leading to and sustaining such a state' (UN, 2016). The consequences for those who are excluded are multidimensional, often culminating in poverty, deprivation, hardship and reduced quality of life (Crous & Bradshaw, 2017). This potential negative result has led to widespread acceptance of the need for concerted global effort to tackle exclusion in all its forms in every part of the world (Hartley, 2016).

Among groups that are often exposed to social exclusion are children. Child social exclusion comprises many different forms, ranging from exclusion from family social activities and school play groups to deprivation of access to amenities, utilities and resources essential to the growth and well-being of children (Mohanty et al., 2016). In 2015, children were identified as the age group at the highest risk of social exclusion across the world. An estimated 26.9% of children within the 28 countries in the European Union are deemed at risk of poverty and social exclusion compared to 24.7% of adults aged 18–64 and 17.4% of elderly people aged 65 and over (Eurostat, 2018). In Sub-Saharan Africa, the United Nations Children's Fund (UNICEF) estimates that about 48.7% of children live in extreme poverty making it the region with the world's highest share of ex-

---

43 Lecturer, Department of Psychology, University of Ghana.
44 Associate Professor, Department of Health Promotion and Development, University of Bergen, Norway

tremely poor children (UNICEF, 2016). With poverty and social exclusion known to be mutually reinforcing (See Department of International Development, 2005), it also means that the region has some of the highest proportions of children at risk of social exclusion. The consequences of exclusion can be negative for children's growth and wellbeing and can also affect their future life trajectories (Crous & Bradshaw, 2017). During the negotiation process to determine the content of the UN Sustainable Development Goals (SDGs), the participation of children was seen as essential for reducing exclusion and achieving a sustainable future for all (UNICEF, 2017). Increasing children's participation is also in line with SDG 10, which aims to reduce inequalities.

Factors that predispose people (including children) to social exclusion vary widely. Factors both internal and external to the individual or group such as age, ethnicity, disability status, place of residence or gender, play roles in determining access to resources and level of participation in social and cultural life (United Nations, 2016). In the specific case of children, their vulnerability to social exclusion is often exacerbated by their dependence on the situation of their families and significant others (Mohanty et al., 2016). For example, type of family, type of household, monetary poverty, living conditions and migration background of parents are listed as specific factors influencing the risk of poverty and social exclusion for children (Eurostat, 2018). The probability of participation or nonparticipation of children significantly depends on economic and political conditions as well as adult interpretations and worldviews regarding the roles and value of children in specific contexts (Hitti et al.2011). This observation suggests that a child's position (often determined by how adults perceive them) within their socio-cultural context is an important determinant of their participation in or exclusion from social life. In this chapter, we present findings from a qualitative study that focuses on a specific group of vulnerable children, namely, children in residential institutional care in Ghana. We explore how adult expectations and perceptions of children in this context expose the children to risk of exclusion.

Children's homes and the Ghanaian social context

In Ghana, Children's Homes (CHs) are residential institutions that provide pseudo-parental care to Children Without Parental Care (CWPC). According to the United Nations Guidelines for the Alternative Care of Children (UNGACC), CWPC are all children not cared for overnight by at least one of their biological parents (United Nations General Assembly, 2010). Ghanaian CHs operate by admitting such children into residence and employing caregivers to care for them within the confines of the CHs (Darkwah et al., 2018). Although described by the government as a 'last resort' alternative care measure, evidence shows that these homes are often at the forefront in providing care for CWPC (see Better Care Network, 2014). The job of caregivers in children's homes is to serve as pseudo-parents for CWPC placed in their care and oversee their total development and well-being (SOS Kinderdorf International, 2004). In performing their jobs, these 'parents' are obliged by law to follow the principles outlined in global children's rights laws. The framework for these laws is the United Nations Convention on the Rights of the Child (UNCRC) which has been ratified by Ghana and is backed by local legislation such as the Ghana Children's Act 560 (Darkwah et al., 2018; Department of Social Welfare, Ghana, 2008).

Although there have been some considerable successes in the implementation of the UNCRC in Ghana, following UNCRC principles in raising children in the Ghanaian context has been found to be problematic. Conflicts and clashes still exist between child rights advocates and local communities regarding perceptions of children, adult-child interactions and expectations of how children should behave (see Ame et al., 2011; Darkwah et al., 2018). The outcomes have consequences for both children and adults (Ame et al., 2011). Ghanaian traditional society, like many in Africa, has expectations of children especially regarding their behaviour and responsibility towards their family and adults (Twum-Danso, 2012; Darkwah et al., 2018). Ghanaian parental expectations resonate more with the African Charter on the Rights and Welfare of the Child (ACRWC) than with the UNCRC, particularly concerning the responsibilities of children (African Union, 1990). Table 1 highlights some of the differences between the two charters:

Table 1. Comparison of relevant articles from the UNCRC and the ACRWC

Issue	UNCRC	ACRWC
Parental rights and duties	Article 5: States Parties shall respect the responsibilities, rights and duties of parents ..., to provide, in a manner consistent with the evolving capacities of the child, appropriate direction and **guidance in the exercise by the child of the rights** in the present Convention. Article 18: Parents ... have the primary responsibility for the upbringing and development of the child. The best interests of the child will be their basic concern. *(nothing on discipline of the child)*	Article 18: Protection of the Family *(before addressing role of parents)* The family shall be the natural unit and basis of society. *(not specified whether nuclear or extended)* Article 20: Parental Responsibilities: Parents ... shall have the primary responsibility of the upbringing and development the child ... to ensure the best interests of the child; ... **to ensure that domestic discipline is administered** with humanity ...
Responsibilities of the child	*No article included on this, but under* Article 29 Education shall be directed to ... (*listed third out of five*): The development of respect for the child's parents, his or her own cultural identity, language and values, for the national values of the country in which the child is living	Article 31: Responsibility of the Child Every child shall have responsibilities towards his **family and society**, ... The child, subject to his age and ability, ..., shall have the duty; (a) to work for the cohesion of the family, to respect his parents, superiors and elders at all times and to assist them in case of need; (b) To serve his national community by placing his physical and intellectual abilities at its service? (d) **to preserve and strengthen African cultural values in his relations with other members of the society**, in the spirit of tolerance, dialogue and consultation and to contribute to the moral well-being of society

Children who behave contrary to expectations often risk some form of social sanction (Danvers & Schley, 2014; Twum-Danso, 2012). Children's rights are perceived to contain 'foreign' values that lead children to behave badly, i.e. not according to local expectations, such that they may be exposed to stigma and possible exclusion. For example, children raised in children's homes under a child rights framework are perceived as 'foreign', 'disrespectful', or 'different' from children raised in local family homes, and thus, as not belonging to the Ghanaian social context (see Darkwah et al., 2016; Darkwah et al., 2017; Darkwah et al.,2018). The authors demonstrate how these perceptions have negative implications for the caregivers' job performance and expose the children to neglect and alienation (Darkwah et al., 2016). The evidence raises key questions regarding the extent to which children raised in children's homes are able to integrate, participate and feel included in social life beyond institutional care. Existing literature does not provide adequate answers to these questions. This study explores the inclusion/exclusion of children raised in children's homes. Within the particular socio-cultural context of Ghana, there were two aspects of social inclusion/exclusion that we focused on: Firstly, the role of international law and norms; and secondly, adult expectations.

Research questions

The study was conducted to answer two main research questions:

1. How are children raised in CHs perceived in their local social context?
2. How do community/adult perceptions of CH children in the Ghanaian socio-cultural context affect the children's inclusion/exclusion chances?

Method

Data for this study

The data used in this paper were collected as part of a bigger qualitative project that explored work-related experiences of caregivers in children's homes in Ghana. In that project, field observations, participant accounts, caregivers' perceptions and accounts from adults who were former residential institution children hinted at risk of social exclusion for CWPC growing up in CHs. This risk of exclusion, it seemed, was a result of adult interpretations of the UNCRC guidelines being used to raise the children. This prompted us to look deeper into the data for answers to the research questions stated above. Our idea was to use adult narratives to show how adult perceptions and interpretations can expose children to risk of exclusion. Our data approach therefore focused on adult caregivers. The methodology described here was also followed in the bigger project.

Approach and design

We used a qualitative approach with a phenomenological (interpretive and explanatory) design for the project with a view to delving deep into the lived-experiences of residential child caregivers regarding the phenomenon of residential caregiving as a job. The design fits the objective to explore, in-depth, participants' subjective experiences with children in residential institutions. The issues we explored include: How such children are perceived; what motivates caregivers in their jobs; the stressors that confront them; the resources on which they rely to perform their jobs; their relationships with the children; and the influences of international children's rights on their jobs within the Ghanaian socio-cultural context.

Setting:

The project was carried out in three regions of Ghana, West Africa. The regions have some of the country's largest government-owned and privately owned CHs which receive funding and resource support from different sources. The local communities within which the CHs are located have a mix of the various ethnic groups in Ghana. The regions were purposefully selected in order to obtain data that would provide a broader understanding of the dynamics of the Ghanaian socio-cultural context in relation to perceptions and reaction to CWPC growing up in children's homes.

Participants:

A total of 57 caregivers drawn from three children's homes located in the three selected regions in Ghana participated in the bigger project. However, accounts from 28 of the 57 caregivers are particularly relevant in this chapter. They highlight the risk of social exclusion for the residential children within the Ghanaian socio-cultural context. The data analysis conducted in this study and the subsequent conclusions are therefore based on the data obtained from these participants. The remainder of the data in the bigger project were not relevant for the topic of this chapter. Considering that adult caregivers in the institutions are part of the local communities having grown up and having raised their own children outside the institutions and within different local communities across the country, we were convinced that information obtained from them would adequately reflect popular norms and perceptions of children in the local communities. Three of the 28 caregivers were former institutional children who had returned to the institutions to work as volunteers and their accounts provided insights into integration experiences of children leaving the institutions. Table 2 presents detailed demographics of the 28 participants:

Table 2. Demographic characteristics of participants

Item	Category	Number
Sex	Male	6
	Female	22
Age Range	25–35	3
	36–45	8
	46–55	11
	56–58	6
Education	Post-Graduate	1
	Bachelor level	3
	Professional/Vocational/Diploma[45]	11
	Middle school	13
Work Role	Manager/Director	2
	Mother	12
	Assistant Mother/Auntie[46]	7
	Former CH child/Volunteer	3
	Resident Nurse	1
	Teacher	2
	Social Worker	1
Length of Service (in years)	0–10	7
	11–20	14
	21–30	6
	31–40	1

Data procedures

The project data were collected using a combination of participant observation, focus group discussions and individual interviews in that order. Only mothers took part in the focus groups. The order in which the data collection techniques were deployed was deliberate and was intended to

---

45 Vocational education often involves crafts and hand work skill training. This kind of training and Diploma certificates are ranked below bachelor degree level education in Ghana.

46 Mothers are principal caregivers placed in charge of the home units where the children live. Each home has an Assistant mother whose role is to assist the mother in their duties. These assistant mothers are called Aunties in some of the institutions.

increase rigour through systematic process. The participant observation data were collected during a one month stay or frequent visits by the project's lead investigator to each of the selected institutions. The observer recorded his observations in a separate field journal for each institution following an observation guide. Three focus group discussions (one in each institution) were conducted with the mothers. 'Mothers' are individuals acting as pseudo-parents for the children and living temporarily or permanently with them within the institutional compounds. The discussions were organized to place the mothers in a group situation to discuss shared experiences and also to seek confirmation, clarifications and explanations to the observations made during the participant observation. There were a minimum of six participants in each discussion group. The final data set for the project was obtained through individual, in-depth interviews involving participants serving in different capacities including institutional directors, nurses, social workers, assistant mothers or aunties, former institutional children now serving as volunteers in their institutions and teachers. There was one interview session per participant. The interviews were conducted to seek additional information, corroborations, diversions, or expansion on observation and focus group data.

For the analysis that appears in this chapter we explored each project data set to identify observation notes, participant accounts and focus group discussion outcomes that reflected how the residential children fared outside the institution; how the caregivers (as representatives of local adults or parents) perceived and reacted to the children in the institutions; and how the local communities perceived and reacted to the children. We paid particular attention to information in the data that highlighted risk of social exclusion for the institutional children and picked out any information that elaborated how socio-cultural norms and expectations of the local communities impacted the inclusion/exclusion chances of the children.

Ethics

Ethical clearance for the project was obtained from the Norwegian Social Sciences Data Services (NSD). The Department of Social Welfare (DSW) of the Government of Ghana reviewed this institutional clearance and deemed it satisfactory for the study to be conducted before data collection began. Permissions were also obtained from the authorities of the individual institutions involved. Project participants were fully informed about the nature and purpose of the project and about their right to refuse participation or withdraw participation at any point without any sanctions. Those who agreed, signed informed consent forms before being involved in the study. The focus group discussions and interviews were audio-recorded with the full consent of the participants. All collected data were stored in a password-protected folder on the personal computer of the project lead investigator. Co-authors and co-coders had access only to anonymized forms of data.

Data analysis

We began the data analyses process for this paper by first going through the data transcripts to identify and select observation notes, participant interview accounts and focus group data that provided any answers to our stated research questions. We were particularly interested in any information that related to local norms of child upbringing, the norms of child upbringing within the residential institutions; caregivers' own experiences with regards to raising children in the local communities, outside the institutions, versus within the institutions, using the child rights approach; and local community folk reaction and attitudes toward children raised with child rights. We also looked out for accounts from former institutional children who now live in the local communities. After identifying transcripts with such accounts, we coded the data by picking out small units of information expressing ideas about the topic to obtain a coding frame. We followed this coding process with a deductive thematic network analysis following Attride-Stirling's approach (Attride-Stirling, 2001). The use of this approach enabled us to identify emerging themes in the text by clustering the codes. This gave us a better understanding of the complexities of participant experiences and perceptions, and helped us uncover the underlying meanings and interconnections between the various emerging themes. We clustered codes that expressed similar meanings into basic units or Basic Themes. Basic themes expressing similar meanings were then put together into Organizing Themes and the same procedure was used to further cluster organizing themes into a larger umbrella theme called Global Theme. The Global Theme captures the essence of the entire data-set used in the analysis. Table 2 presents the systematic thematic analysis process we adopted:

Table 3: Thematic Network Analysis of Data

Codes	Basic themes	Organizing themes	Global theme
… They always told me I was a bad influence … Local parents don't want our children here close to theirs … They teach your children to disrespect you … I won't let them teach bad manners to my kids	CH children are a bad influence	Perceptions of CH children within the socio-cultural context	Influences of socio-cultural context on CH children's exclusion/inclusion
… Children here get frustrated when they go out there … the way they are, our society won't accept them … In our culture, children don't talk back to adults … They don't know our culture, how can they live with us … I don't see myself as their parent, I only serve them … In our culture, children serve parents not the other way round	CH children don't fit in our cultural environment		
… these children are very disrespectful, they won't survive out there … The don't do any work here, they are just lazy … We are not allowed to train them, so they are lazy … Those children only know rights, not respect	CH children are lazy & disrespectful		
… I just felt I don't belong in this place … They treat you like a foreigner … They gave me the best food and the other children normal food … Everyone called me the white man's child	CH children Feel alienated		
… Our children here are not spoken of as good children … Some face exclusion at school … I don't see them as mine so I don't include them in my plans	Not likely to be included	Effect of community perceptions on the children's inclusion/exclusion chances	
… they should take them to live in white people's country … I don't buy those UNCRC ideas so I refuse to take any of those kids … we are trying, but still some local communities reject them … we have had a lot of our children returned to us	Social rejection		
… because you are from a children's home, everyone treats you different … They think the children here are only spoilt … they say we just rear kids and don't train them	Inherent stigma		

Results

Our data analysis yielded some interesting insights into how adult and community perceptions of children in children's homes influence the children's exclusion risks. It also reveals the role that international child rights laws play in this risk exposure in the Ghanaian social context. Perceptions of the caregivers—regarding who the children were, their behaviours, their positions in the local communities and likely reactions to them within the socio-cultural context—were overwhelmingly negative and pessimistic. For clarity, we present the results in accordance with the organizing and basic themes that emerged from the analysis. The themes and quotations presented here highlight perceptions that were recurrent and quite prevalent in all three data sets (i.e. observation notes, focus groups data and individual interviews data). Some of the quotes also reflect experiences that are personal to some of the participants and not necessarily shared by others.

Perceptions of CH children within the socio-cultural context

1. *Bad influence*

One commonly reported perception (perceptions reported by most participants during interviews and focus groups) were that the children being raised in children's homes turn out to be 'bad' influences or seen as such, for local children because of their rights-consciousness and tendency to stand up to adult authority and insist on their rights:

> "… the children from here only know about their rights. They do not respect and they do not obey … they challenge your authority anytime … the community often has difficulties dealing with them because when a child like that comes around your child, they spoil them and your child begins to behave badly as well …" (Aunty, CH institution)

A teacher in one of the institutions testified to such negative local community perception of CH children being a bad influence when he said he once questioned a local parent why she was driving a CH child away from playing with her kids:

> "… When I saw her reaction to the kid from the CH, I was angry and I questioned her. She said she suffers to take care of her children and wants them to behave properly like Ghanaian children so she didn't want any foreign bad influence from those spoilt children we raise in the CHs …" (Teacher, CH)

Interestingly, a different reason was given by one local parent in informal conversations during the participant observation in one institution. The parent had come to visit a friend of hers who was working as a caregiver in the institution.

> "… It's not because they behave so badly … but in these institutions, foreigners give them money so the children get everything they want. In my house, no one gives me money so my children can't get everything. In that case my children often complain that their friend has this and that and they do not have it. That is stressful for me so I have stopped them from playing with my children …" (local community mother)

2. Not fit for the cultural environment

A perception that children from the institutions do not fit the socio-cultural environment was quite common among the caregivers. Almost all participating caregivers perceived the children as too foreign-mannered (apparently due to the use of international rights-centred approaches in their up-bringing and the children's perceived assertiveness) and therefore ill prepared for the Ghanaian socio-cultural environment:

> "... the way they force us to raise these children here, well, I would say it would be good if they would take them to live in those western countries ... because here, they won't fit. They just won't fit in ..." (Mother, CH)

This 'unfit for the environment' argument was corroborated by one of the former institutional children now volunteering in the institution who participated in the research:

> "... some people in the community call me "obroni ba" (white man's child) because one day I challenged an adult who took my seat at a function ... they said I should go and live in the white man's country if I can't respect adults ..." (former institutional child now volunteering)

The perceptions that the children growing up in CHs do not fit in the Ghanaian socio-cultural environment seemed to come in tandem with participant understandings of the Ghanaian culture and behavioural expectations of children:

> "... These children barely know our culture. Sometimes, they don't even greet adults ... at least here, our director allows us to require them to greet us after school, but in other CHs, the children don't even greet. All they know is eat and play and sleep ..." (Aunty, CH)

Despite the overwhelming negative perceptions, the caregivers, especially in the private institutions, stressed that their institutions' focus on academic training of the children allowed their children to obtain high academic achievements, which could compensate for their lack of culturally-apt behaviour:

> "... well, they know book because here, thanks to our foreign donors, they get whatever they want for school. And in this country, those who know book become rich, so maybe they will become rich and pay people to do stuff for them. They will be accepted and respected if they become rich ..." (mother, CH).

3. Lazy and disrespectful

Another commonly reported perception of the CH children was that they are lazy and disrespectful. This seemed to stem from the caregivers' observations of the children's behaviour in relation to adults and institutional norms that allowed the children to avoid what caregivers saw as compulsary household work. For example, the institutions had norms that allowed children to sleep after school and not be involved in housework right away. The caregivers saw such norms as based on the institution's adherence to children's rights laws (which they consider to be foreign) and thought such norms made the institutional children lazy as compared to children living in the local communities. Perceptions of the children as lazy and disrespectful stood out in accounts provided by institutional authorities (directors), caregivers and former institutional children who were now working as volunteers in their institutions:

> "... yes I can confirm it doesn't help us. When I first went out there it was really tough. I was lonely often because everyone shunned my company that I was lazy and I don't respect. The problem is, I didn't know exactly what I was doing that was disrespectful ..." (former inst. Child now volunteering)

During the focus group discussion, in all three institutions, majority of the participating caregivers seemed to perceive that the children in the institutions will face higher risks of exclusion in the local communities because, in the caregivers' judgement, they were spoiled and lacked respect for adults:

> "... well, back home a child takes instructions, here it's almost the opposite... like they are the bosses ... they don't respect. So yes, when they get out there it will be tough for them ... if they speak like they do to us to an adult out there, they will either likely get beaten up or completely excluded ..." (mother, CH)

Another participant said:

> "... they are lazy, they only want to sleep when they come back from school because that is the rule here ... out there in the community children have to help after school ... that is good training ... the ones here can't do half of what children out there do ... (mother, CH)

The director of one of the institutions had this to say during his interview:

> "... well, it depends on how you define respect. You see, when a child asks questions, it doesn't necessarily mean they are disrespectful, but in our social context, a child who asks a question in response to an instruction is seen as disre-

spectful. So in that way they will have problems with the local community ... but we need to follow the rules to get the funding so we can't change it much ..." (Director, CH).

Community perceptions and the children's inclusion/exclusion chances

The data regarding how the caregivers' and community perceptions of the children affect their inclusion/exclusion chances revealed recurring themes of alienation, less inclusion chances, rejection, and stigma. There seemed to be low optimism for the inclusion chances of the children in the local socio-cultural context on the basis that their behavioural tendencies developed through a rights-oriented approach to upbringing would put them on a collision course with local community expectations.

1. Alienation

In the institutions themselves, a picture of the alienation of the children was painted throughout the data (observation, focus groups and interviews) as caregivers gave accounts that suggested they do not relate to the children as their own and treat them with some form of ambivalence both because of the children's behaviours and also to save themselves and their jobs:

> "... the way we use the child rights in this institution will harm these children when they go out there. All the mothers know this but everyone is afraid to talk for fear of losing their jobs. So we just leave the children ... when they get out there it will be their problem not mine ..." (Mother, CH)

Another mother shared this opinion:

> "... I mean these are different from normal Ghanaian children. My own child can never slam a door in my face ... they know better ... But these ones here follow child rights so they can slam a door in your face. The only reason I go near them is because I need a job ..." (CH Auntie)

A social worker had this to say:

> "It would be good to allow the mothers some room to at least blend some local parenting styles with the child rights ... but the rules don't allow it ... It's my job to make sure the mother's obey the UNCRC ... sometimes I feel bad ... but it is the children who will suffer not me ..." (social worker CH)

Another mother said:

> "… Oh I don't see these children as my children at all, my children are well behaved. They show respect. These ones here are white people's children … they are special …" (mother CH)

2. *Not likely to be included*

During participant observation, it became clear that the institution encourages the mothers to develop bonds with the children so that even after the mothers have retired or the children have left the institution, the mother-child bond would remain. While some mothers testified that some of their previous institutional children were in contact and still called them mothers, others refused to include their institutional children in any future plans:

> "… These ones? no … I don't see them as mine so I don't include them in any of my plans …" (Mother, CH)

For other participants, their concern was that the negative community perceptions of the behaviour of the institutional children would be a barrier to their inclusion chances

> "… Our children here are not spoken of as good children … so I think their inclusion in the local communities would be hampered when they finally leave this place and have to find a space out there …" (Mother, CH)

3. *Rejection*

Accounts from institutional directors, social workers and former institutional children showed that among the effects of the negative perceptions of CH children is social rejection:

> "… well, what can I say, we have rules and we have to obey them. The way we raise them with those child rights rules do not help them much after they leave this place. We have had several cases in which children who were taken from here by foster parents have been returned with complaints that they challenge authority and do not show any respect …" (Manageress, CH institution)

An account from a social worker showed how previous experiences by some local community members who adopted children from CHs have led to a blanket negative description of such children and the rejection they face:

> "… Once I tried to convince a rich woman I know to adopt a child from this home … she told me she has tried twice and the children gave her so much problems that she in each case she returned them. She said: "CH children are simply not good, I would rather live alone …" (social worker CH)

For a former institutional child now working as a teacher in her former institution, the cost of being tagged 'rights-conscious' had been quite high for her, outside the institution:

> "... My marriage broke down because my husband said I behave like a white woman. Always talking back at him, insisting on rights and showing him no respect when he is the one who married me ... I can't say this institution made me so because I am an educated woman and understand human rights ... but this was the beginning of it ... and here I am, back at the institution to help these children do better out there than I did ..." (former institutional child)

Data from the participant observation revealed that the institutions had programmes that tracked the biological relatives of residential children and maintained contact with such relatives by allowing the children to visit the relatives, sometimes for long holidays. However, there were accounts of difficulties experienced by some of the children who visited. One caregiver shared a situation when one such child came back and never wanted to go to the family again:

> "... when he came back, I asked him how he fared with the family and he said he would never step there again ... When I asked why, he said he questioned the man of the house why he was sending him on so many errands and the man caned him for being disrespectful ... I just smiled and shook my head at him ... they have been so spoiled over here ..." (Mother, CH)

4. *Inherent stigma*

Some of the narratives provided by the caregivers and former institutional children also seemed to suggest some inherent stigma attached to being a child from a children's home. This seemed to be particularly the case for those raised in homes sponsored by foreigners:

> "... When a child from here misbehaves in the local community, the reaction of the people is quite harsh ... they even extend the reaction to us ... because they say we only rear the children here and don't train them ... but I don't blame them ... if it were left to us, we would train them properly ... but we get money from abroad so we work with rules from abroad ..." (Mother, CH)

One of the former institutional children now volunteering shared this experience:

> "... because you are from a children's home, everyone treats you different ... it's like everyone is watching for your mistakes to confirm their already negative expectations and perceptions of institutional children ... you feel stigmatized ..." (Former institutional child now volunteering)

Overall, the emerging participant accounts and experiences paint a gloomy picture of inclusion chances of children growing up in CHs in the Ghanaian socio-cultural context, suggesting possible exposure to exclusion and rejection as a result of perceived breaches of cultural expectations. In the next section we discuss these findings and their possible implications in relation to the literature on social exclusion.

Discussion

In this chapter, we have explored the influence that the socio-cultural context within which some children live has on their exposure to social exclusion. Putting into perspective a particular group of children—children in residential care—we set out to obtain insights into how local community perceptions and reactions to this group of children affect the extent to which they integrate, participate and feel included in local social life. The perceptions towards the children that emerged in our findings were often negative with the negativities seemingly stemming from local interpretations and reactions to international children's rights laws, which serve as the main guiding principles for raising them.

The participant narratives that we gathered suggest that despite observations in the literature about successes in the implementation of children's rights in Ghana (see et al., 2011), aspects of international children's rights norms through which children are trained to be assertive and insist on their rights, for example, are still interpreted within the cultural context negatively. Such aspects are seen (at least from the perspectives of some trained child caregivers) as spoiling children and making them disrespectful. The stories of a broken marriage (attributed to objection to insistence on rights) and children being branded as disrespectful in the local community when they question adult behaviour buttress this observation and emphasizes that such perceptions may not only be prevalent within peculiar institutional settings. Our findings show that such behaviours of children are seen as 'foreign' and are thought to be more common among the institutional children as compared to the local community children because of the reliance on children's rights approaches to child rearing in the institutions. Twum-Danso (2012: p. 140) observes that many Ghanaian parents reject child rights (especially the ban on physical punishment) because "'this is how we do it here' and that ultimately they felt that Ghanaian children were 'better behaved than those elsewhere' (i.e. in

Western Europe or North America)". This negative interpretation of children's rights and the consequent negative attitude demonstrated towards children seen as rights-oriented are a problem for the inclusion of "all children" in the communities.

First, this observation raises questions regarding the extent to which international children's rights laws are accepted and utilized in local Ghanaian communities and, perhaps, communities elsewhere that share similar customs and belief systems regarding adult-child interaction. As demonstrated in the findings, local perceptions and expectations of children within the Ghanaian socio-cultural context places emphasis on children's behaviour in relation to adults in their communities. Thus inclusion/exclusion chances were confirmed to depend on the extent to which the community perceives that a child fulfils these behavioural expectations.

Within the rights framework, the findings suggest that the local perceptions resonate more with the ACRWC which makes provisions for domestic discipline, guiding children to be respectful and a child's responsibility towards the family and community. This contrasts with the UNCRC, which emphasizes individual rights of the child with no mention of responsibility or discipline (See Table 1). This finding also complements earlier findings in the literature regarding how international human rights laws can cause social tensions and expose some vulnerable groups to social rejection and exclusion (see Burman, 2003; Darkwah, et al., 2018; Deater-Deckard et al., 1996; Snipstad et al., 2010). The social tension raised by implementation of children's rights makes a case for the rethinking of workable strategies for blending modern human rights into local norms and customs. In this context, Twum-Danso (2012, p. 137–9) observes that there is rapid social change in Ghana. He shows that gradually, an emerging group of parents (although small) claim to be more open with their children and try to find alternative ways of guiding them, increasingly recognising them as rights-holders. This implies that increased efforts by the government and a more integrative approach to implementation could be more successful and less resisted.

Second, and more importantly, the observed negative perceptions, attitudes and responses to this group of vulnerable children as a result of their institutionalization adds to existing arguments in the literature regarding the negative implications that institutionalization of CWPC has on their growth and future life trajectories (Crockenberg et al, 2008; Gwenzi, 2018; Yendork & Somhlaba, 2015). The findings show the CH institutions as different 'foreign worlds' located within the local socio-cultural context but separated from it normatively; the values and principles in the CHs are perceived to be different from those in the context within which they are located. In this sense, there is a perceived lack of or inadequate socialization of the children into the local Ghanaian social context. Not only are the children *not* taught the customary way to respect and relate to adults, but what they *are* taught is seen to 'spoil' them. Consequently, the children living within the CH are labelled 'foreign' and different from their local cohorts who live outside the institution. This is exemplified by the sense of confusion shown by the returned residential child who did not know exactly what he was doing that was disrespectful in the eyes of the local folk (see results section). This situation contributes to the argument that separating CWPC from local communities and placing them in institutions exposes them to later integration challenges and consequent risk of exclusion within their local communities (Gwenzi, 2018; Dziro & Rufurwokuda, 2013; Meyer, 2008). Frimpong Manso (2012) studied young people leaving institutional care in Ghana and found that they felt they did not fit in with the wider society because they had been brought up in a different way, i.e. socialized differently. The participants in his study attribute this to being raised with 'European standards and values' rather than 'Ghanaian collectivist values' (Frimpong Manso, 2017, p. 6).

Our findings show that children raised in children's homes in Ghana have already experienced social rejection. Examples from our findings show children who have been returned from foster placements, and adults (who grew up in the institution) choosing to volunteer back in the institution as the only place they felt comfortable. Existing literature portrays social exclusion as a significant pre-cursor to poverty in that social exclusion reduces excluded people's chances to fully function in their social context through, for example, reduced chances of accessing employment, social support, etc. (Crous & Bradshaw, 2017; Frimpong Manso, 2017). The themes of lack of acceptance, social rejection, alienation and stigma shown in our findings suggest that children in CHs face social exclusion within their communities. Frimpong Manso (2017) reports that care alienates CHs children from their extended families who believe that they lack nothing. With such exclusion, the chances of these children to fully function in their communities in the present and in the future, including accessing employment and social support, are lowered. Following the logic of the relationship between exclusion and poverty, it may not be too far-fetched to argue that the findings make a case for suggesting that children growing up in children's homes in Ghana may possibly face greater risks of poverty as compared to their cohorts growing up in local family homes in the communities.

Further, the experience of alienation, negative social reactions, rejection and stigma has been found to be related to poor mental health and social wellbeing (Morgan et al, 2007; Payne, 2011). In this sense the findings suggest possible mental health consequences for children in residential care brought on by reactions they face in their socio-cultural context. The need therefore arises for stakeholders and intervention to pay significant attention to the socio-cultural context and its roles in exposing children in residential care to exclusion. The links between social exclusion, poor mental health, difficulty finding employment and living in poverty found in the literature, are also reflected in the SDGs. Nilsson, et al. (2016) show how each SDG can influence the outcome of other SDGs in a reinforcing or a counteracting manner. Social exclusion (SDG 10 and its targets 10.2 and 10.3) of children raised in CHs in Ghana, may reinforce alienation and mental health problems (SDG 3 and its target 3.4) which in turn would make it harder for them to find employment (SDG 8 and its target 8.5) increasing the likelihood they will live in poverty (SDG 1 and its targets 1.1, 1.2 and 1.3).

Limitations

This study is mainly limited by the small number of participants and the lack of involvement from members of the local community who were not working in the institutions. Generalization of the findings is therefore limited and must be done with care. Nonetheless, the findings give insight into some of the consequences that a socio-cultural context can have for the inclusion/exclusion chances of the specific group of children involved. Moreover, like all qualitative studies, the involvement of the researchers in co-creating the knowledge carried in this study implies higher levels of subjectivity in the conclusions drawn. Future studies in this area should consider involving more local community members in order to obtain a more comprehensive picture of the socio-cultural reactions to children raised with child rights and the implications for their inclusion/exclusion.

Conclusion

With the aim to highlight the role of socio-cultural context in the risk of social exclusion, this study explored the perceptions and experiences of caregivers for residential institutional children to obtain insight into how local communities react to such children and how the reaction affects their inclusion/exclusion chances. We found that the children are perceived in negative ways due to the rights-centred approaches used in raising them in their institutions. The negative perceptions lead the residential children to experience rejection, alienation and stigma within the local communities, which increases their risk of social and economic exclusion in the communities. These interlinkages are reflected in interactions between SDGs too: In order to achieve the goal of 'no poverty' (SDG 1), good health and well-being are needed to promote employment which, in turn, will reduce inequalities (SDG 10). A rethink of strategies to improve the blend of cultural norms and human rights as well as an increased consideration of the socio-cultural context in inclusion/exclusion conversation for children are recommended.

References

Adelman, L., & Middleton, S. (2003). *Social exclusion in childhood: why and how it should be measured. Some thoughts from Britain.* Paper presented at the Australian Social Policy Conference, University of New South Wales, Sydney.

African Union. (1990). *African Charter on the Rights and Welfare of the Child.* Addis Ababa: African Union.

Ame, R. K., Agbenyiga, D. L., & Apt, N. A. (2011). The future of children's rights in Ghana. In R. K. Ame, D. L. Agbenyiga & N. A. Apt (Eds.), *Children's rights in Ghana: Reality or rhetoric.* Plymoyth, UK: Lexington Books.

Attride-Stirling, J. (2001). Thematic networks: an analytic tool for qualitative research. *Qualitative Research, 1*(3), 385–405.

Better Care Network. (2014). Collected viewpoints on international volunteering in residential care centres, Country focus: Ghana. Retrieved 9th February, 2016, from http://www.bettercarenetwork.org/bcn-in-action/better-volunteering-better-care/activities-and-documents/collected-viewpoints-on-international-voluntee ring-in-residential-care-centres-country-focus-ghana.

Burman, S. (2003). The best interests of the South African child. *International Journal of Law, Policy and the Family, 17,* 28–40.

Crockenberg, S. C., Rutter, M., Bakermans-Kranenburg, M. J., Van IJzendoorn, M. H., Juffer, F., & Team., T. S. P. U. O. (2008). The effects of early social-emotional and relationship experience on the development of young orphanage children. *Monographs of the Society for Research in Child Development, 73*, 1–298.

Crous, G., & Bradshaw, J. (2017). Child social exclusion. *Children and Youth Services Review, 80*, 129–139. doi: doi.org/10.1016/j.childyouth.2017.06.062.

Danvers, K., & Schley, D. (2014). Better discipline for Ghana's children: A Comparative Thematic Analysis of Attitudes to and Experience of Corporal Punishment in Ghana to Inform Advocacy on Ending Violence Against Children. Retrieved 13th September, 2018, from Challenging Heights, at: http://challengingheights.org/wp-content/uploads/2014/11/Better-Discipline-for-Ghanas-Children.pdf.

Darkwah, E., Asumeng, A., & Daniel, M. (2017). Caring for "parentless" children: An exploration of work stressors and resources as experienced by caregivers in children's homes in Ghana. *International Journal of Child, Youth and Family Studies (8*(2), 59–89. doi:http://dx.doi.org/10.18357/ijcyfs82201717850.

Darkwah, E., Daniel, M., & Asumeng, A. (2016). Caregiver perceptions of children in their care and motivations for the care work in children's homes in Ghana: children of God or children of whitemen? *Children and Youth Services Review, 66*(C), 161–169.

Darkwah, E., Daniel, M., & Asumeng, A. (2018). The impact of organizational structure and funding sources on the work and health of employed caregivers in children's homes in Ghana. *Occupational Health Science*. doi:https://doi.org/10.1007/s41542-018-0020-x.

Darkwah, E., Daniel, M., & Yendork, J. S. (2018). Care-'less': exploring the interface between child care and parental control in the context of child rights for workers in children's homes in Ghana. *BMC International Health and Human Rights, 2018*(1), 13. doi:10.1186/s12914-018-0151-9.

Deater-Deckard, K., Dodge, K. A., Bates, J. E., & Pettit, G. S. (1996). Physical discipline among African American and European American mothers: Links to children's externalising behaviours. *Developmental Psychology, 32*(1065–1072).

Department for International Development, (2005). *Reducing poverty by tackling social exclusion: A DFID policy paper*: London, United Kingdom, Department for International Development.

Department of Social Welfare (DSW) Ghana. (2008). *Regulations for care and protection of children without appropriate parental care in Ghana*. Accra: Ministry of Manpower, Youth and Employment.

Dziro, C., & Rufurwokuda, A. (2013). Post-Institutional Integration Challenges Faced by Children who were Raised in Children's Homes in Zimbabwe: The Case of 'Ex-Girl' Programme for One Children's Home in Harare, Zimbabwe *Greener Journal of Social Sciences, 3*(5), 268–277.

EUROSTAT. (2018). Children at risk of poverty or social exclusion Retrieved 13th September, 2018, from EUROSTAT at: https://ec.europa.eu/eurostat/statisticsexplained/index.php/Children_at_risk_of_poverty_or_social_exclusion.

Frimpong Manso, K. A. (2012). Preparation for young people leaving care: The case of SOS Children's Village, Ghana. Child Care in Practice, 18(4), 341–356.

Frimpong-Manso, K. (2017). The social support networks of care leavers from a children's village in Ghana: formal and informal supports. Child & Family Social Work, 22(1), 195–202.

Gwenzi, G. D. (2018). The Transition from Institutional Care to Adulthood and Independence: A Social Services Professional and Institutional Caregiver Perspective in Harare, Zimbabwe. *Child Care in Practice*. doi:10.1080/13575279.2017.14 14034.

Hartley, D. (2016). Poverty and social exclusion. In L. Platt & H. Dean (Eds.), *Social Advantage and Disadvantage* (pp. 3–24). Oxford, UK: Oxford University Press.

Hitti, A., Mulvey, K. L., & Killen, M. (2011). Social exclusion and culture: The role of group norms, group identity and fairness. Anales de Psicología, 27(3), 587–599.

Meyer, I. J. (2008). *The experience of a late adolescent state care leavers: A phenomenological study* M.A. (Masters dissertation, Department of Psychology, University of Johannesburg, RSA.), Johannesburg.

Mohanty, I., Edvardsson, M., Abello, A., & Eldridge, D. (2016). Child Social Exclusion Risk and Child Health Outcomes in Australia. PLoS ONE, 11(5), e0154536. doi:10.1371/journal.pone.0154536.

Morgan, C., Burns, T., Fitzpatrick, R., Pinfold, V., & Priebe, S. (2007). Social exclusion and mental health: conceptual and methodological review. British Journal of Psychiatry, 191, 477–483.

Nilsson, M., Griggs, D., & Visbeck, M. (2016). Map the interactions between Sustainable Development Goals. Nature, 534, 320–322.

Payne, S. (2011). *Social Exclusion and Mental Health—Review of Literature and Existing Surveys*. London, UK: Poverty and Social Exclusion UK.

Snipstad, M. B., Lie, G. T., & Winje, D. (2010). Child rights or wrongs: Dilemmas in implementing support for children in the Kilimanjaro Region, Tanzania, in the era of globalized AIDS approaches. In T. Thelen & H. Haukanes (Eds.), *Parenting after the century of the child*. UK: Ashgate Publishing Limited. 205–222.

SOS Kinderdorf International. (2004). Manual for the SOS Children's Village organisation: SOS Kinderdorf International, Innsbruck.

Twum-Danso, A. (2012). "This is how we do it here": The persistence of the physical punishment of children in Ghana in the face of globalization ideals. In A. T.-D. Imoh & R. K. Ame (Eds.), *Childhoods at the Intersection of the Local and the Global*. United Kingdom: Palgrave Macmillan.

United Nations Children's Fund (UNICEF). (2017). *The 2030 agenda for sustainable development: Group of friends of children and the SDGs*. Retrieved 30th May, 2018 from https://www.unicef.org/agenda2030/69525_100608.html.

United Nations Children's Fund (UNICEF), & World Bank Group. (2016). *Ending Extreme Poverty: A Focus on Children*. Retrieved 13th September, 2018, from United Nations Children's Fund (UNICEF) and the World Bank Group, at: https://www.unicef.org/publications/index_92826.html.

United Nations General Assembly. (2010). *Guidelines for the alternative care of children: Resolution/adopted by the General Assembly*. Retrieved 18th January, 2015 from http://www.unicef.org/spanish/videoaudio/PDFs/100407-UNGA-Res-64-142.en.pdf.

United Nations Organization. (2016). *Who is being left behind? Patterns of social exclusion*. Zurich: United Nations Organization.

Yendork, J. S., & Somhlaba, N. Z. (2015). Do social support, self-efficacy and resilience influence the experience of stress in Ghanaian orphans? An exploratory study. *Child Care in Practice, 21*(2), 140–159.

PART III

SOCIAL AND CHILD PROTECTION, CHILD WELL-BEING

Child-Sensitive Non-Contributory Social Protection in the MENA Region

Anna Carolina Machado[47] and Charlotte Bilo[48]

1. Introduction

Children in developing countries are more than twice as likely to be living in extremely poor households as adults. They account for half of the estimated 767 million people living in extreme poverty worldwide, even though they only represent around a third of the world's population (UNICEF & World Bank, 2016). Children experience poverty differently from adults: Not only are they more vulnerable to malnutrition, disease and abuse, they are also more dependent on others for support (UNICEF, 2012). Yet, child poverty cannot be gauged in monetary terms alone, as children experience poverty in multiple dimensions that are crucial to their well-being, including access to nutrition, health, water, education, protection and shelter.

In the Middle East and North Africa (MENA) region,[49] levels of child poverty remain alarming. According to a recent study covering 11 Arab countries, one in four children experiences acute poverty, lacking basic rights in two or more of the following dimensions: Decent housing, health care, water, sanitation, nutrition, basic education and information (League of Arab States et al., 2017; UNICEF, 2018). As Figure 1 shows, the incidence of multi-dimensional poverty is especially high in Sudan and Yemen, but a significant share of children in Morocco and the State of Palestine (SOP) also live in moderate multi-dimensional poverty.

---

47 MSc. in Public Policies, Researcher at the International Policy Centre for Inclusive Growth (IPC-IG).
48 MA in Poverty and Development, Researcher at the International Policy Centre for Inclusive Growth (IPC-IG).
49 Based on UNICEF's definition of the MENA region, this chapter covers the following 20 countries: Algeria, Bahrain, Djibouti, Egypt, Iran, Iraq, Jordan, Kuwait, Lebanon, Libya, Morocco, Oman, Qatar, Saudi Arabia, State of Palestine, Sudan, Syria, Tunisia, United Arab Emirates and Yemen.

Figure 1. Incidence of moderate and acute deprivation for children aged 0–17

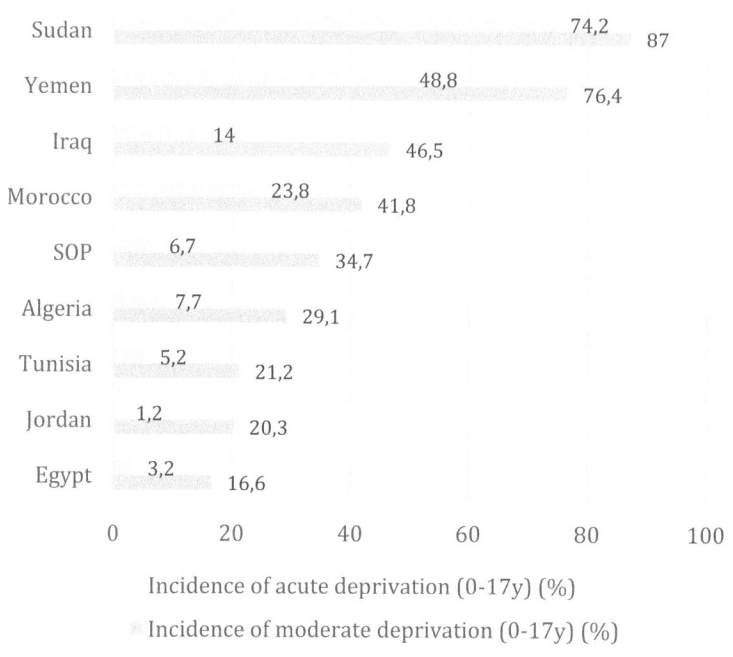

Incidence of acute deprivation (0-17y) (%)
Incidence of moderate deprivation (0-17y) (%)

Source: Authors' elaboration based on UNICEF (2018).

Social protection systems[50] can play an important role in reducing both monetary and multidimensional child poverty, given their potential to contribute towards breaking the inter-generational cycle of poverty, improve outcomes in children's nutritional, health and educational status, and reduce socio-economic barriers to children's well-being. However, it is crucial for social protection systems to respond to children's specific rights and needs. To this end, the design, implementation and evaluation of programmes should consider age- and gender-specific vulnerabilities, as well as the different dimensions of children's well-being (UNICEF, 2012).

---

50 Social protection as a set of public policies is generally classified into three broad categories: social assistance (non-contributory social protection), which is tax-financed and mostly targets poor people; social insurance (contributory social protection), in which benefits are linked to direct contributions; and labour market programmes.

Sustainable Development Goal (SDG) 1 ('End poverty in all its forms everywhere') highlights the role of social protection in the reduction of child poverty. Importantly, Target 1.3 calls for governments to implement national social protection systems and to achieve substantial coverage of poor and vulnerable populations—including children—by 2030. Effective coverage is reported as the proportion of the population benefiting from social protection floors, disaggregated by age, sex and socioeconomic status. In addition, it is known that social protection can play an important role in reducing inequality (see United Nations Economic and Social Commission for Asia and the Pacific, 2015), which makes it a crucial tool in achieving SDG 10 ('Reduce inequality within and among countries'). Target 10.2 calls for the social and economic inclusion of all people, irrespective of age.

However, little is known about the share of children covered by the social protection systems in place in the MENA region. Assessing the benefit incidence of social protection programmes is still an incipient practice in the region and few—if any—assessments consider the coverage of different age groups (Van Diesen, 2017). Administrative data on programme coverage—particularly the coverage of children of different ages—is often not readily available. This information is crucial for enhancing the child-sensitivity of social protection systems, so that they may reach all vulnerable children and respond to their age-specific needs.

Against this background, this research aims to contribute towards filling in the gaps, by assessing the child-sensitivity of non-contributory social protection in MENA and by identifying features that can improve the potential of programmes to enhance children's well-being. In addition, the analysis provides a preliminary estimation of the share of children covered by flagship programmes, which may incentivise countries to report on SDG 1.3 and assess social protection policies in terms of their child sensitivity.

This research is based on a comprehensive inventory of programmes, prepared in partnership between the International Policy Centre for Inclusive Growth (IPC-IG) and the UNICEF Middle East and North Africa Regional Office (MENARO) (Machado et al.,, 2018). This inventory focused on programmes implemented by national governments or those that are, at least in part, publicly funded. In total, more than 100 social protection programmes were mapped in the region. Mapping efforts focused on the following types of non-contributory schemes: Cash and in-kind transfers (conditional and unconditional); school feeding programmes; public works programmes; educational fee waivers; housing benefits; non-contributory health insurance; health care benefits; and food and energy subsidies.

After this introduction, a short synopsis of the context and key features of social protection in the MENA region is provided (Section 2). The research methods used are summarised in Section 3. Section 4 entails an overview of the main design features of existing programmes in the region, including the most prevalent programme types, target groups and targeting mechanisms. In Section 5, cash transfers, in-kind transfers and school-feeding programmes are analysed regarding their child-sensitive design features. The first two types were selected for being the most prevalent in the region, and the latter for presenting comparatively better coverage levels. In addition, an estimation of the share of children covered by these programmes is provided. Finally, the main findings and key gaps identified are summarised in the conclusion.

2. Context, key features and challenges of social protection in the MENA region

Social protection in the MENA region has traditionally been characterised by a reliance on universal food and energy subsidies and on contributory insurance schemes. However, there is a growing consensus that non-targeted subsidies disproportionally favour wealthy people and have little effect on poverty reduction. Social insurance funds and pension schemes are available for civil servants and those working in the formal sector. However, it is estimated that only one-third of the workforce in MENA is covered by formal social insurance systems (Silva et al., 2013).

In recent years, budget constraints—largely due to decreasing government revenues and a decline in oil prices—have contributed to a change in the composition of social protection spending in Arab countries (Verme & Araar, 2017). Universal or quasi-universal energy and food subsidy schemes have been undergoing significant reforms. For instance, in 2010 the Iranian government introduced one of the largest cash transfer programmes of its kind—the Targeted Subsidies Reform Act—to ameliorate the impacts of its subsidy reform, reaching almost universal coverage in 2011 (cf. Shahyar, 2017). In 2014, the Government of Egypt launched substantive fossil fuel price reforms and announced the allocation of nearly 50% of the savings resulting from these reforms (USD 3.6 billion) in health care, education and social protection programmes, including the targeted cash transfers *Takaful* and *Karama* (World Bank, 2015).

Social assistance programmes in the MENA region, particularly those that target citizens who are unable to work due to old age and disability, in need of protection (i.e. orphans), or dependent household members who have lost their household provider/breadwinner (i.e., widows and their children, divorced women, or even women who are single after a certain age), have traditionally made use of categorical targeting. The categorical approach is sometimes further complemented by some type of means-testing and, more recently, proxy means-testing (PMT), to prioritise poor and vulnerable individuals. However, even in high-income countries with generous social assistance programmes, large segments of the population remain uncovered. In the Gulf region, for example, countries are characterised by large numbers of foreign workers (up to 80%). Nevertheless, most social security and social assistance schemes are only available for nationals, often excluding children of foreign low-skilled workers.

In addition, the region has recently seen a dramatic increase in the number of internally displaced persons and refugees. Conflicts and violence are widespread in parts of the region, leaving millions of children in need of humanitarian assistance. In some countries, such as Iraq, Syria, Turkey and Yemen, humanitarian cash assistance programmes have been designed to make use of parts of national social protection systems. The Syrian crisis has underlined the importance of improving the shock-responsiveness and resilience of social protection systems and to use cash schemes established in the context of the humanitarian crisis to strengthen local systems (cf. Smith, 2017). Yet, most social protection programmes in MENA are not accessible to refugees, leaving those families largely dependent on temporary humanitarian support (Bilo & Machado, 2018).

The role of non-state actors and private networks in tackling poverty and economic shocks is an important peculiarity of the region, and an important example is the role of *zakat* funds. One of the five pillars of Islam, *zakat*—the compulsory giving of a portion of one's wealth to charity—is considered a religious duty for all Muslims with a minimum standard of wealth and functions as an important wealth redistribution mechanism. In some countries, *zakat* collection is regulated by the State and distribution has been merged with social protection systems. In Sudan for example, the Zakat Fund supported over 2.1 million families with social transfers and other benefits in 2016 (Zakat Fund, 2016).

3. Research methods

Two types of methodological approaches were used to collect information. First, an extensive literature review was conducted to assess the design features of non-contributory social protection programmes. This included reviewing reports from international organisations and development think-tanks. Programme-specific information made available on official government websites was also consulted. Most sources accessed were available in English or French and, to a lesser degree, in Arabic. Information gathered during the literature review phase was shared with UNICEF country offices for validation and supplementing.

Second, to assess the number of children covered by programmes, the following estimation was conducted. For some programmes, the number of beneficiaries is reported as total individuals.[51] In this case, the share of children in the country's population was applied to estimate the number of children among the total beneficiaries. When the number of beneficiaries was reported as households, the total number of individuals benefitting from a given scheme was computed by multiplying an estimate of the country's average household size by the overall number of households covered by the programme. Once the number of individual beneficiaries was estimated, the share of children in the country was applied to obtain an estimate of the number of individual children covered.[52] This number was then compared to the total number of children in the country as well as to the estimated number of multi-dimensionally poor

---

51 All sources from which the coverage numbers referred to in this chapter stem are referenced in Machado et al. (2018)
52 Most programmes in the region do not report on the number of children covered. Estimations were based on the overall share of children (population under 18 years of age) in the country in the year in which the coverage figures are reported using World Bank's Health Nutrition and Population Statistics (World Bank, 2017) and the average household size. To obtain the average household size, sources such as the Demographic and Health Surveys (DHS), Multiple Indicator Cluster Surveys (MICS), or government statistical agencies were consulted.

children. For the latter, the recent study on multi-dimensional child poverty in 11 Arab countries by UNICEF (2018) was consulted.[53] In a final step, the percentage share of poor children that could be potentially covered was estimated by dividing the number of children covered by the programme by the total number of multidimensionally poor children in the country. This figure helps illustrate the size of the programme relative to both the overall population of children and of poor children in a given country. For programmes that target specific age groups (such as those available only for school-age children), the share of children covered was compared to the total number of children in the respective age group.

Several limitations related to this methodology must be discussed: (i) this procedure's primary assumption is that the share of children relative to the total number of beneficiaries is equal to the overall share of children relative to the overall population. Similarly, it assumes that the average size of beneficiary households is the same as the average household size in any given country, not accounting for the fact that poorer households are often larger in size and have more children; (ii) figures used to indicate the average household size refer to a different year than the reported beneficiary numbers. However, it was assumed that although the population size in these countries may change, the average household size remains fairly stable over a certain period of time—here considered as 5 years, on average.[54]

Third, some programmes can have a cap per household and the overall number of people reported as beneficiaries may only refer to the number of people below this cap—which means that this number is possibly smaller than the total number of individuals living in the household. In other cases, such as in old-age pension schemes, it was assumed that the benefit structure accepts only one beneficiary per household—which could lead to an overestimation of the total number of beneficiaries, in cases where multiple individuals receive the benefit in the same house.

---

53 Using the Multiple Overlapping Deprivation Analysis (MODA) approach, the report applies a cross-country MODA (CC-MODA) methodology. For two age categories, five dimensions of children's well-being are analysed: Water, sanitation, housing, health, and nutrition are considered for children aged 0–4, and water, sanitation, housing, information, and education are considered for children aged 5–17. A child is considered poor if deprived in at least two of these dimensions (UNICEF, 2018).

54 For Djibouti and Syria, lack of more recent data makes it imperative to use older figures (from 2006 and 2003, respectively).

Finally, is not possible to perfectly match the number of children covered to the number of poor children in the country, as it cannot be assumed that children covered by a programme are indeed the poorest ones. Therefore, in this research we have opted to use the concept of 'coverage capacity', meaning that *if* the programme were able to perfectly target the multi-dimensionally poor, it would have the 'capacity' to reach X percent of them. A further discussion on the adequacy and impact of benefits disbursed is not included in this analysis. This coverage estimation is nevertheless important, as it aims to serve as a starting point for a discussion on whether existing social protection schemes have the capacity (in terms of size) to reach the most vulnerable children in any given country.

4. Overview of non-contributory social protection programmes in the MENA region

Programme types

In total, 117 non-contributory programmes were mapped in the 20 MENA countries. Algeria had the most schemes mapped (14 in total), followed by Morocco (9). Fewer programs were mapped in countries such as Lebanon and Iraq (4 and 3, respectively). However, these figures require some clarifications.

First, some of the schemes are large umbrella programmes, which include several sub-programmes. For instance, the National Aid Fund (NAF) in Jordan provides several different cash transfer schemes as well as non-contributory health insurance.[55]

Second, programmes can differ significantly in scale, benefit value and delivery frequency. For example, Iran's Subsidy Reforms Act, features almost universal coverage and Yemen's Social Welfare Fund covered 35% of the population in 2013 (IPC-IG & UNICEF, 2014). Other programmes have a significantly smaller scale or are limited to certain regions. In the United Arab Emirates (UAE), for instance, four out of five programmes are only available for nationals residing in Dubai. Thus, having a larger number of programmes does not necessarily suggest a more

---

55 In total, 155 programmes and sub-programmes were mapped and included in the inventory. For more information on the number and types of programmes at the country level, please see Machado et al (2018).

comprehensive social protection system and can even reflect segmentation and lack of clear targeting criteria. Moreover, the level of benefits further determines the relevance and impact of schemes. In Iran, for example, transfers from the Targeted Reform Act amounted to 6.5% of the GDP and about 29% of the median household income in 2011 (Salehi-Isfahani & Mostafavi-Dehzooe, 2017). The benefit level of many other programmes, however, is much smaller. It should also be noted that delivery frequency can vary significantly. Certain programmes—including most emergency cash transfers—are usually paid on an ad-hoc basis.

As can be seen in Figure 2, unconditional cash transfer (UCT) programmes are the most prevalent form of non-contributory social protection in the region by far, more than half of which target poor households. This is followed by unconditional in-kind transfers, mostly in the form of food distribution programmes, and energy and food subsidies. School feeding programmes and conditional cash transfer (CCT) programmes come next. The former is targeted at school-age children, but the latter also tends to cover them extensively as they have conditionalities related to school enrolment or attendance.

A significant number of countries also provide non-contributory health insurance, such as Morocco's Regime for Medical Assistance (RAMED), as well as health care benefit programmes,[56] such as the National Poverty Targeting Programs (NPTP) in Lebanon. Cash-for-work programmes and educational fee waivers were only mapped for a few countries.[57]

---

56 Health care benefits refer to free or subsidised health care services.
57 Note that the low number of educational fee waiver programmes can also be explained by the fact that some countries do not consider them as part of their social protection system, but rather as part of educational policies. Moreover, in some countries fee waivers may not be very common because of free education.

Figure 2. Number of programmes by type.

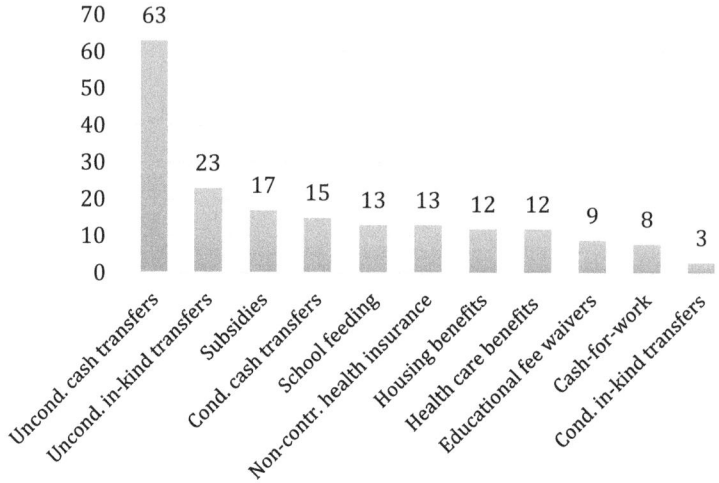

Note: A programme can be classified as more than one type.
Source: Authors' elaboration based on Machado et al. (2018)

Targeting methods

As shown in Figure 3, categorical targeting is the most prevalent targeting mechanism in these schemes, commonly used to identify families without a male breadwinner or whose adult members—particularly the head of household—are unable to work (including the elderly, people with disabilities and widows). This is followed by means-testing, which is often used in addition to categorical targeting. Geographical targeting is the third most common targeting mechanism. Morocco's CCT *Tayssir* programme, for example, targets students in rural schools with poverty rates above 30% and drop-out rates of at least 8% per year (see also Gyori et al., 2017. Proxy-Means Testing (PMT) is gradually becoming more common in the region. For Yemen's Social Welfare Fund, for example, PMT was introduced at a later stage in programme implementation to improve the accuracy of geographical and categorical targeting. However, there are also cases where PMT was used since programme inception, as with *Takaful* in Egypt or the Palestinian National Cash Transfer Programme.

Figure 3.   Number of programmes by targeting mechanism

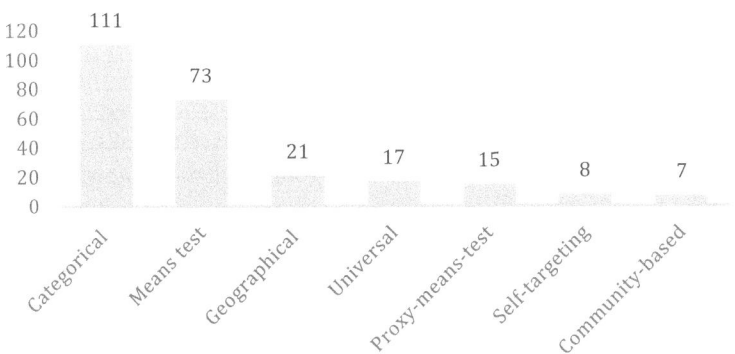

Note: A programme can use more than one targeting mechanism.
Source: Authors' elaboration based on Machado et. al (2018)

Target population groups

Figure 4 illustrates the prevalence of different target population groups by programme type. It is important to keep in mind that programmes may target more than one group. Most target poor households, followed by children. Women are the third most commonly-targeted population group. Fewer programmes were mapped for the chronically ill or designed explicitly for children with disabilities.

Figure 4.   Most prevalent target population groups.

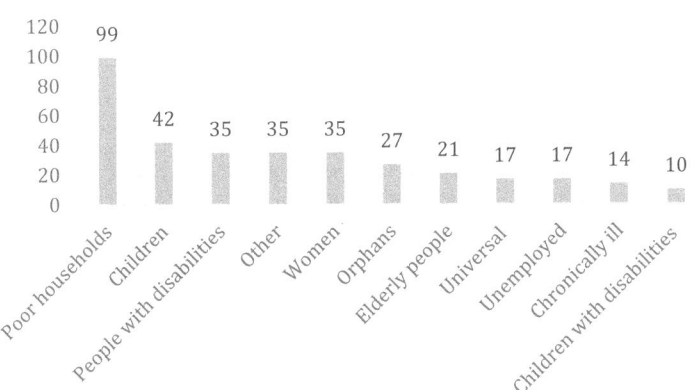

Note: A programme can target more than one population group.
Source: Authors' elaboration based on Machado et al. (2018)

5. Programme analysis—Child-sensitive design features and coverage of children

The authors consider a social protection programme to have a child-sensitive design if it has at least one of the following five key features: (1) directly targets children or households with children; (2) supports children's food and nutrition security; (3) supports children's access to health; (4) supports children's access to education; and (5) provides additional benefits to children and/or other members of the household beyond the direct beneficiary of the programme.[58] Of course, many programmes—such as food or cash transfers to poor households—can have indirect positive effects on children's well-being without explicitly including child-related features in the programme's design. However, the focus of this chapter is on explicitly child-sensitive features linked to programme design. These five features are not mutually exclusive, and some programmes are classified under more than one category.

At least one programme in each country and more than half (81) of all programmes mapped present at least one child-sensitive design feature. Many schemes classified as child-sensitive are related to education (37), including cash transfer programmes that are conditional on children's school enrolment and/or attendance, as well as school feeding programmes and educational fee waivers up to secondary school (see Figure 5). About 21 programmes aim to improve child nutrition, and 11 were found to directly support children's access to health care. In 17 countries, 34 cash transfer programmes were identified for which benefits are either paid per child or the benefit level increases according to the size of the household—a prevalent feature among countries in the Gulf region.

---

58 The approach used to assess child sensitivity in this research draws on the study conducted by Marcus et al., (2011). In 'programmes targeting children', all programmes that explicitly target children through at least one component were included (e.g. cash transfers paid only to households with children and programmes targeting lactating or pregnant women). In 'supporting children's access to education', programmes designed to increase children's access to education were considered (e.g. cash transfers conditional on children's school attendance, school-related in-kind transfers or school feeding programmes). The category 'supporting children's access to nutrition' includes programmes that provide food items to children to ensure their food security; similarly, 'supporting children's access to health' includes all programmes that explicitly support children's access to health care services, such as non-contributory insurance with a specific component for children (i.e. under 5 years old), and programmes with health-related conditionalities. Finally, the classification 'benefits increase with the number of household members' includes cash transfers whose benefit levels increase with the number of children/members in the household.

Figure 5. Number of programmes with child-sensitive design features, by dimension.

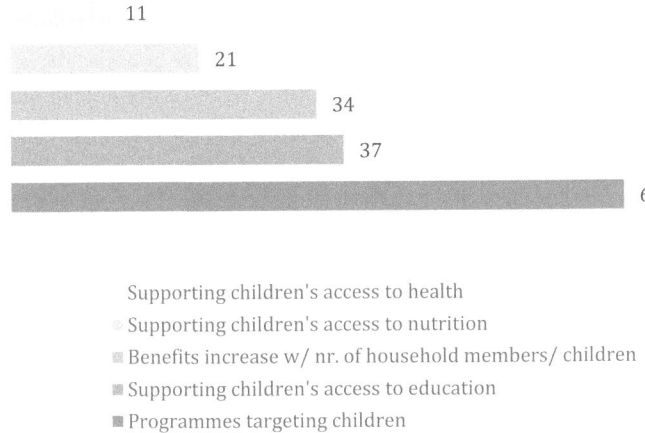

Supporting children's access to health
Supporting children's access to nutrition
Benefits increase w/ nr. of household members/ children
Supporting children's access to education
Programmes targeting children

Note: Programmes can have more than one child-sensitive design feature.
Source: Authors' elaboration based on Machado et al. (2018).

We will discuss in further detail the child-sensitive design features of the following programs types: cash transfers, in-kind transfers and school feeding programmes. It is important to note that other programme types can also be classified as child-sensitive—examples include the Social Safety Net Project in Djibouti, a public works programme that also offers nutrition sessions and micronutrient powders for pregnant women and pre-school-age children, and the Civil Insurance Programme in Jordan, which offers non-contributory health insurance for both Jordanian and non-Jordanian children under the age of 6.

Cash transfer programmes

Design features

Most cash transfer schemes in the region are unconditional (63) and only 15 are conditional. All 20 countries implement at least one cash transfer scheme, varying in scale, benefit value and delivery frequency. Of all programmes targeting children, children with disabilities and/or orphans (68 in total), about half are cash transfer schemes (35). Eighteen of these cash transfers target orphans but not all target children or children with disabilities. This indicates a relatively high prevalence of financial support programmes for orphans compared to cash transfers specifically targeting children or households with children in general. Moreover, financial support programmes targeting widows and unmarried women are present in more than half of the countries mapped. As previously discussed, UCT programs in MENA are often designed to support households without a male breadwinner or those wherein the head of the household is unable to work, which explains why children are not usually the focus of these programmes (except for orphans and children with disabilities). Cash-based schemes targeting lactating women and younger children are still incipient in the region.

Twelve countries were found to have one or more CCT programmes. The majority of CCTs are linked to educational conditionalities. Education-related CCTs include cash transfers for families with school-age children, which are conditioned on school attendance or enrolment (whether verified or not), but also educational scholarships and student grants paid to individual students, with an implicit conditionality. Some of the more recent CCT programmes include the *Takaful* program in Egypt for poor households with children and the Direct Assistance to Widows programs in Morocco, both introduced in 2015.

In fact, scholarships and/or financial support to purchase school materials as well as CCTs linked to school attendance are the two main ways through which cash transfers tend to be linked to education. Algeria's *Allocation Spéciale de Scolarité*, for example, was created to incentivise school attendance among children from poor households. Similarly, Morocco's *Tayssir* was designed to minimise school drop-out rates in the most impoverished regions of the country. Two CCTs are also tied to health-related conditionalities: *Takaful* in Egypt requires four visits a year to health clinics by mothers and children under the age of 6, and the Recurring Cash Assistance of the National Aid Fund in Jordan requires immunisation (among other conditionalities). A further review on the impact of cash transfers on improving children's health and education status can be found in Bastagli et al., 2016.

While the benefit levels of different cash transfer schemes vary, it can be observed that they often increase according to the size of the household and, to a lesser extent, to children's age or school grade. In comparison with programmes that pay a fixed benefit amount per household, they are considered child-sensitive here, as they take into account the higher expenditure levels of larger families (and with older children). Examples include *Takaful* in Egypt, wherein the benefit level depends on children's age and school grade, and most cash transfer schemes in the Gulf region, such as in Oman, Saudi Arabia and the UAE. In these countries, the level of financial support is commonly determined by the number of dependents (children and wives) in the household.

Child coverage estimations

Cash transfers vary greatly in size, covering from 2.9% of all children under the age of 18 in Jordan (National Aid Fund Cash Assistance), up to 34% in Yemen (Social Welfare Fund, recently suspended due to conflict) and 32% in Sudan (*zakat*-funded cash transfers), based on the authors' estimations. However, most cash transfer programmes are rather small in size and reach less than 2% of the respective national population of children. Figure 6 illustrates the estimated share of the children covered by selected programmes as well as their estimated capacity to assist multi-dimensionally poor children—if they were perfectly targeted.

Provided that there are no overlaps,[59] the share of children covered by *Takaful*, *Karama* and the Social Solidarity Pension in Egypt combined is estimated at 12.5%, which is high in absolute terms, as the country has one of the largest under-18 populations in the region, but lower in relative terms when compared to other countries such as the State of Palestine, where the Palestinian National Cash Transfer Programme alone reached 13.5% of children in 2013.

When comparing programmes' coverage capacity to reach the poorest in the country, different poverty levels in each country have to be considered. In Tunisia, the *Programme National d'Aide aux Familles Nécessiteuses* (PNAFN) targets poor families whose head is not able to provide for the household. As of 2016, more than 225,000 households benefited from the programme (Centre de Recherches et d'Etudes Sociales, 2017). We estimate the coverage at 7.12% of all children in the country, with the potential to reach almost 34% of all multi-dimensionally poor children. This is explained by the fact that multidimensional poverty levels in Tu-

---

59 Note that *Karama* was designed to gradually replace the Social Solidarity Scheme. A residual group will remain under social pensions, including poor separated and divorced women.

nisia are relatively low (21%) compared to other countries in the region (UNICEF, 2018). Sudan is the country with the highest poverty incidence: 87% of all Sudanese children are estimated to be multi-dimensionally poor (ibid). Based on our estimations, the Sudanese Zakat Fund reaches about one-third of all children in the country, with the capacity to reach 37% of all multi-dimensionally poor children.

Figure 6. Estimated coverage capacity of multidimensionally poor children by selected cash transfer programmes.

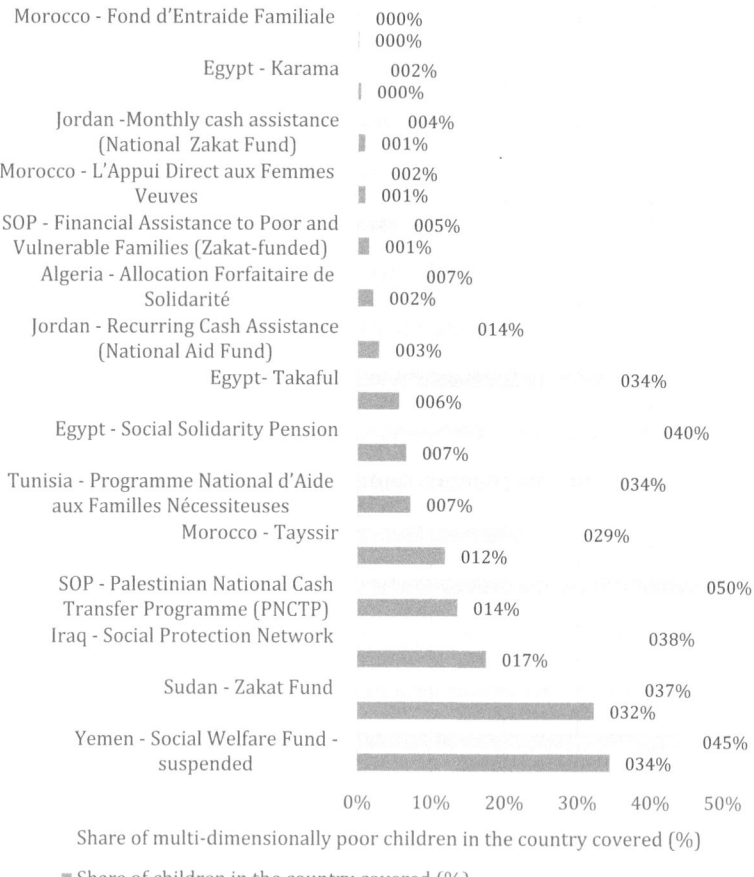

Source: Authors' elaboration based on Machado et al. (2018)

In-kind transfer programmes

Design features

There is a long-standing debate about whether to use cash or in-kind (food) transfers in social protection, which has been receiving renewed attention (for a recent review, see Alderman et al., 2017). While increasingly more countries have been implementing cash transfers, food-based transfers remain a common staple of social safety nets. Food transfer programmes have been criticised for being less efficient and providing less choice to beneficiaries. In comparison, cash- or voucher-based transfers can boost local markets and are generally perceived as less paternalistic (Gentilini, 2015). While the costs of cash and voucher transfers are usually lower than those of in-kind transfers, it cannot be generalised that they are always more effective in combating the various forms of poverty, especially when looking at their impact on malnutrition. As Gentilini (2015) argues, design and context—including duration, frequency of transfers and price volatility—are important factors determining the impact of any programme.

In-kind transfers[60] are less common than cash transfers but 15 countries still have at least one type of either unconditional or conditional in-kind transfer (the latter is less common and usually includes school supply transfers conditional on school attendance). In-kind transfers are commonly provided in the form of food. Food transfer programmes are especially common in countries with higher levels of food insecurity such as Iraq, where the near-universal Public Distribution System (PDS) provides basic food items to improve the nutritional status of the population. In 2016, 90% of Iraqi households (33 million people) received subsidised food items (International Monetary Fund, 2017). Food transfers can cater to the specific nutritional needs of children. Iraq's PDS, for example, includes milk among other items. A few in-kind transfer programmes, such as the Palestinian Food Assistance Programme, also offer accompanying measures and nutrition awareness sessions to mothers.

Child coverage estimations

Overall, in-kind transfer programmes tend to have lower coverage than cash transfer programmes. They can also vary considerably in size, ranging from quasi-universal—such as the PDS in Iraq, which is estimated to

---

60 Note that in-kind transfers do not include food subsidies or school feeding programmes. Also, in-kind transfers include those that are distributed directly as well as those using a voucher or card system.

have reached 88.7% of all children in 2016—to small-scale programs, such as the Emergency Food Assistance and the Relief Assistance programmes in Djibouti (both part of the General Food Distribution Programme), which are estimated to cover only 2.26% and 2.55% of all children under 18 years old.

When it comes to food transfer schemes, tentative findings show that benefits paid out through Zakat Funds in Palestine and Jordan had the potential to reach around 15% and 20% of poor children, respectively. Looking at the Palestinian Food Assistance Scheme, we observe a higher rate, which indicates that almost one-third of the moderately poor under-18 population could have benefited from the scheme in 2016.

In addition to the provision of food, school supplies are another common form of in-kind transfers. They are particularly relevant for children, as they help households with education-related expenditures. In Morocco, the *Initiative Royale Un Million de Cartables* reached more than 4 million children in schools (Ministère de l'Economie et des Finances, 2017), covering half of all school-age children in the country. In Algeria, the *Fournitures Scolaires* and *Manuel Scolaire* scheme supports households with children in school. Based on the authors' estimations, roughly a third and half of all school-age children benefited from these programs in 2011 and 2014, respectively.

School feeding programmes

Design features
While other actions such as water, sanitation, and hygiene (WASH) initiatives, as well as feeding practices, are also critical for improving children's nutritional status, school feeding programmes have the capacity to not only improve the nutritional status and learning capacity of school-age children but also to incentivise their school attendance (World Food Programme, 2013). In total, 11 countries in the region have State-led school feeding programmes. They are implemented by both high-income countries, such as Kuwait and Saudi Arabia, as well as by low-income countries, such as Djibouti and Sudan. Some have a long tradition, dating back to the 1950s such as in Egypt and Morocco. The World Food Programme (WFP) often supports countries financially and/or institutionally, as in the case of Djibouti and Tunisia. Conversely, Algeria's main school feeding programme is fully implemented and financed by the State.

In addition to categorical targeting, geographical targeting is used in some countries to target beneficiary schools, such as in Djibouti, Egypt, Morocco, Sudan and Tunisia. In Sudan, the national school feeding programme targets states with higher poverty rates. School feeding programmes can also help foster local agricultural production. In Tunisia, the school feeding programme is implemented in a decentralised manner. Schools oversee food purchases, thus favouring the participation of local smallholder farmers in the provision of school meals, and potentially having a positive impact on the local economy. A noteworthy feature of the school feeding programme in Djibouti is that it provides extra take-home rations for families of selected girls as an incentive for parents to send their daughters to school and maintain their enrolment and attendance.

In general, it can be observed that school feeding programmes are the most common example of how social protection programmes can be directly linked to child nutrition. While they play an important role in supporting children's access to nutrition, most of these programmes reach children attending school, excluding those who are out of school and those at pre-school age. However, data shows that the latter (children under 5) are especially vulnerable to malnutrition (UNICEF, 2018), suggesting that there is still significant room to improve linkages between social protection programmes and nutrition interventions.

Child coverage estimates

In general, school feeding programmes reach larger shares of children across all countries. For the analysis of school-related social protection schemes, coverage estimates always take into consideration the size of the programme relative to the total school-age population in the country (children aged 6–17). Algeria's *Cantine Scolaire* for example, reached 45% of the country's school-age population in 2013. Considering the most recent figures from 2016, Egypt's School Feeding Programme reached more than half of the school-age population. Other school feeding programmes, however, reach significantly lower numbers, such as in Djibouti or Tunisia, where the national programmes reached only about 15% and 12% of the target population, respectively.[61]

---

61 The potential coverage of multi-dimensionally poor children was not estimated for school feeding programmes as they usually do not target poor or vulnerable children specifically, but at all school-age children who receive formal education at a public school. However, it is worth highlighting again that, by design, they already include those children who do not attend school, and those who are of pre-school age.

6. Conclusion

Countries in the MENA region have a long tradition of social provision for poor and vulnerable people, including those who are chronically ill, have disabilities or are elderly, children, orphans and widows. Many countries in the region are now reducing or phasing out food and energy subsidies and reallocating parts of the accrued budget savings to targeted cash transfer programmes. The region has introduced many new flagship programmes, some of which specifically target households with children. Nevertheless, many schemes still target individuals who are unable to work or live in households without a male breadwinner. Over-reliance on programmes based on these traditional target groups can jeopardise the child-sensitivity of social protection systems by excluding the children of poor families.

Many programmes identified as having child-sensitive design features support children's access to education. However, programmes supporting children's access to health care or nutrition are less common. Except for school feeding programmes, few were found to directly address malnutrition. Pre-school-age children, especially, are rarely covered by nutrition-related programmes. Given the importance of addressing children's needs at early stages of development, more schemes targeting lactating women and younger children (under 6 years old) should be promoted in the region.

The limited data availability in MENA presents a great challenge for any incidence analysis of social protection schemes. An assessment based on the comparison between the child coverage estimations and the number of poor children in any given country shows that programmes are often not large enough to reach all vulnerable children. Even large-scale programmes would only have enough scope to reach less than half of all multi-dimensionally poor children in each country. In general, school feeding programmes and in-kind provision of school supplies have larger coverage levels when compared to cash transfer programmes, which could be linked to the fact that the implementation mechanisms of a cash transfer require more technical tools (such as a beneficiary information system disaggregated at the household level or more elaborated delivery mechanisms—such as facilitated access to ATMs and the banking system).

There is a strong need to expand existing schemes—particularly cash transfer programmes in the form of child allowances—to reach all children. The recent subsidy reforms have cleared some fiscal space for more child-sensitive social protection. Other options to increase spending on social protection initiatives include the introduction of more progressive tax systems.

Moreover, given the context of conflicts and humanitarian crises in the region, it is of utmost importance that national social protection systems can respond effectively in times of crisis through the inclusion of shock-responsive measures. In this regard, the establishment of appropriate regulatory frameworks to ensure refugees' access to a baseline level of social protection is deemed essential (Bilo & Machado, 2018).

Despite increased efforts by governments in the region, more effort is required from policymakers, researchers and the international community to improve the child-sensitivity of existing social protection systems. Considering the relevance of reporting progress on SDG 1—especially target 1.3—it is important that gender- and age-disaggregated data on all programme beneficiaries is collected through comprehensive household surveys, making use of administrative databases and integrated single registries. Moreover, there is a strong need for regular child poverty studies and in-depth programme evaluations to better understand the impact of policy interventions on the different dimensions of child poverty. More rigorous targeting analyses are needed to better understand how current mechanisms can be improved to better reach vulnerable children. This will be especially important to the attainment of SDG Target 10.2, which calls for the social and economic inclusion of all, irrespective of age, sex, disability, race, ethnicity, origin, religion, or economic or other status.

More research is therefore needed to understand how particularly vulnerable groups, including refugee children and children with disabilities, are covered by social protection mechanisms. Likewise, information and evidence need to be further and more efficiently shared across the region to facilitate learning.

Investing in social protection alone will not be enough to achieve social transformation. Ensuring the availability and quality of basic services is crucial for the achievement of the SDGs, especially in the areas of health and education. While the consolidation of a child-sensitive social protection system is possible, this demands a change in perspective. The information and findings in this chapter serve as a useful starting point to further support the production of evidence and encourage the constant development of social protection systems in the MENA region to better address children's needs.

References

Alderman, H., Gentilini, U., & Yemtsov, R. (2017). *The 1.5 Billion People Question: Food, Vouchers, Or Cash Transfers?* The World Bank.

Bastagli, F., Hagen-Zanker, J., Harman, L., & Barca, V. (2016). *Cash transfers: what does the evidence say*. London: ODI

Bilo, C., & Machado, A. C. (2018). *Children's Right to Social Protection in the Middle East and North Africa Region—an Analysis of Legal Frameworks from a Child Rights Perspective*. Retrieved from International Policy Centre for Inclusive Growth and UNICEF Middle East and North Africa Regional Office website: https://ipcig.org/pub/eng/RR24_Children_s_Right_to_Social_Protection_in_the_Middle_East_and_North_Africa_Region.pdf (Accessed June 2020)

Centre de Recherches et d'Etudes Sociales. (2017). *Évaluation de la performance des programmes d'assistance sociale en Tunisie pour optimiser le ciblage des pauvres et freiner l'avancée de l'informalité*. Retrieved from http://www.cres.tn/uploads/tx_wdbiblio/Rapport_CRES_mai_2017.pdf (Accessed June 2020)

Gentilini, U. (2015). Revisiting the "Cash versus Food" Debate: New Evidence for an Old Puzzle? *The World Bank Research Observer*, *31*(1), 135–167.

Gyori, M., Veras Soares, F., & Lefèvre, A. (2017). Tayssir: the first conditional cash transfer programs in the MENA region. *Policy in Focus*, *40* pp. 59–63.

International Monetary Fund. (2017). *Iraq : Selected Issues* (No. Country Report No. 17/252). Retrieved from https://www.imf.org/en/Publications/CR/Issues/2017/08/09/Iraq-Selected-Issues-45175 (Accessed June 2020)

International Policy Centre for Inclusive Growth, & United Nations Children's Fund. (2014). *Yemen National Social Protection Monitoring Survey (NSPMS): 2012–2013 Final Report*. Retrieved from the International Policy Centre for Inclusive Growth website: http://www.ipc-undp.org/technical-paper-08-yemen-national-social-protection-monitoring-survey-nspms-2012-2013-%E2%80%93-final-report (Accessed June 2020)

League of Arab States, United Nations Economic and Social Commission for Western Asia, United Nations Children's Fund, & Oxford Poverty and Human Development Initiative. (2017). *Arab Multidimensional Poverty Report*. Retrieved from https://www.unescwa.org/publications/multidimensional-arab-poverty-report (Accessed June 2020)

Machado, A. C., Bilo, C., Soares, F. V., & Osorio, R. G. (2018). O*verview of Non-contributory Social Protection Programs in the Middle East and North Africa (MENA) Region through a Child and Equity Lens.* Retrieved from International Policy Centre for Inclusive Growth and UNICEF Middle East and North Africa Regional Office website: https://ipcig.org/pub/eng/JP18_Overview_of_Non_contributory_Social_Protection_Programsrs_in_MENA.pdf (Accessed June 2020)

Marcus, R., Pereznieto, P., Cullen, E., & Jones, N. (2011). Children and social protection in the Middle East and North Africa. *A Mapping Exercise.(No. ODI Working Paper 335).* London, UK.

Ministère de l'Economie et des Finances. (2017). *Rapport Economique et Financier*. Retrieved from Ministère de l'Economie et des Finances website: https://www.finances.gov.ma/Docs/DB/2017/ref_fr.pdf (Accessed June 2020)

Salehi-Isfahani, D., & Mostafavi-Dehzooe, M. H. (2017). *Cash transfers and labor supply: Evidence from a large-scale program in Iran.* Working Paper No. 1090.

Shahyar, S. (2017). Social protection in modern Iran: a historic perspective. *Policy in Focus, 40,* pp. 51–54.

Silva, J., Levin, V., & Morgandi, M. (2013). *Inclusion and resilience: the way forward for social safety nets in the Middle East and North Africa.* Retrieved from World Bank website: https://openknowledge.worldbank.org/bitstream/handle/10986/16157/730060BRI0Quic0C0disclosed010010120.pdf?sequence=1 (Accessed June 2020)

Smith, G. (2017). Linking Cash Transfer Programming with National Systems in Humanitarian Settings. *Policy in Focus, 40,* pp. 48–50.

United Nations Children's Fund. (2012). *Integrated Social Protection Systems—Enhancing Equity for Children.* Retrieved from United Nations Children's Fund website: https://www.unicef.org/socialprotection/framework/files/Full_Social_Protection_Strategic_Framework_low_res(1).pdf (Accessed June 2020)

United Nations Children's Fund. (2018). *Child Poverty in the Arab States: Analytical Report of Eleven Countries.* Retrieved from https://www.unicef.org/mena/sites/unicef.org.mena/files/2018-03/Child%20poverty%20full%20report%20-%20English.pdf (Accessed June 2020)

United Nations Children's Fund, & World Bank. (2016). *Ending Extreme Poverty: A Focus on Children.* Retrieved from https://www.unicef.org/publications/index_92826.html (Accessed June 2020)

United Nations Economic and Social Commission for Asia and the Pacific. (2015). *Time for Equality: The Role of Social Protection in Reducing Inequalities in Asia and the Pacific.* Retrieved from https://www.unescap.org/resources/time-equality-role-social-protection-reducing-inequalities-asia-and-pacific (Accessed June 2020)

Van Diesen, A. (2017). Social protection for children and their families in the Middle East and North Africa: where child rights meet smart economics. *Policy in Focus, 40,* pp. 23–26.

Verme, P., & Araar, A. (2017). *The Quest for Subsidy Reforms in the Middle East and North Africa Region: A Microsimulation Approach to Policy Making* (Vol. 42). Retrieved from https://openknowledge.worldbank.org/bitstream/handle/10986/25783/Book%20MENA%20Subsidies.pdf?sequence=1 (Accessed June 2020)

World Bank. (2015). *Project appraisal document on a proposed loan in the amount of US$400 Million to the Arab Republic of Egypt for a Strengthening Social Safety Net Project.* Retrieved from World Bank website: http://documents.worldbank.org/curated/en/944911468023332501/text/PAD6110PAD0P14010Box385454B0 00UO090.txt (Accessed June 2020)

World Bank. (2017). Health Nutrition and Population Statistics | DataBank. Retrieved May 6, 2019, from https://databank.worldbank.org/data/reports.aspx?source=health-nutrition-and-population-statistics

World Food Programme. (2013). *State of School Feeding Worldwide.* Retrieved from World Food Programme website: https://www.wfp.org/content/state-school-feeding-worldwide-2013 (Accessed June 2020)

Zakat Fund. (2016). *Annual Performance Report 2016*. Khartoum: Zakat Fund.

Child Poverty and Quality of Life: Material and Non-Material Domains of Well-Being

Ismael Cid Martinez (New School for Social Research and UNICEF), Enrique Delamonica (UNICEF), Jose Luis Espinoza Delgado (University of Goettingen), Aristide Kielem (UNICEF), Mohamed Obaidy (New School for Social Research and UN DESA)[62]

Introduction

The SDGs opened up an opportunity to strive for an ambitious development path cutting across many (all) dimensions of well-being as well as pushing the frontier for data collection and measurement of progress across the world. This entails refinement and expansion of data collections efforts. Also, the conceptualization and definitions of new indicators. This chapter tackles this last point in order to deepen the analysis of the situation of children and adolescents.

During the last two decades, as research on, and measurement of, multidimensional poverty and quality of life (in general and for children specifically) has expanded several-fold, two quasi-parallel strands of literature exist. One of them looks at material deprivation and is associated to the issues of (multidimensional) poverty. The other one provides a wider perspective but loses focus of the central issue of poverty (in particular in developing countries) as it includes aspects like happiness and safety from violence and severe physical punishment. This chapter attempts to bridge and combine the two literatures without creating a new index or indicator but by combining existing ones. Also, unlike most poverty or well-being indices, in this proposal all indicators are measured at the individual-level (i.e. not at the household or country-wide levels) and, most importantly, the measurements have been adjusted to account for the same child across the different indicators.

Relying on the most recent national household surveys (none more than two years old, roughly 10,000 households in each of them), information covering both child poverty (material deprivation) and other important aspects of children's quality of life such as birth registration, dis-

---

62   The opinions are sole responsibility of the authors and do not entail an official position of their respective organizations.

ciplinary violence at home (including severe physical punishment), or subjective well-being is available for a few large and small developing countries. The Multiple Indicator Cluster Surveys (MICS), sixth round, used in this analysis are for the following countries: Iraq[63] (2018), Pakistan, only the state of Punjab[64] (2018), Sierra Leone (2017), and Suriname (2018). These countries were chosen because they have all the indicators we are interested in, no other surveys with this information are available yet. Although this is not sufficient for covering all world regions, the above countries do come from a range of them as well as being spread out in terms of levels of child poverty.

Before showing the results of these estimates, however, the framework for understanding Quality of Life is introduced, along with a summary of international experiences (mostly in rich countries of the Global North) at measuring it and indicators usually incorporated in those estimates. The adaptation of this framework used for the estimates presented here is also included. This discussion is mirrored by one on the measurement of child poverty, followed by how to combine the two of them. Some conclusions and ideas for further research close off the chapter.

The many dimensions of Quality of Life

In the next section and the following two sections, three issues are addressed. First, the concept and components of the Quality of Life paradigm are briefly introduced. Based on previous experiences constructing indices of child well-being (second issue), a discussion of the choice of indicators used in this chapter is explained (third issue).

What is "Quality of Life"? What is it made of?

The concept of Quality of Life could be traced back, in the Western literature, at least to Classical Greek philosophy and the concept of a "Good Life". Interestingly, in spite of diverse origins, different conceptual frameworks, and the elapsed 25 centuries since then, there are similarities between the

---

63 Unfortunately, in this case, the questions about happiness are only asked of women. Intra-household gender differences in poverty (or among boys and girls for child poverty) are very important. However, the issue is not explored here for lack of space.

64 In Pakistan, one of the five countries with the largest child population in the world, MICS has been carried out sequentially by state. As of the time of writing this chapter, only the database for Punjab is available.

Classical Greek concept and the "Living Well" approach emanating from Latin America[65] and to the Gross National Happiness Index from Bhutan.

Ideally, the Good Life encapsulates a myriad of topics covering a mix of material and objectives conditions as well as subjective ones (Michalos, 2014). The latter could be internal (related to hopes, experiences, or happiness) or external (relationships with friends and family, participation in the community, or social constraints and opportunities).[66] Schemas to measure quality of life also differentiate elements which are considered "inputs" (e.g. public policies, individual market position, access to economic resources, or individual characteristics like personality) from "outputs" (e.g. good health, safety, job satisfaction, etc.) to measure well-being (Hagerty et al, 2001).

A common thread through the quality of life literature is the small to non-existence correlation between income/wealth and quality of life. Across countries and continents, spanning years and decades, and using variegated methodological tools, this is a very consistent result. This is one of the motivators of this chapter: To tease out (and measure separately but present together), child poverty within the quality of life framework in order to distinguish it from other important aspects of child wellbeing (e.g. avoiding violence, participation, family relationships, or emotional balance), which do not require necessarily a material goods or services.

Previous attempts to measure quality of life among children

UNICEF has a tradition of measuring well-being of children in rich countries. It started in 2007 with a Report Card[67] (UNICEF, 2007), shortly after the EU launched the European Quality of Life Survey (EQLS) in 2003

---

65 In Spanish it is 'vivir bien' or 'buen vivir' and in the local indigenous language (Quechua) it is 'Sumak Kawsay' or 'Suma qamaña' (Guendel, 2012; Acosta and Martinez, 2009; Escobar, 2010; Gudynas, 2011). One of the main differences with the Classical Greek approach is the role and connection to nature and the environment, which is central in the good living literature and seldom included in quality of life indices.

66 Walther (2020) proposes a multidisciplinary framework (labelled POZE) that places these elements in a four-layered model encapsulating humans' purpose, emotions, thoughts, and behaviours. These four layers interact with each other and, when properly aligned, lead to life satisfaction and inner peace.

67 The Report Card series tackles a different topic in each issue regarding the well-being of children in industrialized countries. The Report Cards monographs include a league table ranking the countries of the OECD related to the topic addressed in each issue.

(which is not centred on children). This was followed up four years later (UNICEF, 2011). Currently, a third version of these Report Cards is being produced.

In the United States, the Child Well-being Index (CWI) comprising 28 indicators has been estimated since 2004. It contains, a time series which has been estimated with annual data going back to 1975.

While all of these experiences are in rich countries, Hoelscher et al. (2012) estimated an index of child well-being for Eastern Europe and Central Asia. Quantitative analysis of child well-being and quality of life are also available for Latin American countries (Rojas, 2008 and 2016, Watkins Fassler, 2014, Tonon, 2016, Born et al. 2019).

One element all these efforts have in common is that (like the Human Development Index) they aggregate results from various sources for a particular geographic location (usually a country, but also sub-national estimates are available sometimes). For example, prevalence of violence would come from once source while adolescent pregnancy would come from another one.

Another element in common is the domains. Usually these include material or employment situation of the parents as well as subjective well-being and safety/exposure to violence (measured in different ways). The following list covers the labels most often used for each of the seven domains (the first words are for adults and then the terms most commonly used for children)[68]:

1. Material Well-Being—Family Economic Well-Being
2. Personal safety—Safety/Risky Behavior
3. Family and friends—Social Relationships/Family and Peer Relationships/Family Forms and Care
4. Emotional Well-Being—Emotional/Spiritual/Personal/Subjective Well-Being
5. Local community—Community Engagement
6. Work and productivity—Education
7. Health—Health and safety

In the next section, the explanation of the way this framework has been applied for the estimates in this chapter is presented.

---

68 UNICEF Report Cards of 2007 and 2011 grouped them differently in six and five domains respectively (UNICEF 2007 and 2011)

Challenges measuring quality of life among children

The main challenge in measuring quality of life among children, in a consistent way to measure the situation for the same child across the various domains, is lack of data. Fortunately, in recent years, the UNICEF supported Multiple Indicator Cluster Surveys (MICS) program[69] has included indicators that cover most of the domains discussed above such as subjective well-being, satisfaction with family and friends, material well-being, health and education, work, safety and violence, and participation in the local community.

In particular, in this chapter, we use six indicators covering most of the quality of life domains throughout the life-cycle of the child from birth to adolescence[70] (see Annex I for further details). We start with birth registration. Although, it is not a typical indicator in the quality of life literature, it functions as a "gate-keeper" (e.g. to determine age, and thus eligibility for social protection interventions geared towards the family of children and for entering schooling as well as preventing recruitment in the army or being treated as an adult in court). Consequently, it partly provides information about the strength of the local community, i.e. the relationship or engagement of the child (or the child's family) with the state and its institutions.

In order to obtain information about aspects of both family relationships and safety, neglect or inadequate care is included. It is measured by the time young children have been left without adult supervision.

Another element of family relationships is centred on adult caregivers and parents spending time for interaction with children. It measures the number of times mothers and fathers have read books or looked at picture books, told stories, sang songs, played or spent time naming, counting, or drawing things with children. Pointedly, because of the type of activities, this indicator also sheds light on aspects of recreation and play.[71]

---

69 Out of the over 200 Global SDG indicators, around 70 % cannot be generated by household surveys due to their characteristics and definition. Out of all household survey-based SDG indicators, almost half (33) are covered by MICS in its entirety or partially. Further information about MICS, such as countries covered, questionnaires, reports, data sets, etc., can be found at www.mics.data.org

70 As it will be discussed below, material well-being as well as health and education (given that material objects are needed to deliver those services), are part of the measurement of multidimensional child poverty, so they are not included here but below (under the analysis of child poverty).

71 Although in this particular case the activities are measured in the discreet number of occasions that the activities took place, clearly these activities do take time. Time

Support for children doing homework (among those who have been assigned homework), is another indicator of family relationships. It measures support from parents and caregivers.

Issues of safety and security are indicated with information on disciplinary violence at home. There are various types of violence against children. It could be physical (as in beating), emotional (as in insulting), or sexual (as in molesting). Violence against children should be differentiated from maltreatment, which is a wider concept. According to the definitions by WHO and ISPCAN (International Society for the Prevention of Child Abuse and Neglect) maltreatment also covers neglect and abandonment. In other words, unlike violence, acts of omission that also harm children. Unfortunately, children can be subjected to violence everywhere, even in the places that should be safer for them like home, playground, and school. One of the most common forms of violence at home is when it is used for disciplinary purposes. The different categories of violence against children for disciplinary purposes include corporal (physical) punishment, spanking, forcing to do something, shaking, slapping, hitting the child's bottom (or somewhere else) with belt (or stick or other hard object), or hitting or slapping the child's hand, arm, or leg. Severe physical punishment involves hitting or slapping in the head, face, or ears, beating repeatedly, as hard as possible, and with an implement. The focus on violence for discipline in this paper is due to data availability to combine with analysis of the other deprivations suffered by the same child. All types of disciplinary violence at home, physical (including severe) and psychological, are used in our estimates.

Life satisfaction is measured using a 5-point scale of subjective well-being. It ranges from very happy to very unhappy.

Admittedly, these six indicators do not cover everything that should be included for an extensive analysis of quality of life. In particular, social cohesion and work[72] which are important components of quality of life (Helliwell, 2008, Johansson, 2002, Sirgy et al., 2006). Nevertheless, they

---

(or 'time poverty'), in particular within the gender and poverty literature, is a crucial non-material deprivation (Antonopoulos and Memis, 2010).

[72] It must be remembered that this is a difficult topic when dealing with children, as they should not engage in labour activities. However, under certain conditions (to protect their safety, time for recreation, and opportunities to study) older children (adolescents) could work and this could be good for their personal development. Lack of space prevents delving further into these issues. Thus, although the information is available in MICS, it was not included in this exercise.

do cover sufficient ground across the main domains. In addition, as it was mentioned above, all of these indicators are measured for each child in order to capture their individual experience (as opposed to national prevalence rate for different sources for different domains as it is usually done). As it is explained below, this allows for a cross-tabulation with child poverty.

In addition, although for lack of space a summary index across these elements is not done in this paper, having these measurements for the same child[73] permits the estimation of how many of these issues affects each child to obtain an estimation of how pervasive their constraints are.[74] Also, their most common simultaneous occurrences can be estimated which could be important for designing interventions and policies.

A common problem bedevilling quality of life measurement is to concoct an index guided by the availability indicators instead of by a proper conceptual framework (Rojas, 2014). Consequently, an index is not constructed in this analysis. The objective is to offer a way to jointly analyze quality of life and poverty. In other words, the attempt is to show how within the quality of life framework,[75] child poverty (based on material deprivations) can be presented together but separately from the non-material aspects of quality of life[76] in order to highlight its intrinsic importance as well as the conceptual distinction between material and non-material (emotional, family-based, etc.[77]) determinants of child well-being.[78]

---

73 It could have been done for a subgroup of children due to the nature of the indicators (e.g. neglect, captured by being left alone or under the care of another young child) which are measured for children under 5 years of age.
74 Simply put, if there are three domains, and in each domain 30% of children are found wanting (which could be aggregated to calculate a national level of quality of life for children), it is very different to say that the 30% of children suffering in each domain are different children (meaning 90% of the children are affected albeit in "only" one domain) or if it is always the same 30% of children. When different sources of data are used, it is impossible to make this important distinction.
75 This includes among its domains elements which are part of the poverty and child poverty conceptual definitions and metrics.
76 In order to aggregate across these domains, we will consider children suffering shortfalls in any of these six domains to be deprived in their non-material aspects of well-being. This is done in order to maintain symmetry with the measurement of child poverty (see below).
77 Interestingly, although within UNICEF this has been promoted for over a decade (UNICEF, 2005; Fajth et al., 2012) it has not been measured so far.
78 Another reason to eschew and index is that these countries are very dissimilar in terms of history, institutions, and culture, which would make the task of constructing an index a questionable exercise (Veenhoven, 1996 and 2005).

Defining Child Poverty

It has been well understood for several decades that children experience poverty differently from adults. Thus, for instance, it is possible to observe (when measuring national averages) improvements in access to health care, household income, and literacy campaigns, yet children are not taken to clinics, children are exploited or neglected, and children are not going to school. As children make up from a third to almost half of the population in most developing countries, unless child poverty is specifically measured,[79] policy makers may be lulled into believing much progress is made to reduce poverty when actually half of the population is stagnating or worse off.

This is one of the main reasons why the SDGs have set up a specific target (1.2.2) to measure Child Poverty.[80] Moreover, the target explicitly mentions that this measurement should be multidimensional.

While it is important to note the amount of resources available in the household in which the child lives, Child Poverty is to be conceptualized and measured directly. This means that in order to have a general assessment of the opportunities children *could* theoretically have to satisfy material needs and attain a minimum standard of living, it is useful to estimate the proportion of children living in households with income/consumption below the poverty line.[81] However, this is nowhere nearly sufficient to understand Child Poverty.

Household income could surpass the poverty line because children beg in the streets or are engaged in hazardous work. Household income could increase because parents work extremely long hours, leaving children abandoned, neglected, and without any adult supervision, comfort, or guidance. Household income may be above the poverty line, yet if social services are not available (e.g. in rural areas), it does no good to children

---

79 The issue is not to pit children against adults. It is only to recognize the specificity of the rights of children and, thus, the need to have Child Poverty explicitly measured as such and then combined with overall poverty.
80 The exact wording of Indicator 1.2.2 is: 'Proportion of men, women and children of all ages living in poverty in all its dimensions according to national definitions'
81 This measurement should be at the national poverty line level, because the so called 'international' poverty line ('a dollar a day') is not aligned with the actual cost of a minimum basket of goods and services in most developing countries (even when taking Purchasing Power Parity, PPP, conversations into account). Thus, for national planning and policy design, the national poverty lines should be used.

who will still be left without schooling or health care. Thus, Child Poverty should be measured directly by measuring deprivations in specific rights (dimensions) relevant for children independently of family income or financial wealth.

The measurement must be aligned with the concept that Child Poverty is not about lack of income but should rather be centred on deprivations of Child Rights. In this respect, the literature on Human Rights and Poverty is very clear: not all rights violations constitute poverty—only those clearly associated with material shortcomings. In other words, when discussing poverty from a Human Rights perspective, the deprivation or violation of certain (constitutive) rights constitutes poverty, i.e. it makes the person poor. This is independent of income. Thus, it is not that multidimensional poverty is a proxy or a substitute or a marker or cause or a consequence of lack of income. Actually, Child Poverty could be either or both a cause and consequence of monetary poverty. Just as monetary poverty could be a cause and consequence of Child Poverty. There are intricate feedback loops between the two in the short term as well as in the long run (across generations). The important issue is that Child Poverty is not measured because it could be a cause or a consequence of monetary poverty. We measure it because it is important in and of itself and it directly affects children today (independently of any possible causal relationship with their parents' income). Consequently, its correct measurement is crucial for proper policy design. The deprivation in these dimensions is what makes the child poor (Gordon et al., 2003, Minujin and Nandy, 2012).

Methodological issues measuring Child Poverty

As a result, the dimensions of multidimensional Child Poverty are only those rights considered constitutive of poverty. These are clearly associated with material shortcomings and/or the absence of public goods and services that are needed to satisfy basic human needs.[82] In other words, not everything that is bad that happens to children constitutes or is poverty. In particular, Child Poverty is about material deprivation, not inappropriate behaviour. For instance, no proper handwashing is a bad habit.

---

[82] Thus, there is a relationship between the Human Rights approach to poverty and the earlier literature on Basic Needs.

However, it does not constitute poverty (while lack of access to water or to sanitation is a material deprivation that constitutes poverty). Similarly, when a child is not breastfed, it is not due to material deprivation but (usually) due to lack of knowledge or cultural barriers, so no breastfeeding does not constitute poverty.

In addition, early and preventable child deaths do not constitute poverty either (as the dead child is dead and not poor). Other examples are central to this chapter: disciplinary violence (which is well-known, it is quite common among the wealthiest households all over the world) and neglect are child rights violations that do not constitute poverty as they are not determined by lack of material resources (similarly to spending time with parents).

Moreover, all rights are equally important. This means that there should be no differentials in weighting the different dimensions. This is congruent with the capabilities approach. As Dixon and Nussbaum (2012) express it: "A Capabilities Approach is generally committed to the equal protection of rights for all up to a certain threshold. Any trade-off that leaves some people below this threshold will thus be a clear failure of basic justice under a Capabilities Approach". Weighting the dimensions, which in this case does not add information from a statistical point of view, is equivalent to providing an exact numerical value to trade off one right for another one (e.g. health is 1.618 times more important than nutrition) and leads to the distinct possibility that children suffering from three or even four constitutive rights violations would not be considered poor, a clear failure of basic justice. (Ghiselli et al 1981, Hagerty and Land, 2007, Gordon et al 2012, Abdu and Delamonica, 2018).

In addition, Child Poverty is about the experience of the whole child. This means, on the one hand, that Child Poverty ought to be measured at the child level (i.e. all the dimensions must be assessed simultaneously for the same child) and on the other hand, consequently, it cannot be estimated using different sources of information (i.e. all the information about the individual child must come from the same household survey).

Thus, in this chapter, for the estimation of the relationship between Child Poverty and children's non-material elements of quality of life, the following dimensions were used to estimate Child Poverty: Education, Health, Housing, Information, Nutrition, Sanitation, and Water. For each of them a threshold of severe deprivation was established (see Annex II).

Then, all the children suffering severe deprivation in at least one of the dimensions was considered poor. This provides an estimate of prevalence.[83]

Searching for a combined measure

As it was mentioned above, the purpose of this chapter is not to promote a new quality of life index. There are too many of those already. Instead, the idea is to show the salience and specificity of both material and non-material aspects of well-being, and then to present them jointly.

Methodologically, the proposed step is very simple. It consists of a cross tabulation between a self-standing measure of child poverty (based on the long tradition of rights-based, multidimensional child poverty estimation) and the combination of the non-material aspects of child well-being.

Findings: Analysing the relationship between child poverty and no-material deprivations

As explained above, quality of life or well-being for children encompasses both material and non-material aspects. Both are important and should be measured. However, they are qualitatively different and it is useful to keep them separate for monitoring the situation of children. For the few countries for which data are available to carry out the exercise central to this chapter (i.e. estimate both aspects of children's quality of life separately and then combine them), the prevalence of child poverty and non-material deprivations are depicted in Graphs 1 and 2 respectively.

---

83 While it is possible to also estimate depth/breadth and severity, those results are not included in the findings section due to space constraints.

Graph 1: Child Poverty, selected countries

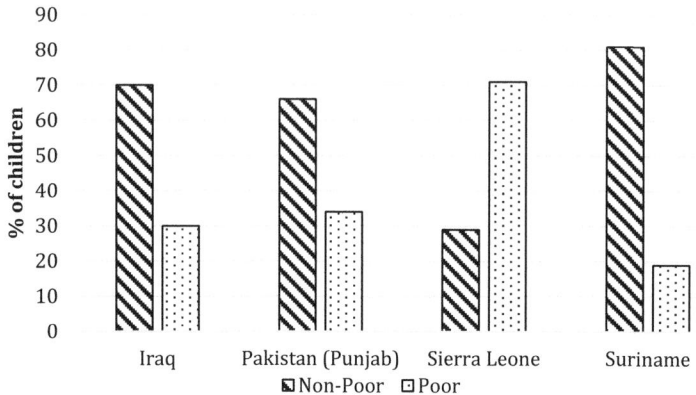

Source: Own calculation based on MICS

It can be observed that child poverty ranges considerably in these countries. It goes from less than 20% in Suriname to over 70% in Sierra Leone. However, non-material deprivation ranges considerably less. It ranges between 30 and 60%.

Graph 2: Non Material Deprivation, selected countries

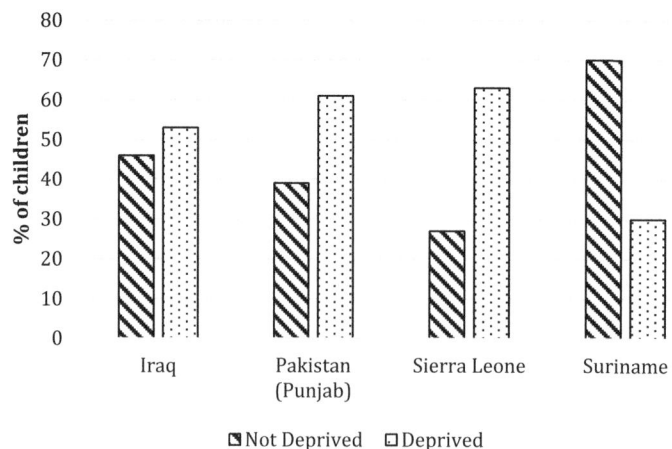

Source: Own calculation based on MICS

In graphs 3 through 6, the cross-tabulation of material (child poverty) and non-material deprivation can be found. Children suffering deprivation in either domain ranges between 44% (Suriname) and 89% (Sierra Leone).

Another element to consider is the range of the prevalence of children suffering deprivation in both domains simultaneously. It goes from 5% (Suriname) to 47% (Sierra Leone). This result is mirrored by the percentage of children who are deprived in neither domain. It ranges from 11% (Sierra Leone) to 55% (Suriname). It is not surprising that Suriname fares in this way as it is the country with the lowest overall material deprivation (child poverty).

Graph 3: Combining material (child poverty) and non-material deprivations: Iraq

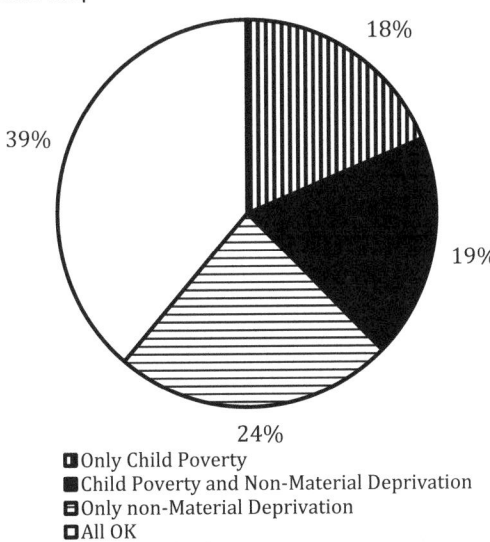

◨ Only Child Poverty
■ Child Poverty and Non-Material Deprivation
▤ Only non-Material Deprivation
☐ All OK

Source: Own calculation based on MICS

Graph 4: Combining material (child poverty) and non-material deprivations: Punjab, Pakistan (2018)

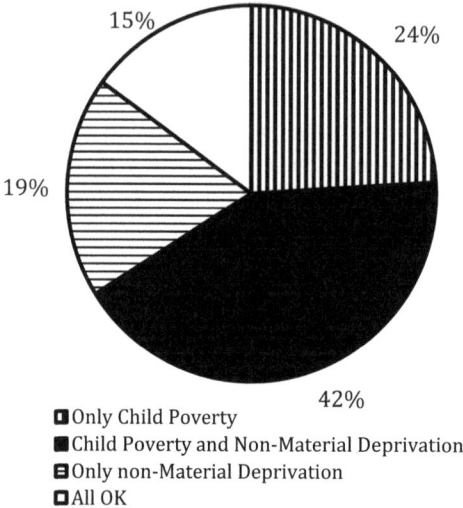

☐ Only Child Poverty
■ Child Poverty and Non-Material Deprivation
☐ Only non-Material Deprivation
☐ All OK

Source: Own calculation based on MICS

Graph 5: Combining material (child poverty) and non-material deprivations: Sierra Leone (2017)

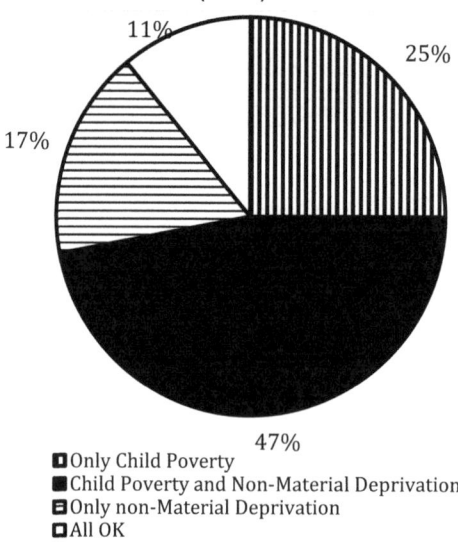

☐ Only Child Poverty
■ Child Poverty and Non-Material Deprivation
☐ Only non-Material Deprivation
☐ All OK

Source: Own calculation based on MICS

Graph 6: Combining material (child poverty) and non-material deprivations: Suriname

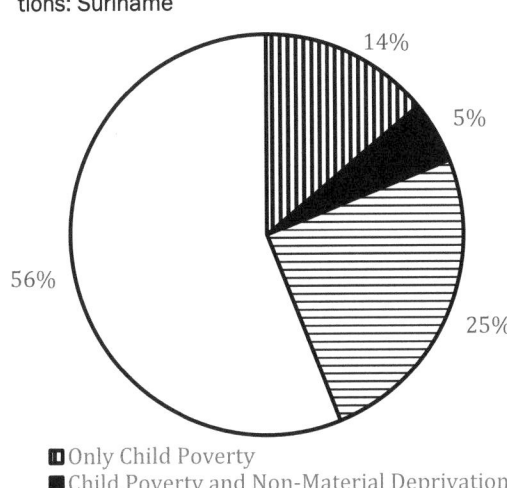

■ Only Child Poverty
■ Child Poverty and Non-Material Deprivation
■ Only non-Material Deprivation
□ All OK

Source: Own calculation based on MICS

The main conclusion from the assessment of these four countries is that material deprivation seems easier to address. Moreover, the overlap between domains seems to disappear.

Nevertheless, the main conclusion is methodological.[84] It is possible to provide a holistic assessment of children's quality of life combining (but estimating and presenting separately) the material and non-material domains of well-being.

Conclusion and further research

Three conclusions can be derived from the previous analysis. First, the prevalence of both material (child poverty) and non-material deprivation among children varies widely among countries. Secondly, child poverty varies more than non-material deprivation (both in terms of its minimum as well as its maximum observed values).

---

84 There are too few available countries to establish global or regional conclusions. The country results are merely illustrative.

Thirdly and most importantly, from a methodological point of view, it is possible to combine the material (child poverty) and non-material domains of children's quality of life. This provides a holistic view of how their well-being maintain separately elements which are conceptually distinct.

In terms of next steps for future research, it may be interesting to explore and test for time trends. This may not be feasible going backwards but household surveys like MICS may continue to include the questions used in this analysis, which would allow intertemporal comparisons (assuming the questions are kept the same through the various rounds). Also, the specification of the non-material deprivation elements could be altered to capture older data. For instance, the fifth round of MICS had additional questions regarding subjective well-being and satisfaction with peers and family members.

Additionally, it may be worth to explore further the combination of levels of deprivation (in both domains). In other words, combining not only the prevalence of child poverty with the prevalence of non-material deprivation, but also their depth/breadth and severity.

References

Abdu, M., Delamonica, E. (2018) Multidimensional Child Poverty: From Complex Weighting to Simple Representation. *Social Indicators Research* 136, pp. 881–905.

Acosta, A. and Martinez, E. (eds) (2009) *El Buen Vivir. Una vía para el desarrollo*, Abya-Ayala, Quito; Escobar

Antonopoulos, R. and Memis, E. (2010) Time and Poverty from a Developing Country Perspective, *Bard College Levy Economics Institute Working Paper No. 600*

Born, D., Colamarco, V., Delamónica, & Minujín, A. (2019) South American Children's Quality of Life: Intra-Urban Disparities along Life-Cycle Indicators. *Applied Research Quality Life* 14, pp. 799–817 DOI: https://doi.org/10.1007/s11482-018-9607-2

Escobar, A. (2010) Latin America at a Crossroads: Alternative modernizations, post-liberalism, or post-development? *Cultural Studies* Vol. 24, No. 1, pp. 1–65

Fajth, G., S. Kurukulasuriya, and S. Engilbertsdóttir (2012) "A multidimensional response to tackling child poverty and disparities: reflections from the Global Study on Child Poverty and Disparities" in A. Minujin and S. Nandy (eds.) *Global Child Poverty and Well-being: Measurement, concepts, policy and action*, Policy Press, UK

Ghiselli EE, Campbell JP, Zedek S. (1981) *Measurement Theory for the Behavioral Sciences*. San Francisco: W.H. Freeman

Gordon, D., Nandy, S., Pantazis, C., Pemberton, S., and Townsend P. (2003), *Child Poverty in the Developing World*, The Policy Press, Bristol

Gordon, D., L. D. Howe, B. Galobardes, A. Matijasevich, D. Johnston, O. Onwujekwe, R. Patel, E. A. Webb, D. A. Lawlor And J. R. Hargreaves (2012) "Authors' Response to: Alternatives to principal components analysis to derive asset-based indices to measure socio-economic position in low- and middle-income countries: the case for multiple correspondence analysis", *International Journal of Epidemiology*. 41 (4), pp. 1209–1210

Gudynas, Eduardo. (2011). Buen Vivir: Today's Tomorrow. *Development*. 54. 441–447

Guendel, L. (2012) Thoughts on the concept of Vivir Bien and human rights: A pragmatic point of view, *Integra Educativa* Vol. V/Nº 133–156

Hagerty, M.R., Land, K.C. (2007) "Constructing Summary Indices of Quality of Life: A Model for the Effect of Heterogeneous Importance Weights", *Sociological Methods and Research*, Vol. 35, n. 4, pp. 455–496

Hagerty, M. Cummings, R., Ferris, A., Land, K., Michalos, A. et al, (2001). Quality of Life Indexes for National Policy: Review and Agenda for Research. *Social Indicators Research* 55, pp. 1–96

Helliwell, J. (2008). Life Satisfaction and Quality of Development. Working Paper 14507, NBER *Working Paper Series*. Cambridge, MA

Hoelscher, P. D. Richardson and J. Bradshaw (2012) "A snapshot of child well-being in transition countries: exploring new methods of monitoring child well-being" in A. Minujin and S. Nandy (eds.) *Global Child Poverty and Well-being: Measurement, concepts, policy and action*, Policy Press, UK. 179–206

Johansson, S. (2002). Conceptualizing and Measuring Quality of Life for National Policy. *Social Indicators Research* 58, pp. 13–32

Michalos, A.C. (2014) "Quality of life, two variable theory". In A.C. Michalos (Ed.), *Encyclopedia of Quality of Life and Well-Being Research*. Dordrecht: Springer, pp. 6427–2429.

Minujin, A. and S. Nandy (2012) *Global Child Poverty and Well-being: Measurement, concepts, policy and action*, Policy Press, UK

Rojas, M. (2008). "The Measurement of Quality of Life: Conceptualization comes first". *A four-qualities-of-life conceptual framework and an illustration to Latin America*. Facultad Latinoamericana de Ciencias Sociales, Sede México & Universidad Popular Autónoma del Estado de Puebla, Mexico

Rojas, M. (2014). Quality of Life, Conceptualization. In A. Michalos (Ed.). *Encyclopaedia of Quality of Life and Well-Being Research*. Springer, pp. 5360–5363

Rojas, M. (Ed.) (2016). *Handbook of Happiness Research in Latin America*. Springer

Sirgy, J., Michalos, A., Ferris, A., Easterlin, R., Patrick, D., & Pavot, W. (2006). The Quality-of-Life (QOL) Research Movement: Past, Present, and Future. *Social Indicators Research* 76, pp. 343–466

Tonon, G. (Ed.) (2016) *Indicators of Quality of Life in Latin America*. Springer

UNICEF (2007) An overview of child well-being in rich countries: A comprehensive assessment of the lives and well-being of children and adolescents in the economically advanced nations, Innocenti Research Center (now Office of Research), Report Card number 7.

UNICEF (2011) Child well-being in rich countries A comparative overview, Office of Research, Innocenti Report Card number 11.

Veenhoven, (1996). Happy Life-Expectancy: A comprehensive measure of quality-of-life in nations, *Social Indicators Research* 39, pp. 1–58

Veenhoven, (2005). Apparent Quality-of-Life in Nations. *Social Indicators Research* 71, pp. 61–68

Walther, C. (2020) *Development, Humanitarian Aid and Social Welfare: Social Change from the inside out*, MacMillan Palgrave.

Watkins Fassler, K. (2014). "Gender Considerations on Income and Health in Latin America". In L. Eckermann (Ed.) *Gender, Lifespan and Quality of Life: An International Perspective*. Springer, pp. 173–182

Annex I: Non-material Deprivations, Definitions and Categories Used for Quality of Life Domains[85]

Domain	Deprivation Definition	Unit of Analysis
Community strength/engagement	Children without birth certificate	Child under 5
Family Relationships (Neglect, inadequate care)/Safety	Children left alone or with another child for more than one hour at least once during the past week	Child under 5
Recreation/Family Relationships	Adult household members have engaged in less than 4 activities with the child during the last 3 days	Children age 3–5
Family (Interaction)	Child was not supported with homework (among those children who have been assigned homework)	Children age 7–14
Safety, security, and violence	Children who experienced any violent discipline method (physical or psychological) during the last one month	Children age 1–14
Emotional well-being/Life satisfaction	Children who answer being neither happy nor unhappy, somewhat unhappy, or very unhappy in a 5 point scale of happiness	Children age 15–17

---

85 Health and Education are included under material deprivation and work is not included

Annex II: Material Deprivations, Definitions and Categories Used for Child Poverty Dimensions

Dimension	Severe Deprivation Definition	Unit of Analysis
Shelter	Children living in a dwelling with five or more people per room, a mud floor, or one made out of waste material.	Children 17 and under
Sanitation	Children with no access to a toilet facility of any kind.	Children 17 and under
Water	Children using surface water such as rivers, ponds, streams and dams, or who trek 30 minutes or more (round trip) to collect water.	Children 17 and under
Information	Children with no access to radio, television, or a mobile phone at home.	Children age 3–17
Nutrition/Food	Children who are more than 3 standard deviations below the international reference population for stunting, or wasting, or underweight.	Child under 5
Education	Children who have never been to school or are not currently attending school	Children age 6–17
Health	Children who did not receive immunization against any diseases or who did not receive medical advice or treatment for a recent illness involving diarrhoea, an acute respiratory infection, or malaria.	Children under 5

Protection Risks and Protective Factors of Vulnerable Young Children Through the Study of Community-Based Child Protection (CBCP) in Rural Western Kenya

Martin Hayes, Melissa Kelly and Darcy Strouse

Introduction

Violence against Children (VAC) is one of the most pervasive, harmful, and costly public health epidemics of our time. VAC—defined as 'the intentional use of physical force or power, threatened or actual, against a child, by an individual or group, that either results in or has a high likelihood of resulting in actual or potential harm to the child's health, survival, development or dignity' (Krug, et al., 2002, p. 59)—includes all forms of physical and sexual violence, emotional abuse, neglect, negligent treatment, and exploitation that is perpetrated against children aged 18 or under (Leeb, et al., 2011; UNICEF, 2014). VAC transcends all social, economic, geographic, and cultural boundaries, affecting over 1.5 billion children globally—more than half of all children in the world (Hillis et al.2016). The estimated economic damage of physical, psychological and sexual violence alone is in the magnitude of $7 trillion, up to 8 percent of global GDP (Pereznieto et al., 2014), making VAC one of the leading burdens on the global economy.

Among children, infants and young children ages 0–5 years (IYC) are victims of some of the most severe forms of violence due to the physical dependency and socio-legal vulnerability that makes this group of children ill equipped to mitigate risks, defend themselves, report abuses, or advocate for their rights in the same ways as older children (Belsky, 1980). Violence in the home and directly against IYC compounds this risk to children's development and well-being by increasing the number of cumulative risk factors during the early years (Walker Wachs, Grantham-McGregor, Black, Nelson, Huffman, Baker-Henningham et al., 2011). Persistent or severe forms of stress, such as violent discipline, can become 'toxic,' and, without intervention, results in negative and life-long effects, including impacts on physical, mental, and reproductive health, as well as social and cognitive development (Krug et al., 2002; Shonkoff & Garner, 2012). Globally, more than 250 million children under five years in low and middle-income countries may not reach their full potential due to poverty, lack of access to services, and inadequate caregiving practices (Black et al., 2016).

Recent data from the United Nations Children's Fund (UNICEF, 2017) highlights the pervasiveness of violence against young children around the world. Three in four children globally aged 2 to 4 experience some form of violent discipline on a regular basis. This is confirmed in the United States, where infants account for more than half of the severe cases of child hospitalizations resulting from abuse (Leventhal & Gaither, 2012). Data also highlights that infants experience violence early in life. Data from 29 countries show that 47 percent of one-year-old children are disciplined by shouting, yelling, or screaming and 30 percent are disciplined by spanking (UNICEF, 2017).

The true prevalence of violence in the early years is not known because physical abuse, neglect and interpersonal violence affecting IYC take place in the privacy of the home setting, and are therefore invisible to the public eye (UNICEF, 2014). While nearly all countries have ratified the United Nations Convention on the Rights of the Child (UNCRC), only 60 out of 182 countries have adopted legislation that fully prohibits the use of violent discipline (physical punishment and/or psychological aggression) at home. This means that more than 600 million children under age 5 around the world do not have legal protection (UNICEF, 2017). While many cases are not reported to legal authorities (less than 10 percent in high-income countries), global evidence reveals that the self-reported prevalence of child sexual abuse incidents is more than 30 times higher than official reports and self-reported physical abuse victimization is more than 75 times higher (Gilbert et al.,2009; Stoltenborgh et al.2011; Stoltenborgh et al., 2013).

To better understand the protection harms and risks, as well as the corresponding available child protection mechanisms and services for IYC in resource-limited settings, ChildFund International (ChildFund) conducted ethnographic case studies in two rural villages in Western Kenya. Specific research questions examined by the study in this context were: (a) What are the community-level child protection issues, including risks and protective factors for IYC?; (b) What do the community-based child protection systems, in terms of mechanisms or support structures, look like for IYC?; and (c) How can we use the information from the first two questions to inform and improve community responses?

The results of this research will help inform the realization of the Sustainable Development Goals (SDGs) 1.3, which aims to 'implement social protection systems; 5.2, which aims to 'eliminate all forms of violence against women and girls'; and 16.2, which aims to 'end abuse, exploitation, trafficking, and all forms of violence against children,' (United Nations, 2015, p. 20–30). The study is unique in two ways. First, in that it focuses on deriving context-specific knowledge on how child protection systems serve IYC. And second, in that it investigates not only contextual perspectives on developmental aspects for this special age group but also specifically on harms, risks, and protective factors for IYC.

Contextual background

Siaya County comprises of one of the six counties in the Nyanza region of Kenya, with a population of 885,762. Siaya County has among the highest HIV prevalence rates in Kenya, which at 24.9% is four times the national average prevalence of 5.9% (National AIDS Control Council, 2016). Over half of the population is composed of children below 18 years of age (UNICEF, 2013). In the age cohort 0–4, the number of male children is higher than that of female children. Over 80% of households in the county are considered food insecure. Changing weather patterns characterized by frequent droughts and intense rainfall further constrain agricultural productivity and food security in the county (Government of Kenya, 2016). As a result, nearly 25% of children in Siaya County are stunted because of chronic malnutrition in early life (Kenya National Bureau of Statistics, 2015). Some of the contributing factors of poverty are dependence on subsistence agriculture with increasingly poor soil, accompanied by lack of innovative farming techniques, lack of infrastructure and the continued high rate of HIV and AIDS affecting heads of families (Obonyo et al., 2016). These factors are not dissimilar to the rural challenges facing families across Kenya and more broadly in the east and southern Africa region.

The two Kenyan villages targeted for this ethnographic research are situated in the Nyanza region of Kenya's Siaya County's Sub-County X.[86]

---

86 The two villages and Sub-County are not named in this paper in order to protect the anonymity of research participants.

Similar with County-level data, these two villages are characterized by high levels of poverty and unmet health needs. Sub-County X has an infant mortality rate three times higher than the country average, making it one of the highest in the country. Most sub-county residents are mixed subsistence farmers, with the rural poverty rate reaching 60% (Obonyoa et al.2016; County of Siaya, 2016). These factors are not dissimilar from the rural challenges facing families across Kenya and more broadly in the east and southern Africa regions.

Historically, to address the multi-faceted IYC challenges in these resource-limited, high-risk communities in Siaya County, ChildFund and its local implementing partner have engaged community health volunteers (CHVs), parents and caregivers, and other community members in both villages to support rural families who depend almost entirely on subsistence agriculture. Program interventions have included establishing preschools for children aged 3–5 years in coordination with Sub-County government education officials, including developing learning materials, establishing community preschool management committees, training and capacity building of preschool teachers on the national curriculum, and linking them to available CHVs and other health services. To promote improved health and nutrition of IYC, ChildFund has worked closely with Sub-County X and local government health officials to support CHVs in their efforts to share essential messages and distribute health related information at regular health outreach sessions. Further, ChildFund has trained CHVs on the first 1000 days, most notably providing nutrition practices during this period, with the aim of promoting exclusive breastfeeding and supplementary feeding for pregnant and lactating mothers and children up to 24 months.

Methods

The case studies employed rapid ethnographic methods to address study research questions and to explore, through a grounded methodology, each community's conceptualization and perception of child protection issues and formal and informal child protection systems in their communities.

Site Selection and Study Participants

The two villages of focus for this study were selected from the six villages where ChildFund has ongoing programming. Data from ChildFund's implementing partner were used to inform the selection of two study villages, representing the highest level of economic vulnerability. ChildFund categorized economic vulnerability based on household outcomes on measures of economic and social dimensions consistent to the Household Economic Strengthening Framework (Poverty Outreach Working Group, 2011). On this basis, struggling households were defined as those that: (a) can usually pay for necessities (such as food) but may not regularly afford other necessities (such as schooling and medical fees), especially if they require relatively large lump-sum payments; (b) have somewhat predictable but limited income, often linked to agriculture; and (c) possess some assets (animals, tools, land) or savings that may fluctuate during the year, have some hungry periods, and one productive/working adult. Of the six villages where ChildFund has been conducting interventions for IYC and their families at the time of village selection, Village B showed the highest level of economic vulnerability, while Village A reported the highest number of child abuse cases.

Within each community, ChildFund's implementing partner consulted with service providers and traditional leaders to identify vulnerable sub-groups within the community to be included in the study. This process aimed to ensure that the most marginalized groups, including but not limited to the very poor, disabled, and elderly, participated in the study. For each case study, study participants therefore included both sexes, different age cohorts and residents of different socio-economic status groups. Key informants for interviews also reflected traditional leadership and service providers, such as preschool teachers and community health volunteers.

Study sub-groups were formally categorized as follows: Old women and men; young women and men; teenage boys and girls (below 18 years old); young children (3–5 years-old); and community-based organizations. Participants from non-governmental organization working in the County included representation from county children's services, the Special School Sub-County X, the Sub-County Police Division's crime unit, and a non-governmental organization (NGO).

Data Collection

Qualitative data were collected over a period of 10 days by multi-disciplinary teams in the two selected villages using four primary data collection tools (see Table 1 for a summary). The data collection tools were translated into the local language of Dholuo.

- **In-Depth Interviews:** In-depth interviews explored the community's conceptualization and perceptions of child protection issues for IYC. They explored the respondents' views on the existing support systems, harms to children, response and protection services, and levels of satisfaction with the services. Probing was used to gain in-depth understanding of the community's view of the situation for IYC and community-based child protection mechanisms by asking open-ended questions.
- **Key Informant Interviews:** Key informant interviews were conducted with community members who had specialized knowledge on child protection issues for IYC and/or who had a general representative role in the community. Participants were selected based on their knowledge and experience about the topic under study, as well as the positions held in the community.
- **Focus Group Discussions:** Focus group discussions provided community views and perceptions of child protection risks, response pathways, responsive and protection structures at the community level. Focus groups were held with specific subgroups, including adult women, adult men, and parents with children 5 years of age and under, female youth, and male teenagers with children aged five years of age and under.
- **Timelines:** Timeline generation was used to learn about respondents' conceptualization and understanding of childhood and children's development. The timelines were used to derive a contextual understanding of how the community conceptualizes and comprehends children, childhood, the typical path of children's development, and "normal" children's roles and activities at each stage of development. Respondents were engaged to identify important times, events and activities in the life of children aged 0–5 years. This data collection method was important for ensuring that the research team did not impose an "outsider's" view concerning children and childhood, and, instead, captured the community's understating of what constitutes a child and childhood.

Study of CBCP in Rural Western Kenya   249

Table 1.   Profile of Study Data Collection Tools

Tool	Data	Respondent Group	Number of Sessions/ Interviews	Output
In-depth Interviews	Interview transcripts, tape recordings	Selected community members from each village	**25** • 14 in Village A • 11 in Village B	Description of responses related to child protection issues for IYC from community sub-groups
Key Informant Interviews	Interview transcripts, tape recordings	Selected community Members from each village and the overall county	**28** • 10 on County Level • 9 in Village A • 9 in Village B	Description of responses related to child protection issues for IYC from community members with special and/or expert knowledge
Focus Group Discussions	Group transcripts, tape recordings, fieldnotes	Specific subgroups: Adult Men and women, Parents with IYC, male and female youth, teenagers with IYC	**17** • 8 in Village A • 9 in Village B	Description of responses related to child protection issues for IYC from community sub-groups; understanding of consensus and disagreements within and across sub-groups
Timelines	Narrative transcripts, fieldnotes	Selected community members from each village	**17** • 6 in Village A • 11 in Village B	Contextual understanding of how the communities conceptualize children, childhood, the typical path of child development

Ethical Considerations: 'Do No Harm' Principle and Other Ethical Guidelines

Ethical considerations, including the protection of children from harm, informed consent, privacy and confidentiality, were core tenets of the participatory research. All researchers were trained on and abided by ChildFund's child protection policy as well as ethical guidelines and internal review processes for participatory research (ChildFund, 2010). Structures were put in place to monitor adherence to the code of conduct and to provide channels for support and referral if needed during the research. In accordance with ChildFund's ethical guidelines and review processes, informed consent and assent forms and materials were developed, reviewed, and approved; and researchers were trained on administration of consent and assent forms, as well as on ethical principles to be observed during the data collection. The entire research process was guided by the 'Do No Harm' principle and adhered to the following ethical principles: Respect, non-maleficence, beneficence, best interest of the child, objectivity, and child protection policies and safeguarding policy.

Data Analysis

Data from both sites were analyzed by carefully reading the transcripts from interviews and field notes until themes, patterns, and categories organically emerged from the different texts. The views of study participants were captured through verbatim quotations to support key points. Triangulation was used to confirm, compare, and contrast data from different sub-groups, as well as from key informants, in-depth interviews, focus groups, and timelines. The identified major themes were then coded and assigned descriptive labels and indexed with values of 1 (for identified theme) and 0 (for non-identified theme). The thematic analysis process employed an iterative approach to combine and catalogue related patterns into sub-themes. Overall, the derived themes and sub-themes represent units derived from data patterns that include vocabulary, repeated activities, conversation topics, feelings, and folk sayings and proverbs.

Results

A total of 310 people participated in the study and were representative of all members of the community: Children, men, women, teenage boys and girls, and community leaders. While it was the aim of this ethnographic rapid assessment to increase our understanding of the protection risks facing the specific hidden population of IYC, respondents often offered information about children of all ages even when asked specifically about IYC. The risk factors that affect young children also affect children of all ages. To understand the risk and protective factors of young children, it is necessary to understand how these factors impact families. The emergent findings suggest that the experiences, situations and reactions of adult family members, older siblings and young teenage parents all impact young children's well-being.

Overall, iterative analyses generated three key overriding thematic areas focused on: Risks to IYC's development and well-being in the family setting; the protective factors and needs of young children; and common practices and challenges for accessing child protection services.

Risks to Children's Development and Well-being in the Family Setting

The family is a critical institution for the care and protection of children and in times of prosperity households are generally very stable. However, acute stress on households is caused by the lack of food and when parents are unable to provide sustenance for their family. Risks and harms experienced by IYC in the family setting clustered around the following sub-themes: Domestic violence, corporal punishment, family breakup, and teenage pregnancy (leading to alternative care placements—elderly caregivers and kinship care).

Domestic Violence

An Assistant Chief—a member of the traditional leadership structure at village level—described the causes of high levels of domestic violence: 'What brings this issue is like this season when there is lack of food, and the price of *unga* (maize meal) has also gone up. At the moment, domestic violence is at its highest peak in this village. And one of the reasons is because the poverty level is very high, most of the people live from hand to mouth.' He went on to say: 'We have many cases of domestic violence in this village, especially now that the price of food has increased, and there is no produce from the farms, there is always tension in the family, especially when the fathers cannot provide.'

As mentioned by numerous study participants, alcohol abuse is a significant contributing factor for domestic violence in the communities. Alcohol is widely available and consumed in both communities. Some houses brew *chang'aa*, which is a local beer made from sorghum, maize or millet. An older woman in another focus group talked about violence in her family and in most others that she knows: 'conflicts are mostly brought about by alcohol.' Teen boys in Village A described how sometimes parents under the influence of alcohol commit acts of violence against their children.

Children often witness domestic violence. However, the impact on younger children being exposed to domestic violence may be underestimated by some in the community. As a county social welfare official mentioned, 'on domestic violence, I would say sometimes that the older children suffer more than the younger children who are below five years. This is because the younger ones are still not able to comprehend what is happening around them, they just live their life. They don't know what is going on. The older ones see what is happening and they understand, so they are affected more than the younger ones.'

However, a preschool teacher from Village A who spends a substantial amount of time with younger children had a different perspective in relation to the impact of witnessing domestic violence on younger children. 'When they are in school', he said, 'is when we know that things are like this, and this because sometimes you find that children are not their normal self. And sometimes they are sick; you will only find out when they look dull but when they are at home you cannot tell whatever is going on with them. And you know there are issues in each and every home.'

In a focus group of women in Village A, one woman explained the impact of domestic violence on young children: 'They look tired all the time and you may think the child is sick, but the child is just so stressed [...] even when they eat they don't get satisfied [...]. You know when a child eats, his mind doesn't work normally, whenever you call the child he fears as he might think you want to beat him, so in the house when he sees fights always he really gets scared, at times he might even come to you as a mother and ask "mother does dad always beats you?" or at times ask their father why he loves fighting with mother [...] At times when parents fight in the house and the children are so small, you find that the next day they start abusing other children in the same way they heard.'

Corporal Punishment
Some children were described by several study participants as the direct victims of violence in the home. Corporal punishment is an accepted form of disciplining children in Kenya. In fact, some study participants felt that

the cause of children's misbehavior was due to parents not adequately using this form of punishment. However, as an Assistant Chief explained, '[…] some parents tend to *over punish* their children. You find some of these young children being caned to the extent that they have scars. I had a case of a child who had been sent to the shop and she lost fifty shillings ($0.49 USD). She was thoroughly caned, and her body was swollen, but parents do it out of anger. After doing it, they feel sorrowful. But we had to take the child to the hospital. The child was just 5 years old.'

During a focus group with teen mothers, one mother indicated that harsh corporal punishment is sometimes necessary for effectively disciplining children: 'If a child is indiscipline then you have to beat them *puodo a puoda* (meaning beating a child in anger and excessively).'

One teenaged girl interviewed described how some children are beaten when they consume the families limited resources without permission. An example was provided, 'when their parents leave them home without food. Sometimes their parents go to the funeral and come back very late without leaving them with food to eat. If they eat food, they are caned. The parents think they have done a mistake, but it was because of hunger.'

Family Breakup

An Assistant Chief described that *mpango wa kando* (extra marital affairs) are a big source of conflict in the family. Sometimes women will have extramarital affairs when the husband is unable to provide for the family. Some of the female study participants described occasions when men brought home new women and kicked their wives and children out of the house. The Chief of Sub-County X provided an example of when 'a man locked the mother and all the children out of the house. The wife and children, who some were under five years, were actually living in the bush like wild animals. They could actually time when the father was away so that they could come and live in the kitchen, but sometimes when the father appears the mother would run to the bush with her children.' Despite Kenya's Matrimonial Property Act (Government of Kenya, 2013), which gives women rights in relation to land ownership, traditionally women do not have property rights. The land and all household assets are thought to belong to the husband and the husband's family.

A teacher in Sub-County X described how children get mixed up in marital disputes and the harm it causes them: 'What causes these harms are ... let me say, parenting. It depends on *huyu motto anaishi na nani* (who the child lives with). She lives with the grandmother, or this child lives with the mother, this mother has left the husband somewhere. This also causes the child to be harmed because you find the mother coming to live with the grandmother, the child attends school for three months the goes back to the father. Then when the mother goes back to the father, stays for two years, they fight then she takes the child and comes back with him. Sometimes you find the child stays with the mother and the father wants him back, so you find the father coming here and takes him. Sometimes the father meets him on the road and takes him. I have cases like that have I've handled. A parent comes and waits for the child outside the gate, he takes the child and goes away. So those are the things that badly harms the child."

Teenage Pregnancy: Young Mothers and Care by Other Family Members
A focus group of teenaged girls from Village B explained that one of the biggest problems for girls her age is 'Early pregnancy [...] most girls are being lied to by older boys and even the *boda boda* (motorcycle taxi) people who give them ten shillings to buy *mandazi* (donuts) and sleep with them.' A woman from a focus group in Village A added: 'Children even at 13 years old they know how you stay, they know that a girl can now go get married, you find her staying in another homestead and she is still young, she is saying she is married. Even in schools you just get surprised that a child is pregnant, and you wonder how can this small child get pregnant.' A second woman mentioned the frequency of these early pregnancies: 'So many. Like last year, very young girls below the age of 18 years got pregnant. Cases of girls of 12, 13, 14 and 16 years old getting pregnant were so many.'

A teenaged boy from a focus group in Village A described a similar scenario but indicated that sometimes parents encourage their girls to do this in order to buy food for the family: 'You find that some parents send their girls to go and sell their bodies to help the family buy food to eat and the *boda boda* have money.' A second boy added: 'You can find that a young girl sometimes, one who has not even attained the age of 13, has been left to roam around in the center until 9 pm selling her body.'

The teen mothers discussed the growing phenomena of transactional sex. 'Some children will start acting promiscuous and because of this can be cheated by men who give them money, and this will make them start having sex early.' *Boda boda* were frequently mentioned by study participants in both communities as perpetrators of sexual assault and of luring girls into transactional sex. These are men with some resources (cash and transport) and are quite visible riding around the community. '[Men] like the *boda boda* riders destroy other people's children's lives by giving them money they pretend like they are helping you like when you are in school and you lack something in school they offer you money. This makes you feel that they can help you, so you agree to sleep with them then later on they make you pregnant and you are forced to leave school.'

Teenage sexual activity and the risk that it would result in pregnancy was thus seen as resulting in cohorts of young mothers, often not prepared to take care of an infant or a very young child, as they were still children themselves. This resulted in some young mothers giving their children to their parents to help raise or in some cases, to a residential care center for babies in the county.

A village Chief in Village A described the challenges faced by young mothers: 'These young girls who get children while they are still young [...] some of them don't know how to bathe the child, or to clean the child properly [...] Some don't even buy their children warm clothes, they just leave them to walk naked, and then at some point you find that the child is suffering from pneumonia.'

Grandparental Care of Young Children

The challenges of teenage pregnancy have a direct effect on elderly caregivers. Grandparents often assume the role of caregivers when parents are unable or unwilling to do so. Children who have children are usually ill-equipped to assume this role and turn to their own parents for help. However, grandparents, particularly older grandmothers, also struggle to provide adequate care. An Assistant Chief described this: 'There are also cases where these young girls, because of lack of discipline, they get children at a very young age and dumps the child with their parents. In that case, the grandmother of the child is the one who reports it to me because you find that these old women are very poor and they do not have the energy to go and work and provide for the child, so most of the time they are stressed on where to get food to feed the child, and now that they are also old, some of them find it difficult to start taking care of the young child. I refer such cases to the children's department in Ward A [in Sub-County X].'

A woman from a focus group described her own perspective: 'We are now grandparents and these young girls gives birth and leaves the children with other children who do not know how to take care of children, maybe a mother gives birth goes somewhere leaving a child with the baby so for this child to take care of this baby is a hard task and the baby has to endure a lot.'

An NGO respondent in Sub-County X described how grandparents assume care provision when their own children die: 'Those with dead parents and left under the care of grandparents are not well cared for, they lack proper feeding, sometimes they don't even bathe and also sometimes walk naked without clothes. Diseases such as malaria and measles also affect children a lot in this area. You take a child to the hospital and they test and get malaria then give medication, but nothing changes. This happens when a child has measles. Also, the houses where they live with grandparents are not well smeared on the floor which forms good habitat for jiggers (painful parasites affecting the feet).' Community residents use a soil-cow dung-ash mixture to smear the floors of their homes as a measure to prevent flea infestation. Older residents may have physical difficulties using this method.

This respondent continued to explain how children left in the care of their grandmothers are sometimes mistreated. 'Some of them who are under the age of five years live with their grandmothers who mistreat them and [...] they are neglected. Some of them have parents but you find that the parents have left them under the care of their grandparents. These children suffer a lot from neglect from their parents who sometimes look for livelihoods and in some cases; their mothers go out with other men.'

Kinship Care

In addition to care by grandparents, children being sent from one household to live temporarily in another household is a very common phenomenon in Kenya. In fact, parents sending their children away to other extended family members' households that may have more resources or are closer to schools is a very common coping strategy in resource-limited communities in Sub-Saharan Africa. While these households may be slightly better off financially, their resources are usually still very limited, and the welfare of biological offspring are often prioritized, including for the provision of food and school fees.

Young mothers in a focus group described how children are often treated when they are sent to live with their extended families. 'You are beaten. You are always hungry.' A second woman added: 'You are given a lot of work and very little food.' A third woman added: 'When people are about to eat you are sent to go fetch water and firewood. You are given a lot of work at that time. You will only eat when some food has remained.'

Protective Factors and Needs of Young Children

Given the adverse conditions in the communities of Villages A and B, the odds of surviving the first 5 years of life and going on to have a healthy and productive life is less than optimal. Families in these two communities are both the primary care providers and first line of protection for children. Despite caregivers' great struggle to provide, children are greatly valued and loved in these communities.

As a mothers' focus group participant from Village B put it, 'a child is an angel sent from God.' A woman from Village A in a separate interview had similar sentiments saying that 'a child is a flower, a blessing from God.' These statements are examples from women in both communities of their affection for young children. A male elder from Village A explained how children should be cared for by providing, good food, clothing, bathing, should be loved, parents should be close to their children and that will prevent anyone with an ill motive to reach the child.

Families in the communities celebrate the birth of children. The family typically holds a party that serves as a presentation of the child to the world, known as *golo nyathi oko*. Family and neighbors 'are invited to pray for the child, then people eat, and gift the child.' The event provides neighbors the opportunity to visit and meet the newborn and provide small gifts to the family. Explained by a male elder from Village A, [This celebration of the birth of a child] 'opens ways for the child and also makes a child own a few things of his own.'

In rural Western Kenya, families are the primary source of support and protection for children. Children are cared for by the mothers and fathers, but in a household in rural Siaya County, the household includes more than the nuclear family and traditionally, grandparents, aunts, uncles and older siblings all play important roles in raising children. As one woman from Village A described, 'Family is big. It has a mother, father, and the children. But also extended relatives like grandparents, uncles and aunties can also be called family.' Grandmothers were mentioned by many participating in the study as providing critical care of children when parents are working. In addition, aunts, uncles and older siblings are also expected to provide care to younger children. Older children are expected to escort their younger siblings to and from school.

The Ministry of Health trained and sanctioned community health volunteers (CHVs), within the health system structure, were mentioned by several assessment respondents as the main service provider for children in this age cohort. CHVs and *nyamrerwas* (which are informal traditional birth attendants that some study participants referred to interchangeably with the CHVs) were said to support infants and young children with vaccinations. The CHVs also held information dissemination sessions with community members and home visits with parents to discuss nutritional and hygiene needs of young children and encourage parents with sick children to go to the hospital.

Despite this support from families, neighbors and volunteers, severe food insecurity and very high HIV infection rates in the county have created a very difficult environment for IYC survival. Participants in one focus group discussed the fragility and death of young children and how they are honored when they die by neighbors visiting the house, paying their respects and contributing to the burial. One man mentioned the cultural importance of this ceremony of visiting the grieving family to eat and pay respects, 'Even if he dies today he will be buried the next day because in our culture as Luos, if we don't eat *nyoyo* (maize and beans) then it's like we have buried a dog.' The young child is 'buried the next day, but first we have to eat,' one focus group participant described. A third participant added that neighbors contribute to the family of the dead child, 'so we have to contribute for coffins and tea and some might remain for other things.'

Accessing Child Protection Services: Common Practices and Challenges

Themes that were generated relate to community-based responses to child protection issues. These themes focus on: (a) common practices of how suspected cases of harm of IYC are addressed; and (b) the myriad of challenges for caregivers to access child protection services for IYC, including corruption, family shame, and mob justice.

Common Practices

Kenya's Children Act, ratified in 2001 addresses parental responsibility, fostering, adoption, custody, maintenance, guardianship, care and protection of children (Government of Kenya 2012). Children's Officers, who are employed by the Department of Children's Services, Ministry of Gender, Children and Social Development are based at the County level. They should be providing case management services to children and families in communities in their respective jurisdictions. However, they often fall short of reaching communities. Under the Children Act, Village Chiefs and Assistant Chiefs are recognized as 'authorized officers' with the same statutory authorities as Children's Officers, but generally are expected to refer serious child protection cases to the Children's Officers.

A Children's Officer from Siaya County explained how these service providers rarely enter communities to provide outreach services. She said: 'Most of the Children's Officers are just doing desk report without going to the field to collect data and carry out investigations because you go to the field just for one week and when you come back to the office, you find so many people and so many things waiting for you in the office and you have to do them alone. That is why so many Children's Officers just resort to doing the desk report.' With government social service providers largely out of the picture, most cases are dealt with locally by families and in some cases with the assistance of traditional leaders.

A female village elder from Village A described how she supports families experiencing domestic violence. Serious cases involving physical injuries are referred to the Assistant Chief. She explained: 'Other cases that people report to me are cases of domestic violence. But I only handle cases where there is no blood involved, as long as the mother was beaten, and she has blood anywhere in her body, I refer those cases to the Assistant Chief. There was one case that was brought to me where the husband was not supporting the family, he was not providing food for the child, so we sat the mother and the father down and advised them that children cannot grow up well if the mother and the father keep on fighting, so instead of them fighting, they should learn to live in peace in order for their children to grow up well. After that, I have not seen them fight again. But I also received a case of a woman who was thoroughly beaten by the husband and she had blood all over her face, so I referred the woman to the

Assistant Chief, and the Assistant Chief referred her to the police. I don't know how the case went.'

Community members usually first report incidences of neglect or violence against children through informal mechanisms, including traditional leaders. However, as with the formal service providers, there are also barriers to receiving help from traditional leaders, and there was quite a bit of dissatisfaction expressed. This includes frustration with the way the *Miji Kumi* (the elders), the Assistant Chief and the Chief responded. A woman from a focus group discussion in Village B added: 'There are village elders and the Chief, but they tell you that they can't handle such cases and they send you to the police.' Women in a focus group in Village A explained that 'the cases are reported to the village elder who forwards the same to the Assistant Chief, but no action is taken.'

Challenges: Corruption, Mob Justice, and Family Shame
The results of the qualitative study revealed sub-themes focused on several obstacles to families and children accessing protective services. This included lack of accountability and corruption of leaders and service providers appointed to assist community residents. In this environment, where the punishment of crimes against children is decided by the highest bidder and the poorest in the community ignored, frustration has led to brutal forms of mob justice. In some cases, families attempt to hold on to some semblance of dignity in unimaginable circumstances and resort to handling child protection incidents informally, particularly when the perpetrator is another family member.

Corruption
Families in the two communities are generally reluctant to report to law enforcement. From a focus group discussion in Village B, women explained why people are reluctant to report incidents to the police: 'Police will ask you for fuel and "where is that money?" That makes it difficult to report matters to the police. You are left to sort it out on your own.'

A teen from a focus group discussion with boys described some of the challenges with corruption in his community. 'Yes, in some cases the parents go and report but when it comes to justice for the young girl you find the culprit, or his family have money, so the case discontinues. They just pay the authorities and the cases are dismissed.'

In another interview with a woman from Village A, she explained that reporting is difficult, and the best option is to bring concerns up in a community meeting, 'The only thing you can do is to wait until the day when there is a *baraza* [community gathering] to talk about it.' If a community member would like to report a concern, they find themselves with limited options. Another participant explained: 'You can only report to village elders *Miji Kumi*. Sometimes *Miji Kumi* when you report to them, they in turn advise you to go and report to the authorities yourself. So, I do not understand if they want to be bribed before they go to the authorities or not; that I do not know.'

And, in a focus group with teen mothers, participants described how all supportive structures, informal and formal, require payments for action. 'Even if they report and they have no money it goes nowhere; you are told to give something small first before people start dealing with your case,' one teen mother explained. Another woman added that '[the problem] starts from the village elder [...] the village elders also ask for something small.'

From a discussion about the rape of a young girl with a focus group with mothers of young children in Village A, one mother explained: 'Yes the matter was reported to the Chief. But nothing was done afterwards. Most of the times when things happen people pay their way out especially if you are related to the authorities. People who have money also pay the policemen. If you are poor, you have no choice but suffer in silence no matter how bad the crime was.'

A woman interviewed from Village A reiterated this sentiment about the power imbalance associated with poverty in her community. She explained: 'You know that those who have nothing are not listened to and their complaints not well received. People do not normally listen to those who are poor [...] some people can go and report to the authorities and then action is taken against them, but those action is preferred against are very poor, sometimes they can be given a huge bill to pay and this becomes impossible for them. And after seeing that, you realize that you should try and see if they can pay that bill; if they cannot then come to an understanding amongst yourselves.'

Mob Justice
Mob justice was revealed as a common phenomenon and symptomatic of a lack of trust in the justice system. A woman elder in Village A explained: 'Fathers, especially those abusing drugs, sometimes rape their female

children. Like it happened in a village recently when a man was killed with mob justice after his 9-year old daughter raised the alarm. Villagers broke into the house and saved the child and although the man fought back even cutting one man, he was overpowered and killed.'

Sexual abuse of children is considered a very serious offence in the communities but with the risk of perpetrators escaping justice, communities sometimes resort to very brutal methods of mob justice on those suspected of an offense. In a focus group of teen mothers in Village A, one woman described this: 'If the community finds out, they will beat him to death, or burn him using a tire.' This refers to the practice of 'necklacing,' where a tire from a car is forced around the victim's chest and arms and filled with gas, then lit on fire.

Family Shame Preventing Reporting

Families in these locations fear that public attention will bring shame to them, so they do not report. With little hope of accessing assistance from the formal justice system, many families that experience violent incidents against their children may be attempting to cling to the hope of maintaining some sense of dignity by not reporting the incident. Of course, this limits the opportunity for children to access services and to prevent future transgressions. An elder woman from Village A explained: 'Often no actions are taken as they say *gino brio ketho nyingwa* [it will spoil our name].' This reason was reiterated by a woman in a focus group in Village B, who said: 'We sort them out within the community so as to avoid shame that might accrue from following such cases with authorities.'

Assistant Chief said: 'But again, cases such as children being raped are never reported, some due to ignorance, but most of the community members fear going to court so they would not report. You know the community members have this belief that *watna onge kaka dachung godo e bao* [you cannot stand in court with your relative].' This means that child protection incidents involving family members are generally not reported.

Discussion

This rapid ethnographic research conducted in two communities in Western Kenya revealed many of the harms experienced by IYC and the response challenges faced by community members. Specifically, the results of this qualitative study provide insights into the stresses experienced by families and the corresponding impact on children of all ages. Families tended to talk about their children of all ages, even when responding to questions about protection risks for young children. Thus, much of the data in this paper includes the situation of children older than five years of age. The results also describe the informal and formal child protective service providers' roles and examples of obstacles that prevent children and their families from accessing services. Taken as a whole, these qualitative findings supplement quantitative research from Kenya's Violence Against Children's 2010 National Survey (United Nations Children's Fund Kenya Country Office, US Centers for Disease Control and Prevention & the Kenya National Bureau of Statistics, 2012) which revealed high percentages of children nationwide experiencing various forms of violence, while very few were able to access protective services.

Identifying Harms and Protective Factors

The study's first research question sought to elicit common harms and protective factors that young children experience in these two case study villages. The life of families in the two communities is an overwhelming struggle. Climate change, resulting in the increased frequency of droughts and intense rainfall and flooding, has led to food insecurity due to the subsistence livelihoods prevalent in the communities studied. This is coupled with a staggeringly high HIV infection rate, leading to debilitating illness, and the death of residents of all ages. Both external factors impact caregivers' and families' capacities to protect and care for their children.

Study participants specifically described the impact that exposure to this family stress has on violence towards IYC, as well as children of all ages. These economic stressors have also had negative consequences for older children, including children being encouraged to adapt harmful coping strategies such as engaging in exploitative labor, crime, transactional sex or sex work to access food for themselves and their families. An unintended consequence of these activities includes teen pregnancy—introducing motherhood and caregiving roles to young women who are not able to fully provide and support their own children.

Despite the adverse conditions faced by residents in the rural villages of Western Kenya and the enormous struggle that families endure providing for their children's basic needs, the importance of young lives was clearly articulated by many of the assessment participants. Local traditional customs also reflect the value bestowed upon the lives of children. Children's lives are celebrated at birth and honored when there is a premature death.

While families have the primary responsibility to care for and protect children, governments have the ultimate responsibility for this care and protection. Under the Convention on the Rights of the Child, which the Government of Kenya has ratified, the state has the obligation to step in with necessary services when caregivers are unable to protect their children.

Understanding the Availability of Protective Services

The study's second research question sought to understand the systems and structures in Village A and Village B that are or should be used to protect children. Government law enforcement, justice and social work case management services are essentially inaccessible to community residents. The poorest and youngest residents are the most vulnerable and have the least access to these services. Traditional leaders, who should be assisting community members to access services, also are largely unsupportive, particularly to the poorest in the community. Families in the two communities have largely lost trust in the service providers, both formal and informal, to provide the services. Community residents also do not perceive the services that are offered as particularly relevant to their needs, so they frequently do not report and often take matters into their own hands.

Implications for Practice

The final research question posed by this study focused on identifying how the rapid ethnographic assessment approach and its findings can be utilized to help communities better respond to and prevent violence against IYC. As a next step towards using the case study findings to improve practice at the community level, ChildFund and its implementing partner analyzed the findings and engaged government and community stakeholders in validation and action planning. A validation meeting was held at the county level with 32 participants Sub-County X, and community representatives from the two villages to confirm that the findings were an accurate representation of perceptions and response of child protection for this age group. During the meeting, the participants endorsed the findings and prioritized the recommendation to improve coordination of child protection services in the county, including at the Sub-County, Ward, and community levels. Subsequent validation meetings were held in each village and were attended by local and traditional community leaders, teachers, CHVs, and young, middle, and old caregivers. Before a community action plan could be developed, identified informal actors asked to be trained in the foundations of identification and response to child protection harms. ChildFund engaged the county staff to train using the Government of Kenya's manual for community actors and a community action plan was developed.

Across communities, key thematic areas of action included: integrated parenting education (including child development, health, and child protection); community sensitization on existing child protection services for IYC; activating non-functional community-based structures for child protection; improved coordination of child protection services; and capacity building for the formal and non-formal child protection actors on the protection needs for IYC. A critical component of this action planning was to strengthen local child protection referral and service provision networks and mechanisms of accountability. This involved enabling broader community representation in mechanisms that serve as the checks and balances in the community that hold leadership more accountable for their actions. Overall, the participatory research process conducted in each community enabled collective learning about the harms, risk of harms and protective resources and factors within each community. This learning helped a diverse representation of the community residents develop a plan to prevent and respond to child protection harms.

Based on lessons learned from these case studies, ChildFund has adapted the tools and the methods utilized in this study to inform organizational adoption of a rapid ethnographic approach to community mapping of child protection issues. Modifications include simplifying the number of tools and reducing the data collection period from 10 to 5 days to reduce participants' burden. While this research focused on responsive services, it is equally important to use findings from this kind of ethnographic study to inform strategies and interventions aimed at preventing child protection harms and reduce the risks of harm. The preventive support that children and families need is critical for creating a protective environment for children. This includes programs that address the evolving developmental and protection needs of girls and boys and young adults from 0 to 24 years of age. The rapid ethnographic assessment approach is used by ChildFund and its partners to tailor programs and advocacy actions that are relevant to specific contextual issues. In the coming years, follow-up rapid ethnographic studies will facilitate reflective learning about the impact of the action planning, and other programming strategies in these communities, and perhaps, neighboring communities.

Poverty, SDGs, and Preventing Violence Against Children

The case studies expose the accumulative poverty-related problems faced by families that increase their vulnerability and ultimately the protection risks for their children of all ages. The recurring issue of hunger and food insecurity surfaced in virtually every interview and focus group discussion. This included children having to exchange sex for food or to steal in order to be able to eat. It also included the stress on caregivers who are unable to provide for their children using negative coping strategies such as harsh corporal punishment, substance abuse or coercing children into prostitution.

The SDGs provide an important global framework for reducing the risk factors for children by addressing a range of related harms that families and their children experience. This includes SDG 5.2—the physical and sexual abuse against girls, and 16.2—abuse, exploitation and all forms of violence against children. The SDGs also address the causes and the factors that contribute to these harms, such as poverty and hunger (SDGs 1 and 2); factors that contribute to food insecurity such as climate change (SDG 13); and other factors that contribute to poverty and stress on the family, such as HIV infection and substance abuse (SDG 3).

Dissatisfaction and frustration were vocalized by some participants about the inaccessibility of services, particularly for poorer residents, due to corruption. This is a systemic obstacle for children and families accessing protective services. The SDGs also address this important issue of systemic corruption (16.4, 16.5, 16.10) in promoting the goal of peace, justice, and strong institutions.

The SDGs were framed to reflect the interrelated nature of the social, economic and environmental challenges to sustainable development requiring integrated solutions. Each SDG should not be considered in isolation but part of a larger puzzle. While SDG 16.2 specifically calls for the end of abuse, exploitation and all forms of violence, it is important to understand the SDGs central holistic tenet also applies to tackling violence against children. As described in this paper, broader efforts are required that address the various root causes and contributing factors of the problem.

Conclusion

This research, being qualitative in nature, cannot be generalized beyond the case study context areas. However, the study was unique in that while previous studies have been conducted on strengthening community-based child protection systems, none of these studies have focused exclusively on IYC, thereby filling an important knowledge gap on child protection issues and systems for this vulnerable age group—and doing so based on learning derived first-hand from the community perspective. Furthermore, previous studies have only focused on very young children's development, and narrowly touched on harms, risks, and protection needs for IYC. Future research can expand upon the exploration of utility of rapid ethnographic approach to inform both contextual understanding of the underlying issues, such as poverty and disease, that support toxic environments for developing children and the best methods for scaling this approach to other communities' contexts.

As affirmed by our study participants who often shared information about children of all ages even when asked specifically about IYC, the risk factors and harms that affect young children also impact children of all ages. Thus, it is difficult to separate IYC issues from children's issues across the life course. Our findings also show that IYC are perhaps not 'invisible' but are 'hidden' in an entwined family context—to understand the risk and protective factors of young children, it is necessary to understand how these factors impact families as a whole.

In sum, the findings of this study can be used as a reflection of the trends in protection of IYC in Siaya County—and trends that may be reflective of and/or inform child protection issues for infants and young children in other poverty contexts. This study demonstrates how the protection of children is inextricably tied with the socioeconomic conditions of their families. Families create the environment where IYC come into the world and grow up. The multiple risk factors that contribute to violence in this environment were clearly reflected by the study participants. These compounding factors of poverty, hunger, sickness, alcoholism and marital strife have made the struggle to care for and protect IYC difficult.

Overall, this research shows how a rapid ethnographic assessment approach can be used to, in less than a two-week period, capture data to comprehensively 'map' community-based perspectives for both understanding the context of and shaping the response to child protection issues for the often-invisible infants and young children population. The approach provides an innovative, highly contextualized method for building awareness and engaging stakeholders in a collaborative response to strengthening community-based child protection systems for young children and to inform the creation of inclusive, safe spaces where vulnerable infants and young children feel nurtured and protected and celebrated by their families.

References

Belsky, J. (1980). Child maltreatment: an ecological integration. *American Psychologist, 35* (4), 320–335.

Black, M., Walker, S., Fernald, L., Anderson, C., DiGirolamo, A., Lu, Chunling, McCoy, D. et al (2016). Early childhood development coming of age: Science through the life course. *The Lancet, 389* (10064), 77–90. doi.org/10.1016/S0140-6736(16)31389-7.

ChildFund International (2010). *Child-and-youth friendly participatory action research toolkit.* Washington, D.C.: Author.

County of Siaya (2016). *Siaya County annual development plan 2017–2018.* Siaya: County Treasury. Retrieved from http://siaya.go.ke/wp-content/uploads/20 17/09/SIAYA-COUNTY-2017-18-ADP-FINAL.pdf.

Gilbert, R., Kemp, A., Thoburn, J., Sidebotham, P., Radford, L., Glaser, D., & MacMillan, H. L. (2009). Recognising and responding to child maltreatment. *The Lancet, 373* (9658), 167–180.

Government of Kenya (2012) *Children's Act, NO. 8 OF 2001, revised edition.* Nairobi: National Council for Law Reporting with the Authority of the Attorney-General. Retrieved on December 15, 2018, from http://www.kenyalaw.org.

Government of Kenya (2013). *Matrimony Property Act No 49 of 2013.* Nairobi: National Council for Law Reporting with the Authority of the Attorney-General. Retrieved from http://www.ilo.org/dyn/natlex/docs/ELECTRONIC/97351/11 5471/F-540095358/KEN97351.pdf.

Government of Kenya (2016). *Kenya County climate risk profile series: Climate risk profile Siaya County.* Nairobi: Ministry of Agriculture, Livestock and Fisheries. Retrieved on January 11, 2019, from https://ccafs.cgiar.org/publications/climate-risk-profile-siaya-county-kenya-county-climate-risk-profile-series#.XEWvX1xKjIU>

Hillis, S., Mercy, J., Amobi, A., & Kress, H. (2016). Global prevalence of past-year violence against children: A systematic review and minimum estimates. *Pediatrics, 137* (3), 1–13. Retrieved from http://pediatrics.aappublications.org/cgi/doi/10.1542/peds.2015-4079.

Kenya National Bureau of Statistics. (2015). *Kenya demographic and health survey 2014.* Nairobi: Author.

Krug, E.G., Dahlberg, L., Mercy, J., Zwi, A.B., & Lozano, R. (2002) *World report on violence and health.* Geneva: World Health Organization.

Leeb, R.T., Lewis, T., & Zolotor, A.J (2011). A review of physical and mental health consequences of child abuse and neglect and implications for practice. American Journal of Lifestyle Medicine, 5 (5), 454–468. doi.org/10.1177/1559827611410266.

Leventhal, J. & Gaither, J. (2012). Incidence of serious injuries due to physical abuse in the United States: 1997 to 2009. *Pediatrics, 130* (5), e847–e852.

National AIDS Control Council. (2016). *Kenya HIV county profiles 2016.* Nairobi: Ministry of Health.

Obonyoa, V., Otieno, C., & Ang'awa, F. (2016). Land fragmentation and food security in Uganja, Siaya County, Kenya. *American Scientific Research Journal for Engineering, Technology, and Sciences (ASRJET*S), *19* (1), 53–73.

Pereznieto, P., Montes, A., Routier, S. & Langston, L. (2014). *The costs and economic impact of violence against children.* New York: ChildFund Alliance and Overseas Development Institute (ODI).

Poverty Outreach Working Group (2011). Economic-strengthening pathways for the bottom billion: Connecting the dots e-consultation discussion synthesis. Washington, D.C.: SEEP Network.

Shonkoff, J. P., Garner, A. S., The Committee on Psychosocial Aspects of Child and Family Health, Committee on Early Childhood, Adoption, and Dependent Care, & Section on Developmental and Behavioral Pediatrics. (2012). The lifelong effects of early childhood adversity and toxic stress. *Pediatrics, 129* (1), e232–246.

Stoltenborgh, M., van Ijzendoorn M.H., Euser E.M., & Bakermans-Kranenburg, M.J. (2011). A global perspective on child sexual abuse: Meta-analysis of prevalence around the world. *Child Maltreatment, 16* (2), 79–101.

Stoltenborgh, M., Bakermans-Kranenburg, M.J., & van Ijzendoorn, M.H. (2013). The neglect of child neglect: A meta-analytic review of the prevalence of neglect. *Social Psychiatry and Psychiatric Epidemiology, 48* (3), 345–355.

UNICEF (United Nations Children's Fund) (2013). *Siaya County overview.* Retrieved on August 30, 2018, from https://www.unicef.org/kenya/Siaya.pdf.

UNICEF (United Nations Children's Fund) (2014). *Hidden in plain sight: A statistical analysis of violence against children.* New York: Author.

UNICEF (United Nations Children's Fund) (2017). *A familiar face: Violence in the lives of children and adolescents.* New York: Author.

United Nations (2015). *Transforming our world: The 2030 agenda for sustainable development*. New York: Author.

United Nations Children's Fund Kenya Country Office, US Centers for Disease Control and Prevention, & the Kenya National Bureau of Statistics (2012). *Violence against Children in Kenya: Findings from a 2010 National Survey. Summary Report on the Prevalence of Sexual, Physical and Emotional Violence, Context of Sexual Violence, and Health and Behavioral Consequences of Violence Experienced in Childhood*. Nairobi, Kenya: Author.

Walker, S., Wachs, T., Grantham-McGregor, S., Black, M., Nelson, C., Huffman. S., Helen Baker-Henningham, H., et al. (2011). Inequality in early childhood: Risk and protective factors for early child development. *The Lancet, 378 (9799)*, 1325–1338.

Contributor Biographies

Samantha Cocco-Klein is a PhD candidate in Public and Urban Policy at the Milano School for Policy, Management and Environment at the New School University. She also serves as Senior Advisor to Equity for Children. Prior to joining The New School, she worked for over 15 years as an advocate for children and international development specialist with UNICEF, the UN and International Rescue Committee in countries around the world.

Alberto Minujin is a professor at the Studley Graduate Program in International Affairs at The New School, with a special focus on topics related to social policy and children's rights. He is the founder of Equity for Children and a member of the Observatory on Latin America at The New School. Professor Minujin was awarded the Argentina Bicentennial Medal in recognition of his contributions to the fields of child rights and social policy. Professor Minujin is the author of many books, articles and papers about child rights, social policy and the middle class.

Tomoo Okubo is a Social Policy Specialist at the UNICEF Thailand Country Office. His work mostly focuses on using data and evidence to inform policy and programmes with emphasis on the most vulnerable, through supporting the collection of child-related data and development of child-related SDGs. Prior to working in Thailand, Okubo worked in UNICEF-New York, UNICEF-Nepal and served as a Japanese Overseas Cooperation Volunteer in Mozambique. He holds a Master degree in Public Administration/International Development from Harvard Kennedy School.

Ana Maria Restrepo is an Anthropologist and Political Scientist with a MSc in Social Policy and Planning from the London School and Economics. Ana Maria started her career working in the City Council of Bogotá as part of the team that led the formulation of the local Youth Public Policy. In 2011, she joined UNICEF in Colombia and since then she has worked as Monitoring Officer in Argentina and the LAC Regional Office. More recently, she has been working as Planning Specialist in the UNICEF Thailand Country Office. Currently, she is supporting the implementation of MICS in Argentina and providing technical assistance to other countries in LAC that are conducting MICS.

Chirawat Poonsab is working at the Thailand National Statistical Office (NSO) as a statistician with more than 15 years of professional experience providing technical assistance in all phases of survey implementation, from survey planning, questionnaire and training manual design, staff training, fieldwork logistics, fieldwork monitoring, data processing, tabulation, data analysis to report writing and data dissemination. He has been directly involved in the planning, implementation and completion of the 2012 and the 2015–2016 Multiple Indicator Cluster Survey (MICS). He also participated in the 2010 Population and Housing Census and the 2013 Agricultural Census as a master trainer and field coordinator.

Christina Popivanova is a public policy professional with nearly 20 years of experience with the UN in the field of social policy, monitoring and evaluation. Currently she heads the Social Policy team in UNICEF Thailand. **Popivanova** previously worked in Sub-Saharan Africa, Southeast Asia, Central and Eastern Europe and the USA. She holds Master degrees in Economics from Sofia University, Bulgaria, International Relations from the Central European University and Public Policy from the University Of Minnesota.

Sudeshna Chatterjee has worked in the international development field for nearly twenty years as a researcher, evaluator and technical advisor to government, UN agencies, NGOs and the private sector. She holds an interdisciplinary PhD intersecting public policy, urban planning and design, environment behavior and cultural geography from North Carolina State University. Dr. Chatterjee led the formative evaluation of UNICEF Work for Children in Urban Settings as a consulting senior evaluation specialist to UNICEF, HQ in New York. She is also the founder and CEO of Action for Children's Environments (ACE), a knowledge-based NGO offering research, evaluation, programme planning and design services on child-centered urban governance, planning and programming.

Katie Hodgkinson is a Post-Graduate Researcher at the University of Leeds, working on the Changing the Story project. Her research explores social justice at the intersection of the arts and education in post-conflict contexts. Hodgkinson's background is in International Development Studies, specializing in education and youth issues. Prior to starting her PhD, Katie worked at the University of Amsterdam on projects spanning 17 countries in Sub-Saharan Africa, South Asia, Central America and Europe.

This included research into the social exclusion of vulnerable youth and working as a research partner in a Netherlands Ministry of Foreign Affairs funded SRHR alliance.

Nicky Pouw is an economist with over 20 years of research experience in international development studies, mainly in Sub-Saharan Africa (Ghana, Burkina Faso, Uganda, Kenya, Tanzania, Malawi, Côte d'Ivoire) and Sri Lanka. Dr. Pouw is currently Associate Professor of Economics of Wellbeing at the Governance and Inclusive Development Research Program (GID) or the AISSR at the University of Amsterdam.

Marielle Le Mat is an expert in sexual and reproductive health and rights (SRHR), gender, young people, and education. She is an Advisor at the Dutch Royal Tropical Institute (KIT) and carries out research, training, and advisory work in low- and middle-income countries, particularly in sub-Saharan Africa. She obtained her PhD on comprehensive sexuality education and gender-based violence in schools in Ethiopia, from the University of Amsterdam. Dr. Le Mat is experienced in youth participatory, qualitative, and mixed methods, and comparative research.

Jennifer Seager is an Assistant Professor of Global Health and Economics at George Washington University, where she is an applied microeconomist with research interests at the intersection of development and health, particularly focused on adolescents and sexual and reproductive health and risky behavior. Dr. Seager has been working with research teams evaluating randomized controlled trials and overseeing longitudinal data collection in South and Southeast Asia and Sub-Saharan Africa since 2012, including ongoing projects in Tanzania and Bangladesh.

Sarah Baird is an Associate Professor of Global Health and Economics at George Washington University, where she focuses on the microeconomics of health and education in low- and middle-income countries with an emphasis on gender and youth. Dr. Baird is also a visiting fellow at the Center for Global Development and the Impact Evaluation Lead for the Gender and Adolescence: Global Evidence research programme. Her work has been published in leading academic journals including the Quarterly Journal of Economics and The Lancet and has been featured in media outlets such as The New York Times and The Economist.

Joan Hamory Hicks is an Assistant Professor of Economics at the University of Oklahoma, where she is a development economist focusing on transitions to adulthood among youth in low income countries. Dr. Hicks has been working with research teams evaluating field experiments and actively managing longitudinal data collection since 2004. Her research has been published in outlets such as The Quarterly Journal of Economics, the European Journal of Political Economy, Oxford Economic Papers, and Applied Economics Letters.

Sabina Faiz Rashid is Dean and Professor at BRAC James P Grant School of Public Health, BRAC University. Her research specializes in ethnographic and qualitative research, with a focus on gender, sexual and reproductive health and rights, sexuality and the well-being of adolescents, young women and men, use of social media/digital technology, changing gender relationships, power dynamics, urban poverty, governance, and health services in urban informal settlements. Dr. Rashid has been involved in research for over 20 years, is widely published, and is actively engaged in translating knowledge into action at the grassroots and national level.

Maheen Sultan is a Visiting Fellow and the Head of the Gender Studies Cluster and the Coordinator of the Centre for Gender and Social Transformation at BRAC Institute of Governance and Development, BRAC University. Her work addresses women's leadership; local governance; gender norms and masculinities; women's employment and care work. She has over 30 years' experience working for NGOs, the UN, Grameen Bank and the Bangladeshi government and more than 10 years' experience in the field of research, communications and advocacy. Maheen has a License in Sociology from the University of Geneva and postgraduate diplomas in development studies and gender.

Workneh Yadete has over 15 years of experience in qualitative and quantitative research in Ethiopia. Before GAGE, Yadete conducted research for the Girls' Education Challenge and the Young Lives longitudinal study, in addition to research projects on barriers to girls' education, education quality and primary education completion. He was also Managing Director of SOS ENFANTS Ethiopie, which works on the provision of care and support to orphan and vulnerable children. He has a Master's Degree in History from Addis Ababa University.

Nicola Jones is the Director of Gender and Adolescence: Global Evidence and Principal Research Fellow, Gender, Equality and Social Inclusion at the Overseas Development Institute. Her expertise lies in the intersection of gender, age and social inclusion and social protection, in developmental and conflict-affected settings. Dr. Jones has carried out qualitative and mixed-methods research for a range of funders and her country expertise is broad, having worked in East and West Africa, Asia, Latin America and more recently in the MENA region. She has published widely including six books, more than 30 peer-reviewed journal articles, as well as reports, policy briefs and short communication pieces.

Ernest Darkwah is a lecturer and occupational health psychologist at the University of Ghana, Accra. His research interests include using qualitative exploratory approaches to explore workplace health promotion and occupational health issues surrounding the children's services workforce in Ghana and Sub-Saharan Africa. He also researches general workplace wellness issues as they are related to people who work with vulnerable populations.

Marguerite Daniel is an associate professor in the Department of Health Promotion and Development, University of Bergen, Norway. Her research interests include development-related health promotion, equity and inclusion; vulnerable children, particularly in Sub-Saharan Africa; and resilience among refugees in Norway. Her theoretical approach is strengths-based and methodologically she uses qualitative approaches, especially participatory action research.

Anna Carolina Machado Maciel da Silva holds an MSc in Public Policy from the University of Bristol in the UK, a specialization in Public Administration from the Federal University of Rio de Janeiro and a BA in International Relations from the Federal Fluminense University. Since 2015, Machado has been working as a researcher at the IPC-IG and has contributed to projects in partnership with UNICEF on child-sensitive social protection, the WFP, IFAD and other organizations in Brazil, sub-Saharan Africa and in the Middle East and North Africa.

Charlotte Bilo holds a Bachelor degree in Political Science from University College Maastricht, Netherlands, and a Master's degree in Poverty and Development from the Institute of Development Studies (IDS), Brighton, UK. At the IPC-IG Bilo is currently works on a research project in partnership with UNICEF MENARO on child-sensitive social protection in the Middle East and North Africa regions.

Ismael Cid-Martinez is a Ph.D. student (Economics Department, New School for Social Research), focusing on development and social policy. He serves as research assistant for the American Sociological Association. He has worked as research assistant for the Schwartz Center for Economic Policy Analysis and for Equity for Children. He was also a summer associate for UNICEF (Latin America Regional Office, Nigeria), the National Academy of Social Insurance, and the Social Security Advisory Board.

Enrique Delamonica is a Senior Statistics Specialist working on Child Poverty and Gender Equality at UNICEF Headquarters. He is an economist and a political scientist educated at the University of Buenos Aires, the Institute for Economic and Social Development, Columbia University, and the New School for Social Research. His work has been focused on poverty reduction and human development strategies, social protection, socioeconomic disparities, child poverty, financing social services, equity, and the impact of macro-economic trends on child welfare. He has published and co-edited books on issues of social policy and economic development, particularly as they affect children's rights. He has also taught economics, international development, policy analysis, statistics, and research methods at, among other places, New York University, Columbia University, the New School for Social Research, and Saint Peter's College (New Jersey). He was a Fellow of the Comparative Research Programme on Poverty of the International Social Science Council between 2010 and 2018. Currently he is on the board of the Research Committee on Poverty, Social Welfare and Social Policy of the International Sociological Association.

José Espinoza-Delgado holds a PhD in Economics, Development Economics, from the University of Göttingen in Germany and another PhD in Economics from the University of Zaragoza in Spain. He is currently a postdoctoral researcher of the research center "Poverty, Equity and Growth in Developing Countries" at the University of Goettingen and, since 2018, has been working as a consultant for UNICEF on child poverty, impact of crises on child poverty, and on gender equality. His main research interests include individual-based multidimensional poverty measurement and analysis, health inequality, gender inequality, vulnerability to poverty, and financial literacy.

Aristide Kielem is Senior Programme Analysis advisor with the Government of Quebec in Canada, while also leading independent researches on child poverty. He holds a MSc degree from the *"Centre d'Études et de Recherches sur le Développement International"* (CERDI—School of development economics of the University of Auvergne) and an MPA degree from the National School of Public Administration of Québec in Canada. Kielem has worked for UNICEF and other donor agencies (including UNDP and the World Bank) in Togo, Senegal, Sierra Leone, and Jordan, where he contributed to major humanitarian emergency responses as well as to researches and capacity building on child poverty and social protection. He also works as a consultant for UNICEF on child poverty and gender.

Mohamed Obaidy is a PhD student in economics at The New School for Social Research in New York, USA. His research is in macroeconomics, international finance, development and political economy. He previously worked at UNICEF on child multidimensional poverty before joining the United Nations Department of Economic and Social Affairs (Financing for Sustainable Development Office). In addition, he has been an Adjunct Lecturer at the City University of New York, a graduate Teaching Assistant and research assistant at The New School for Social Research, and a Teaching Assistant at Barnard College of Columbia University in New York.

Martin Hayes is a Senior Child Protection Adviser with ChildFund International, providing technical assistance to programs in nineteen countries worldwide. He has over twenty years of professional experience in the child protection sector in both humanitarian and development settings. A focus of his work has included the development and use of participatory action research methods with vulnerable and hard to reach populations. Previous organizations that Hayes has worked with include the US Agency for International Development, the International Rescue Committee, Save the Children and UNICEF. He has an M.A. in sociology specializing in community development from Concordia University.

Melissa Kelly is the Director, Child Development and Protection for ChildFund International, supporting country programs globally with a focus on comprehensive programming for infants and young children. She serves as the chair of Asia-Pacific Regional Network for Early Childhood's (ARNEC) Executive Committee and as the co-representative for Civil Society Organizations (CSO) on the Executive Group of the ECD Action Network (ECDAN). Prior to joining ChildFund, she served as a global ECD Specialist at Save the Children and managed Save the Children's Early Childhood Development Program in Mozambique. She received her M.A in International Educational Development from Columbia University Teachers College.

Darcy Strouse is the Research Manager for ChildFund International. Prior to joining ChildFund she spent two decades providing research methods and evaluation design and implementation leadership expertise as an independent consultant and research/study director to non-profit and for-profit research organizations. As an applied behavioral scientist, she has led local, national, and international research studies in prevention and health promotion fields, including those focused on physical activity promotion, youth sexual risk behaviors, HIV prevention, child abuse and neglect, childhood injury, and youth peer and parent relationships She received her Ph.D. and M.A. in Human Development from the Catholic University of America.

ibidem*.eu*